I'm a cyclist let me out of here

Published by Phased Publications: www.phased.co.uk
Cover design by Nathan Ryder: www. ryderdesign.studio
Cover Illustration by Olha Voronova

Introduction

"Everyone has a book inside them, which is exactly where it should, I think, in most cases, remain." - Christopher Hitchens 1997

"I'm a cyclist, let me out of here" covers a 24 month period during which I attempted to write a book about cycling. I walked away from a well-paid job, abandoned a promising career and ventured into the world of authorship. A world I knew nothing about. I thought I'd better document the process just in case something went horribly wrong and others could learn from it. I did this via a blog published on my rarely visited website. These posts have been edited into the book you're reading now. It's a book about writing a book written by a bloke who should maybe have listened harder to Christopher Hitchens.

There's an element of structure and order but be prepared for some meandering, tangential observations and bits that have absolutely nothing to do with cycling authorship whatsoever. You'll see a writing style evolve over the pages, as a man tries to find his way in uncharted waters whilst discovering his true writing voice. This includes colourful language, self-depreciation, attempts at humour and the occasional serious crime against the English language. It can be an acquired taste but I make no apologies as I know of no other way to write. There's a prelude telling you how I got into this authoring game, triggered by a swimming pool. This is followed by a series of observations in chronological order that bring you into my time as an author. At the end I've banged out a few conclusions and brought my story up to date. I hope that there is some vague inspiration along the way.

If you were expecting a polished narrative clearly explaining two years of life as an author, I'm afraid it's time to hit the refund button. On the other hand, why not dip into a few chapters and get a feel for the life I led during this period.

Editing these scribblings finds me yearning to return to those times of rapture and frustration delivered in equal measure. I miss the madness of attempting to write a cycling book with no experience whatsoever. I miss having a mission that can only be fulfilled by cycling and writing about it. I miss the people I met, the places I visited, the incidents that happened and I even miss the constant self-doubt that comes with jumping in at the deep end.

You'll have to read to the end to discover how it all panned out for me I'm not going to offer any spoilers but I sincerely hope you enjoy my journey and can use elements of it to plan one of your own.

Dave Barter
January 2021

Prelude

"*Once bitten, twice shy*". What a load of old toss. If that saying were true I'd never stub my toe, drink coffee that's too hot, enter a road race or pay money to watch Swindon Town Football Club. The phrase needs to be reworded somewhere along the lines of "*It takes about ten proper hard run-ins to get the message*". These thoughts were idling through my mind as I fiddled with my tie in an executive board meeting. To my left were some vague noises concerning a recent outage and its complete unacceptability which immediately triggered a new game of spin the management bottle. The participants passed the blame around waiting for it to stick. Each director winced in turn as the neck of the bottle pointed in their direction.

Maybe I should have winced as well, but my attention was captivated by the swimming pool across the road, or to be more accurate, the remainder of the swimming pool. It was being methodically torn down by demolition experts, apparently Leeds had greater need of a car park than a swimming pool and so this 1970's monstrosity had to go. I reflected upon the swimming pool's brief time on this earth.

It had probably been conceived from enthusiasm as a councillor or two fought for the budget to improve the health and fitness of the Leeds population. Many late nights and negotiations resulted in a signature on a piece of paper allowing construction to begin. Local children had watched in anticipation as brick by brick this temple of entertainment had grown in front of them before throwing open its doors to a legion of swimmers undeterred by chlorine and the inability to pet in the pool. This pool would have had a single purpose, to allow people to swim in safety away from murky ponds, trolley filled canals or lobster infested coastlines. It would have been happy with its purpose and as long as its basic needs were catered for, would probably have fulfilled this purpose for centuries.

But ultimately the pool would have been stymied by factors unrelated to swimming. Management decisions would have diverted maintenance funds elsewhere. Other political priorities would have overridden the need for a city centre swimming pool or a set of management consultants would have proposed a more cost-effective/profitable alternative on a cheaper greenfield site out of town. The pool itself would have had no say in these decisions, it would have been quite happy being swum in until one day the water was drained out and chipboard nailed over its windows. The pool had ceased to be a receptacle for swimmers, it was now prime real estate instead. Exercise and entertainment had been driven out in the name of commerce and so the human cycle of tearing down a perfectly serviceable building to replace it with another would begin again.

I saw this cycle of inception, purpose, growth, review, decline in myself. Ten years previously I'd built a career within another large organisation, driven by the enthusiasm to create new products and leverage exciting technologies to fulfil them. The excitement and purpose had waned as I'd climbed further up the ladder. The whiter my shirt, the larger my wage packet, the lower my morale and drive became. Deep challenging technical problems were replaced with senior management politics and game playing. Tedious box-ticking business plans that were never properly read replaced detailed hand-drawn schematics of engineering prototypes. Like the pigs in Animal Farm, I found myself starting to "walk on two legs" and caught myself relaying management speak to colleagues that were supposed to be my friends. A future of balance sheet appraisal, total quality audits, senior management cap doffing and suit-wearing lay in front of me. The fiscal and pensionable benefits certainly had some merit, but I could feel the proper me seeping out of my skin with each further day I endured.

I walked out of that job with a few thousand pounds in savings and no real idea as to what I was going to do. I reassured my wife that "something would come up" and we set off to France with our young family for a long circumnavigation of the country to give me some respite. We were sitting on a beach in Antibes when the planes hit the twin towers. Things were going to change in the world and so we decided to slowly make our way home and find me a job.

A series of consultancy assignments followed by a serendipitous meeting introduced me to Grant, a mischievous sales director in a large American software company. We shared similar motivations and enthusiasms and a few months later our startup technology company was born. Grant and I constructed a large shed in my back garden and our own little Hewlett Packard story began. It's a book in its own right, but to keep the story brief, five years from formation, after the most amazing rollercoaster small business ride we sold a majority share to a larger company. And once again I donned the suit, attended management meetings and began to do the two-legged pig walk.

Remind yourself of the opening sentence. I should have known better, I should have remembered my frustration five years previously, I should have ignored all the zeros on the company offer letter and the short term financial security it would provide. Instead, I signed away the next three years to a set of profit targets, performance measures and compliance documents. The first two years were very exciting. Our new owners gave us autonomy and we expanded from my shed into proper offices and grew the team. We created all sorts of new products and enjoyed the benefit of proper investment into our operation. Our business-within-a-business was doing well and soon it became time to become properly subsumed within the mother company.

I was given a flighty job title, large salary, share options and a place on various boards. Our mother company was sold to venture capitalists, the pace of growth increased, all sorts of industry superstars were being headhunted and once again I found myself in meetings that had no technical content whatsoever.

Watching the swimming pool being torn down made me realise that I'd lost my sense of purpose. I was now well on the wrong side of forty, I'd rediscovered my cycling obsession and spent every free moment travelling about and sampling new sections of road. I'd even conceived a vague plan about writing a book of cycling routes but done nothing to further it. But here I was in a boardroom, discussing outages rather than writing code to prevent them. An ember of discontent flared from the back of my mind and before the sanity firefighters could get to the root of the flames I'd been overrun by an inferno of desire.

Boardrooms were not my future. I needed to get out and write a book about cycling.

Anyone I've encountered will attest to the fact that I am a strange sort of bloke whose thought chains can vary wildly. One minute I'm considering my preferred pot noodle flavour choice, the next pondering whether the big bang really was a bang if there was nobody around to hear it. There's also a darker chain of thought that has stayed with me for many years. I am constantly visualising my funeral. This visualisation is usually a variation around the wife and kids digging a shallow grave in a local allotment. But I sometimes consider what words would be said over my grave. Probably something along the lines of *"I told him brown was the live wire"* or *"Can I have his titanium Omega frame please Helen?"*.

After these words have been said I've always hoped that they'd throw something into the grave after me. Something that I've done that represented my life on earth and the useful contribution that I've made to humanity. At this point, I felt that there was not a lot of useful Dave stuff that could follow me into the earth. The songs I'd written in a punk band many years ago could only really serve a purpose in noise cancellation feedback loops for tractor engines. All of my computer code had become "todo" items in a long list of systems rewrite projects. It seems a bit barbarous to throw my children in as the Egyptian pyramid builders liked to do and the three-legged lathe-turned table I made in woodwork would never survive the journey out of my parent's house.

I needed something that could be chucked in after me. Something that at least one person could have derived some sort of pleasure or satisfaction from. Something that could serve as a tiny legacy to show that my brief existence upon this planet had served some sort of purpose. The swimming pool had served its purpose and a generation would look back upon it fondly and remember the place where they took their first tentative strokes alone in the water or laid their first swimming pool poo. I wanted to serve mine.

This board meeting was timely as I had a week's holiday booked that began the next day. A week's cycling in the Alps with a friend. My wife Helen dreads my cycling holidays. I announced my first resignation to her following a week's mountain biking in Moab. She managed to keep two hands on the wheel as she drove me back from the airport, remarkable restraint as she held back from pummelling my face with balled fists. Every holiday since she's waved me off with a cheery "Please don't come back and resign". This holiday was no different.

The long monotonous French toll roads offered up great spaces for thinking. From Calais to Reims I'd outlined the book I wanted to write, from Reims to Lyon I'd mentally drafted a few chapters and conceived options for the look and feel and by the time we'd arrived in Bourg Saint Maurice there was no turning back. Yet again I was going to walk out of a safe and lucrative job, but this time with a real purpose. I was going to write a book. A proper book that would serve a useful purpose. A book that could be chucked into the hole after I'm lowered into it and land on my coffin with a decent "thud".

The following days saw my thoughts consumed with this new future. At the age of 45, it's tempting to view this as a mid-life crisis, I saw it differently. This was not a crisis at all. A crisis is deemed to be an event that is, or can lead to, an unstable and dangerous situation. I wasn't in any kind of crisis, I was too bloody comfortable. The only crisis in my life was the slight loss of purpose, but now I had it. This was more a mid-life reaffirmation of who I am, which is not a suit-wearing business strategist, more a person who gets out there and does stuff. The sale of my previous business had liberated some funds that could bankroll this new direction. It was supposed to be my pension, but what's the point of having a pension if you spend your later years rolling in regret.

I cycled up mountains and worked on my speech to Helen. This needed clear thought as my plan was entirely selfish. Pack in the job, cycle all over the place for a year and then publish a book in the vain hope that I might be able to recoup some of the outgoings. The more I thought, the harder it got. There was no way to dress this up as a shared benefit. This was definitely about me.

The trickiest part of this speech construction was the knowledge that I had previous form. It would be difficult to present my plan as a once-in-a-lifetime risk as we'd already been through that. I felt empathy with the mountain climbers that I love reading about, I imagined each and every speech made to their partners as they prepared to depart on another hugely ambitious project. "I'll be alright love, it's only K2 and I've packed my thermos". Ultimately you don't climb mountains for the benefit of your family, you do it for yourself and your own personal (in)sanity. It's the same with cycling books, I was well aware of the economics of authorship vs those of IT directorship I'd struggle to build any sort of fiscal or family-based business case.

Things were further complicated by the fact that Helen was in full-time employment within my own company. I'd be leaving a good job and she'd be staying behind to carry on earning a crust. Mulling this over it became clear that I'd have to present my case in the manner of Charles Dickens' A Christmas Carol. I'd lay three Dave's out in front of Helen. The Dave of the past, driven by enthusiasm and boundless energy. The Dave of the present slowly losing the will to live in a confining job. Finally, the Dave of the future sat solemnly behind a large mahogany desk working with HR to dispose of unnecessary employees. The simple question posed would be *"which one would she prefer being married to?"*.

As it happens all of my mentally rehearsed soliloquies were in vain. On my return, I stepped over the threshold muttered something about my job and Helen told me to resign. You see women are far more intuitive than we can ever give them credit for. She'd seen this coming for months and was simply counting the days until I uttered the "R" word. All the signs had been there; the extended reading of the paper in the morning before leaving for work, the lingering glances at maps/

bicycles/P45's and the fact that I'd encouraged her so avidly to take up a full-time position.

We didn't bother with any sums or financial advice, there was no point as we hadn't bothered last time round and things had worked out OK. I had some money in the bank from selling the business, we'd spend it on writing a book instead. Seven years of hard work within a small business also builds a degree of self-confidence in your ability to earn a crust. I'd learnt hard work the hard way. I'd learnt how it feels to be dependent upon your own ability to deliver and what it means to face the consequences of not meeting deadlines. A vein of arrogance told me that I'd make this money back again, better to spend it now whilst I had my relative youth, fitness and drive.

"Dear John,

I am writing to formally resign from my current position .."

There is amazing satisfaction in being a bloke and having a boss called John. Not only did I get to write a letter of resignation, but I also got to write a *"Dear John"* letter. Even more so, it contained all sorts of *"it's me not you"* phrases:

"Finally, I would like to stress that this decision is based upon myself, my goals and a need to spend much more time with my family and other projects than I currently do."

I posted the letter at the beginning of October 2010 and a short period of shitting myself began. I'd read through my contract of employment and come across the *"years' notice"* clause. I had no idea how my decision would be received or whether this clause would be strictly adhered to. A years' notice, how on earth would I cope? What would they make me do? I had visions of becoming the UK's highest-paid potato peeler. Fortunately, it didn't come to that, my company proffered the right amount of regret whilst agreeing to a three month notice period. At the same time, an email circulated Head Office Subject: "YAY He's Off!" A few token efforts were made to get me to stay including the option of a career break. I waved them all away. I knew I'd never deliver on my mission if it came with a huge great safety net.

The next three months proved to be a blur of anticipation and frustration. I simply wanted to get on with the job of writing the book. However, I was duty-bound to sort out all of my loose ends at work (there were a lot), find a successor, keep my area of the business running and write a convoluted paper about IT strategy that would be quietly binned as soon as I walked out the door. Finance sent me papers to sign handing back my shares, I dashed off a signature without thought to what I was doing. Four years later when the company was eventually sold those shares would have bought a lot of bikes quite a few bike shops and maybe the odd flash car to transport them to boot.

The fateful day arrived. The day that answering the phone became optional, support requests were someone else's problem, my pockets were emptied of entry cards and computer security dongles and the alarm clock was set to "when I bloody well feel like it". All I had to do was write a book. A cycling book that conveyed my passion for riding the roads of Great Britain. A book that would challenge and inspire whilst making a decent "thunk" on hitting my coffin. I had a title in mind "Great British Bike Rides", I had a loose idea that it would contain 30-40 road rides and lots of lovely photographs. But that's all I had, an idea.

Being a forgetful soul I wanted to ensure that I'd remember the experience of chasing this mad idea. A diary was out of the question as I have a (yet unrecognised) disability linked to a complete inability to wield a pen. Instead, I'd fire up a blog and keep myself and a few friends updated with progress, hopefully in a semi-entertaining manner.

So let's begin with me sat my desk staring at an empty document that would hopefully become Great British Bike Rides. And without further ado, we'll dive into my blogs. I sincerely hope you enjoy the ride.

Beginning

The house is empty bar myself. Helen's gone to work and the kids have sullenly dragged themselves down the hill to school. Two hours into my new life as the self-unemployed I've delivered a masterclass in procrastination. The kitchen became way tidier than it's ever been, with cups neatly and unnecessarily arranged in cupboards with their handles facing left. I've walked around the house staring at various things in a contemplative manner and then taken this into the garage and contemplated my fleet of bicycles. I'm not sure what this contemplation achieves but it feels better than scrolling up and down the internet looking for cat memes. This procrastination is actually down to nerves. I'm just not sure where to begin? How does one write a book about cycling? I thought it would be pretty straightforward, something along the lines of ride about a bit on a bike, capture a few statistics and photos then assemble them all into some sort of order. A bout of internet searching came up blank with project templates for cycling books and so I'd need to create my own. This was not as easy as I'd thought so I sat at my desk and carried out a few other important tasks.

First, pencils were sharpened. This ate up a decent amount of time as I had to liberate a pencil sharpener from the depths of a child's bedroom. Uranium miners have it easier. Then, as always, each lead broke on the final turn of the sharpener, so by the time the pencil had any semblance of a point it was less than two inches long. I'm not even sure why I sharpened pencils as I'd planned to write the whole book on a computer. It just felt productive and gave me the false impression that progress was being made. After pencils, I managed a bit of desk rearrangement followed by some staring out of the window. I don't normally get the luxury of spying on my neighbours during working hours and today was no exception as they were all at work. The recycling lorry delivered a few moments of vague excitement but all too soon it was gone leaving me with a static view of my driveway covered in leaves. So I wasted another hour sweeping them all up.

Day one was stunningly unproductive. Near lunchtime, my computer's memory was untarnished with words or any other form of useful work. I called myself into my office and delivered a right old fashioned bollocking. This was no way to act if I was to have any chance of success. Procrastination could wait until the book was finished and it was time to do something useful. Sit yourself down and get on with some research man. If you're going to get forty rides in this book you need to carve up the country and work out just where you're going to ride them. You'll need some ride criteria and inspiration. This doesn't just grow on trees. Stop messing about!

And thus my research began in earnest. I stuck a map on the wall and scribbled all over it. Google were forced to add a server or two to their network as I hammered away at them with various questions. *"Best ride in Manchester"* was maybe not a good idea as the results had a distinct lack of cycling flavour. But I began to fall into the swing of things. This researching lark was not quite as hard as I'd thought. Luckily my cycling career has taken me to most of the UK and so I knew where the good stuff was likely to be. There was a myriad of classic cycling events, races and sportives that handed out pointers and finally there was the map itself. Small yellow lines surrounded by contours usually meant there'd be some decent cycling to be had.

Then I got all excited. As it became clear that to get the book finished I had an indecent amount of cycling that needed to be done. Procrastination was kicked right into next year after I had this (obvious) revelation and so the pattern of my first week was set. Get up, fantasise about riding somewhere brilliant in Great Britain, scrawl a series of route options upon a map, cycle a bit in the afternoon (well one needs to keep one's fitness) and deflect the annoying texts from friends in real jobs accusing me of sitting on my arse watching daytime TV.

It's worth mentioning that the media companies provide an excellent service to home workers concerning their daytime TV offerings. I salute their ingenuity in presenting hours of utterly banal and depressing content designed specifically to deter home workers from attempting to watch TV. It takes real dedication to go beyond more than thirty minutes of it without launching a shoe at the screen and I've found more entertainment in the shipping forecast.

So week one is in the bag. An element of progress made and a vague plan as to what to do next. I'm sure Winston Churchill never wrote that in his diary but it felt good to me and so I celebrated by compiling a to-do list for the following week:

- sweep up the leaves that I stupidly left in a pile and did not bag
- buy new pencils
- ride bike a bit more (because I can)
- avoid Manchester
- write a bit more of a book about cycling

Leaving Do

Monday morning was completely written off by the dentist. Two fillings, a crown and a proffered cheque with hardly enough room for the zeros distracted me from any writing. The whole experience had a tint of the surreal about it. My dentist spends his exorbitant fees on gimmicks. Lying in the chair the patient is treated to an LCD screen mounted upon the ceiling, which was aptly showing the Jeremy Kyle show. He also has a stereo system that is permanently tuned to Classic FM. The combination works pretty well, there's a strange sort of beauty in watching those in petty dispute gesticulate at each other set to Tchaikovsky's Waltz of the Flowers. It's like Swan Lake but set in Swindon. The afternoon was spent sitting in front of the computer feeling sorry for myself and not managing to write a whole lot. I planned routes instead and have a big chunk of Lands End - John O' Groats in the bag and ready to be ridden. This was planned to be the centrepiece of my book.

I did manage to do some proper writing later in the week and the word count is now knocking on the door of 5000 which would be good if any of it made grammatical sense, which none of it does. But I have learned a lot of new stuff about Romans, rights of access to the road network and the genesis of the leather saddle. I've also watched some seriously dodgy videos and spent far too much time on internet forums. I think I'll have to install a web proxy and create an internet access policy for weekdays.

Midweek I was travelling up to Leeds for a final meeting with my old work colleagues. I'd agreed to do this final meeting as part of my negotiations for an early exit from my notice period. I attempted the journey by train, always an experience following the government's decision to outsource the housing of psychopaths to Network Rail. I had the luxury of a reserved seat, or so I thought, and as I boarded the train at Cheltenham I made my way to seat C19. On arrival, I was met by a man who looked like a ferret and a suitcase larger than him blatantly occupying my seat. I politely informed the ferret that I had this seat reserved and I would be eternally grateful if the suitcase could be relocated to the luggage rack to facilitate my arse taking its rightful place. To say he went crazy would be an understatement. He completely lost the plot akin to a five-year-old child who has been denied Oreos in a supermarket. "Oh my fucking god" he protested, "It's going to take me fucking ages to move it, for fucks sake mate look at the fucking size of it, Jesus Christ, for fucks sake..anyway there are no reservations, for fucks sake etc....". I looked at my ticket which clearly stated that there were reservations and that I had one. However, I'm no slouch at spotting potential psychosis and decided to locate myself elsewhere. He carried on ranting. His cord had been pulled and he seemed incapable of retracting back to normal behaviour.

I sat next to a normal looking sort of bloke who was plugged into his iPhone and devoid of any outward symptoms of madness. That was until he reached into his bag and pulled out wine gums. He popped one in his mouth and made the loudest, most ridiculous chewing noise ever. How the hell can you do that with wine gums? They are soft, malleable and possess no physical structure that allows them to "crunch" but somehow he managed to make a bleeding racket that got more and more annoying. After 5 more wine gums, I was contemplating going back to the ferret and pushing him to move his case. Luckily the woman on the seat opposite left and so did I, straight into her seat.

The madness didn't end there. I arrived in Leeds at around about 6 pm, checked into my hotel and bought a sandwich. I then settled down in front of the telly trying to while away the time until Shameless came on the box. At 7.30 pm I got a text from one of my ex-colleagues asking me "Are u coming tonight mate?" At first, I thought he was accusing me of watching hotel porn, then he phoned and informed me that they were sitting in a restaurant waiting for me...at my leaving do. They'd forgotten to invite me.

Corporate life certainly has its ups and downs but not being invited to your leaving do surely takes the biscuit. I guess I must have made a real impression in the 3 years that I was there, so much so that they decided to celebrate my leaving without me. I exacted revenge at the next days' meeting by whimsically browsing social media on my phone whilst they were all earnestly hunched over their Blackberries dealing with the usual corporate crises.

First Rides

This week contained some book writing relevance, or as we cycling authors refer to it, bike riding. My business mileage tally says 175 miles in the past five days. I spent Sunday wrestling with the winter bike in the garage. As per usual, my preparation was poor. The day before a big ride I decided to swap all of the Shimano components for Campagnolo. For any non-cyclists reading this, a non-technical analogy would be trading in a reliable Honda car for a swanky Alfa Romeo. The Honda will be cheaper, simpler and infinitely more reliable, but an Alfa Romeo is Italian which sounds better. I'm struggling to justify beyond that. It did not go well. After spending most of the day carefully routing and trimming cables followed by handlebar tape wrapping I decided to test the gears. I discovered that they didn't work. The shifters I'd lifted from an older bike were completely seized.

Helen decided that this would be the optimum moment to enquire whether I would be interested in going for a walk with the neighbours around a lake. The cacophony of swearing and hand mashing answered that query where a simple "*no*" would have sufficed and been more polite. Garages occupied by male cyclists need clear health and safety notices for all daring to enter. Fortunately, I have more than one bike. On Monday I headed out for 75 miles of Wiltshire's finest on my swanky expensive summer race bike. A very wise decision given that it was pissing it down and freezing cold. I rode off armed with a voice recorder and compact camera and quite enjoyed the luxury of stopping every few miles to waffle on about the scenery and take rubbish pictures. It made a refreshing change from the usual frantic training rides that I undertake where I am glued to the GPS screen over-analysing average speeds and heart rates. The voice recorder will certainly prove to be a useful tool, as long as I can learn to say something useful into it. One of the comments I played back later was "Remember to write something about the interesting tree", which would be great if I could recall where the tree was, and what was so interesting about it. I've got a lot to learn.

The day was punctuated by punctures, down to the racing tyres I'd fitted. This was gleefully pointed out to me by several golfers when I stopped to fix one at North Wilts Golf Club. I diplomatically bantered away with these fine, rotund tweed-clad fellows. Resisting the temptation to enquire as to the experience that led to their conclusion? We agreed that racing tyres and winter hedge cutting, never the twain shall meet. Speaking of Twain, wasn't it he that said *"Golf is a good walk ruined"*? I was too polite to ask. I rolled in the door an hour before dark, knackered but with half a chapter in the bag.

Tuesday was more of the same, apart from the glorious sunshine that greeted me as I left the house and stayed with me for most of the day. I had a beautiful ride on traffic-free roads and was starting to eulogise in my fortune at this being my working day until my knee coughed politely then began to shout. I've been suffering from knee pain for several months and thought I had cleared it, but after twenty miles it was announcing itself loud and clear through the layers of lycra. I soldiered on and a few miles later it began to fade leaving me to concentrate upon the task at hand. This went reasonably well, apart from a further three punctures and a poor feeding strategy. With twenty miles to go, I was starving and had nothing left in the jersey pocket. I'd forgotten to compensate for the previous day's riding by taking more food and caught myself eyeing up roadkill as calorific potential. Nevertheless, after 78 miles I fell in the front door and emptied the kitchen cupboards into myself. Surely a fitting reward for a productive two days and enough material for an entire chapter.

Wednesday and Thursday were photography days. Wednesday spent learning about it and Thursday driving around the place and doing loads of it. To be frank the results are pretty crap and will not make it into the book for the following reason. There are no cyclists in the photos which is not a great strategy for a book on cycling. Thursday was a day of clear skies and blazing sunshine, not the best light for capturing contrast in the sparse rolling hills of Wiltshire, the pictures look like they were taken on Mars. I was distracted by the two overturned cars I came across first thing in the morning the first overturned car had a woman next to it. I stopped and walked over to her carefully enquiring if she was ok? *"Yep, I'm fine"* she quipped casually as if nothing had happened and then updated her Facebook status. There are some tough cookies in this world I'll tell you, I'd have been a quivering wreck if I'd just totalled my Fiesta into a ditch. She seemed to be acting as if this happened every day. Maybe it does, if so I'd advise others to avoid Hackpen Hill during rush hour. Friday was a writing day. I'm knocking on the door of 10,000 words already and will soon offer some over to my family for peer review. My 13-year-old son, Jake, asked *"Can we be honest when we give feedback?"*. I'm dreading this.

Software

I've been doing this for a month now and I'm wondering if I've now earned the right to call myself an "experienced cycling author". I doubt it as yet again I find myself dealing with adversity that is entirely of my own making. I began the week on a low, back in the dentist's chair to be precise as he removed a temporary crown placed previously and replaced it with half the UK gold reserves. I got talked into this by him when I had a job. Now, I need to advise my undertakers that the entire funeral can be funded simply by removing half the contents of my gob.

From the dentist, I went straight to my doctor to get my knee looked at. She admired it for a few minutes then asked me if there was anything else. I told her of the niggling pain that has been troubling me for a few months and was despatched to the hospital to have an X-Ray. I'm pretty sure I was victim to a time-honoured hospital prank during this procedure as the staff made me stand in my pants and make poses curiously reminiscent of those shapes thrown by Bruce Forsyth at the beginning of the "Generation Game".

I get the results in two weeks. I suspect the diagnosis will include the words "old", "idiot", "wonky" and probably "overuse" somewhere within. Truth is that it is almost definitely down to my incompetence when specifying the right bike size and subsequently setting it up incorrectly. Luckily, I had squirrelled a bit of cash away for this very situation and Helen will have her head in her hands yet again when the new frame arrives next week. This time it's OK, it's tax-deductible.

Back to the book. This week has involved a lot of fettling, but not of bikes, more computery type fettling. I decided that I would give myself a morale boost by attempting to lay out a full chapter. Contrary to popular belief this is a little more involved than typing into Microsoft Word and importing the odd picture.

I spent Monday and Tuesday getting to grips with Adobe Indesign which I am reliably informed is the industry standard for laying out illustrated books and magazines. I ran it for the first time, navigated to the *"Tools"* menu and looked for the menu item labelled *"Create a great looking cycling book with zero knowledge of typography or layout"*. This didn't exist, so I immediately shat myself and clicked *"Quit Indesign"*.

I mentioned *"adversity of my own making"* and this is exactly the sort of thing we are talking about. I thought that laying out a book would be simple and there would be packages with menu items that were in tune with my needs, for example:

"Place picture where it will look good, size it right and automatically reposition everything else"
"Import text from weirdo authoring package that we've never heard of but I'm sure is good value for a cheapskate like Dave"
"Copy layout from an out-of-print climbing book that sort of looks like the way Dave would like his cycling book to look"

Instead, I'm faced with:

"Layers/Object Styles"
"Conditional Text"
"Clipping Paths, Kerning and Transparencies"

My naivety cost me a day of begging Google to provide me with an insight into the publishing industry. Fortunately, Google loves me and link by link I started to understand what I should be doing. After a few hours I had text on a page, then I broke it into columns and finally I managed to add a picture with the text flowing neatly around it. Late Tuesday evening I was staring at what almost looked like the chapter of a book. Adversity had been overcome and I became quite excited that a small portion had taken shape. I then tried to design some graphics to augment the chapter and yet again my world fell apart. I need to face facts, I can ride a bike for long distances, I can even write semi-coherently about the experience and if I press the shutter enough times, probability coupled with modern technology dictates that I may capture a photo that could go with the writing. But I cannot design graphics. Full stop.

I sodded about with Photoshop Elements for hours and hours to no avail. Everything I came up with was on a par with the Olympic 2012 logo apart from the fact that I couldn't even manage to suggest fellatio within the design. That evening I gave up and texted my hugely talented, graphic designing sister and asked for a bit of help. Sally spent a couple of hours beating my poor designs into submission and the result has given me a real lift.

Putting the words and photos aside, the book is now looking great. I had a vision at the start of this project and Sally has just about nailed it for me. Years in IT management have taught me that I now need to work hard on a strategy for taking 100% of the credit for this, but I've been doing that for twenty years so it shouldn't be hard.

On Wednesday I mounted the bike as a bit of light relief to the IT shenanigans of the previous days. I set the alarm for "bloody early", shoved porridge down my face (and my t-shirt), drove down to the coast waving merrily at the commuters going the other way and bashed out a glorious 80 miles of sea, moors, forest and empty roads in reasonably clement weather. The ride was so good that I forgot to stop. I wittered on into my voice recorder and studiously obeyed the directions of the GPS until after 65 miles I realised I was utterly desperate for a piss. As always, this occurred on an open section of the road with a complete lack of trees, bushes or bus shelters to hide behind. I briefly considered wetting myself and then upping the pace for the final twenty-five miles to dry out. But became worried that it would filter down onto my water bottles and urophagia is not on my tick list. So instead I stopped, faced away from the road and achieved the same result by not checking wind direction.

Tommy Godwin

I'm sure that even the most committed non-cyclist will realise that Coventry is not exactly the heart of pulchritudinous British bike riding. However, it is home to the Coventry History Centre where I spent a fascinating day researching further details of my cycling hero Tommy Godwin. Tommy holds the record for the largest number of miles cycled in any single year, 75,065 of them to be exact. That is over three times around the world, including oceans, an average of over 200 miles every single day for 365 days of the year. Tommy carried this out in 1939 and his bike only had four gears and weighed about the same as my entire collection of steeds. I've now managed to piece together his entire year. Tommy's achievement is stored firmly in my mind locked behind a safety release called *"For Emergencies Only"*. I use this section of memory for the moments on the bike when things become desperate, in my case, usually 60 miles into a ride when I've been a silly boy and ridden beyond my capabilities. At these moments I'm found chewing away at my handlebars and feeling desperately sorry for myself. I tend to slide down that self-pitying slope imagining that nobody in the world can have suffered to the extent that I have at this moment. Then I smash the glass protector and pull the lever of the emergency safety release and Tommy's ride comes flooding out.

I realise that he must have crossed this barrier daily for an entire year, I realise that I am suffering at a point where he had another 140 miles to go, I realise that I've got an armoury of modern cycling weaponry and nutritional supplements at my disposal and all he had was a heavy steel bike, bread, cheese and milk. These simple facts keep the mobile phone in my pocket and remove the temptation to call Helen and feign some obscure and un-fixable mechanical problem with the bike. I can almost hear Tommy (or "The Whip" as his club mates called him) berating me to "Cyclist the Fuck up" and get on with it.

And on Wednesday I reached for this lever.

I'd planned a route through Kent, a fantastic loop steeped in history and parts of which were used in the 1994 Tour de France on one of its fleeting trips to England. The major flaw in my planning was the cursory glance I made at the height profile. This glance should have been a long hard stare as I would have then realised that the route snaked over 7500 feet worth of climbing, or one-quarter of the way up Mount Everest to give it some context. I must have failed to salute a magpie or something as my luck took a further dive the day of the ride. The wind decided to swing around and blow from the southwest knowing full well that the last 30 miles of the ride were heading in the same direction.

Suffice to say I found the ride slightly challenging. No, scrub that, let's tell it how it was, I completely and utterly died on my arse. I'm not used to riding long distances over shed loads of hills this early in the year. Equally, if I am going to do a hard ride I make sure that the wind assists me on the return leg when I'm at my most shagged out. The height profile for the ride adequately describes the dentistry of any large prehistoric predator with the largest tooth right at the end of the ride. Therein lies the ultimate failure in my planning. When the legs aren't quite what you want them to be start hard, end easy.

Some light relief on the final mile. I encountered four riders proceeding at a pace that could only be described as "chatting" and taking up the entire road. I gave my usual merry shout of warning which they ignored completely. Luckily I was able to squeeze through on the right and make progress. Guess what? every single one of them talking at the same time. I'll leave you to stitch together enough stereotypes to derive the sex of the riders. Or were they Italians in drag? They were oblivious to my passing and I was secretly proud of their deep immersion in the ride and/or the conversation. Oh to reach such levels of transcendence myself and not spend so much effort moaning about the final hill.

The rest of the week has been spent writing and I'm pleased to announce that I think I've found the key to the art of being productive. Quite simply you have to sit down and do some work. This was quite a revelation to me when I found that my word count goes up if I do some typing. Often in life, it is the simple most obvious solutions that provide the Eureka moments. And so I'm striding on towards thirteen thousand words worth of content, which is great progress and will be rewarded with the afternoon off today to go away with Helen and the kids in the van. As usual, this has coincided with severe weather warnings.

Dartmoor

If you are going to write a non-fiction book then it is probably quite important that you gather some content. When your book is about cycling that content can be gathered via several different mechanisms:

- listening intently to elders recounting their fascinating tales of the past whilst smelling of wee
- typing "cycling content" into a search engine and mercilessly cutting-and-pasting the results
- thumbing through old books in libraries wishing that Google would finish their grand project to scan and index all the world's information
- riding a bike around the place and gabbling madly into a voice recorder about views

This week I'd run out of elders, exhausted internet searching and was too flatulent for libraries so I resorted to the bike instead. I, therefore, spent Monday planning rides. This is "oh so easy" to do when you have a computer and a screen full of digital maps. Clicking merrily away at the route completely hides the fact that what appears to be a nice yellow line on the screen, is in reality a heinous shite strewn potholed lane littered with hawthorn cuttings and the natural habitat of reckless tractor drivers with huge great pointy pitchforky attachments on the front of their beasts.

And so, lulled into a false sense of security by my computer, I threw an assortment of cycling stuff into the motorhome and trundled off down to Dartmoor for the first big ride of the week. The "adventure" began before I'd even got out of the van, entirely due to my trust in technology namely the blind following of the sat-nav. I'd booked myself into a campsite on a farm, which should maybe be re-advertised as *"a muddy field"* if it is to properly adhere to the Trade Descriptions Act.

There are two approaches to this farm, the sensible wide one and, what can only be described as a *"small thin tunnel through trees"*. Unfortunately, the tunnel takes the direct route, and so did the sat-nav. I'm amazed I got the van through it with the sleeping bits still attached to the chassis. I nearly missed the farm as well. Luckily Mr Giles was waiting for me by the gate swinging a lamp to wave me into his field. How many times have I read of the woes of feckless sat-nav followers, and here I was gaining full membership of their clan.

The shower block advertised on his site needed a few upgrades. The loo had no light, resulting in my scariest ever poo. If I'd had the video camera, I could have taken the Blair Witch Project into new territory But being a hardy sort of fellow, I made the most of it, got a good night's sleep and headed out onto the moor bright and early the next day. I won't dwell too much on the ride as that is for the book. However, I will regale you with an interesting fact. Dartmoor is unusual geographically as it only has uphill. You can try all you like to go downhill but it just won't work. no matter where you cycle, you'll be going uphill. And I did what felt like 70 tortuous miles of uphill.

Going back to the point I made earlier about digital mapping, none of these packages has a setting that allows you to display the ever-increasing amount of pain you will suffer as the ride goes on. If they did, the Dartmoor ride would have started at level *"ouch"*, moved on to *"amputation without anaesthetic"* and ended at *"please leave me here to die, I cannot suffer any more"*.

So, you get the picture that it was quite hard. And what better way to follow it with a short recovery ride in Exmoor. Well, that would have been a good plan if the recovery ride did not involve Porlock Hill. I've been slowly ticking off the climbs from Simon Warren's book *"100 Greatest Cycling Climbs"* and Porlock Hill is in it. Therefore, I planned a brief 25-mile scouting ride starting up this hill. Describing the ride up Porlock Hill without using cliches is almost as hard as cycling up it. The writer is tempted into adjectives such as *"brutal"*, *"fearsome"*, *"impossible"* etc. I'm going to try a different tack.

Imagine that you get on your bike and cycle up to the first corner. As you ascend Chris Tarrant pops up beside the road and offers you five hundred thousand pounds to get off your bike and walk. But, despite this offer you persevere, at the next bend, he doubles his offer to one million pounds, simply to get off and walk. You have to ignore this hugely tempting offer and keep riding but, as you round the corner, he doubles it again and walks beside you up the hill maintaining the offer for nearly three miles.

Hopefully, that conveys how hard this climb is at this time of year. The pain is so intense and the temptation to dismount so huge that only the mind can carry you up to the top. I dragged myself up it by imagining the huge satisfaction of continuously screaming "Fuck Off" at Chris Tarrant. The rest of the ride was a peach. Beautiful empty roads, a lack of rain and an absence Porlock type hills.

Later in the week, I drove to Wells to scout out a long ride that included an ascent of Cheddar Gorge. This was going to be a nice relaxing day out on the bike as Ian Ferguson, the "Points West" weatherman, had assured me that any rain should be gone by the morning.

Well Ian, it is nice to see you upholding the long-standing tradition of the UK Met Office for understatement. A more accurate weather forecast would have read something along the lines of *"Wherever Dave is riding ..it will rain"*

All was not lost as I was able to ride the bike up Cheddar Gorge. Normally I do this in the height of summer and the climb is made even more challenging by the deranged American tourists who block the lower slopes as they scuttle from twee shop to twee shop laden down with fancily wrapped cheese that is one quarter the price in Tescos. On a wet Thursday in February, the shops are mostly closed. The Americans are all safely tucked away in KFC and the gorge is empty.

It was like being in a different Cheddar. In the absence of tourists, the gorge had regained some of its wildness and majesty, despite 70

29

miles in the legs I felt energised. I even attacked a bit, until a little bit of Porlock still locked in the thighs cried *"Whooooa there boy!"*. But the climb is steady enough to gain a proper rhythm, I tentatively clicked down the block, gripped the brake hoods and lifted a Pantani fantasy from the memory bank. I was properly absorbed, engaged and yet lost within the climb. I lamented the end of the gorge as it winds out of the Mendip rock up onto the downs. I was soaked, tired, hungry and a little bit cold but all of these stimuli were overridden by the joy of the climb. I think I might copyright the phrase "The Climber Sutra" for experiences such as these.

It's moments like that which hammer home the privilege I have in my hugely supportive wife and family who enable me to undertake this project. I repaid that privilege by returning home with a black bin liner full of the wet muddy rancid cycling gear and depositing it unopened pleadingly close to the washing machine.

The week ended with writing. Fifteen thousand words in the bank with five thousand other little tinkerings that I've been messing about with. Life is now measured in the word count. I paid a visit to a physiotherapist for some further knee pain investigation. The good news is that there appears to be nothing pathologically wrong. I think this means that the bits are all there as they should be. The bad news is that I'm getting old and in his own words *"Like a car that has been running for years you need a bit of a service"*. The term *"service"* had me scared for a few seconds as he was massaging my leg at the time, but it turns out that this involves sorting out posture and balance. I get the feeling that it is a clever way of making me adopt humiliating positions in a gym and then paying for it.

Magazines

One man's junk is another man's treasure. Through a tangled web of connections, I was privileged to meet Adrian and Jean Cannings who graciously filled my entire car with Cycling Weekly magazines. Now to a household as cluttered as ours this may be seen as a huge backward step, even with the advent of recycling collections our paper mountain continues to grow. I don't understand where it all comes from? It's almost as if we are some sort of paper disposal unit for the rest of society who sneak their unwanted communications through our letterbox. The house is awash with computers, mobile phones, blackberries, iPads and even the fridge can probably tweet yet still people insist upon talking to us via the written medium. Most of these paper-based communications are backing up transactions that were completed electronically anyway. For example:

"Dear Mr Barter, I know you took out your hugely expensive car insurance with us over the internet for a pittance of a discount. You have received and replied to several emails, but here's a bit of paper with some terms and conditions in Times Roman font size 3 so that we can wheedle out of paying any claim you may deign to have in the future."

The rest are adverts for take-aways or even more ironically a leaflet from my local council telling me how well they are doing concerning their recycling target. I read it then recycled it immediately.

I digress. The cycling magazines are a gold mine for some research I

Dave Barter

am doing into the Tour of Britain. I have a cunning plan for a section of the book that will be dedicated to this very topic. Or that's what I'm telling Helen. The reality is that I've now got over three years worth of toilet based reading material in the bag which will make a change to sitting there and straining over a pizza menu. I'd like to write long and hard about all of the fabulous progress that I have made in terms of writing. However, this has been the least productive week of the project. The word count for the past five days stands at exactly zero. Like a naughty boy standing in front of the headmaster, I offer two excuses; mechanical ineptitude and over-ambition.

Let's take the mechanical ineptitude first. I've spent a large portion of the week building up a second bike. The reason I need a second bike is mechanical ineptitude. Despite having been riding for years, I appear to be incapable of properly maintaining a bike. It doesn't matter that I wash it and oil it after every ride, something serious will be overlooked and inevitably fail at the most inopportune moment. The zenith of this ineptitude was the failure to do up the rear wheel quick-release, closely followed by the failure to notice for over ten miles. I turned right onto a main road whilst shifting up and the wheel came out of its dropouts. All sorts of horrible tangly type things happened which resulted in a pile of metal and flesh neatly bisected by the centre line of the road. An oncoming motorist stopped and enquired as to whether I was *"OK"*, which was very polite, as the question I think he had on his lips was *"What the fuck are you doing playing Twister with your bike?"*

The business case for having two bikes stems from the fact that one of them will always be broken in some weird and probably expensive sort of way. Shares in Swindon bike shops were at an all-time high as news of a Dave Barter bike build was leaked. I think I have visited all of them over the past five days to purchase components that I have either forgotten about or broken when trying to install. And in this process I made a fatal mistake, I forgot to reassure the existing bike.

You may be tempted to think that bicycles are inanimate objects with no feelings, you are cruelly mistaken. The old bike sat in the garage brooding over all of the attention that the new bike was getting. It watched me arrive home with new cables, outers, seat posts, chains

32

and gears and sat resentfully as it heard the sound of indexing being properly set and brake block distances being adjusted. Before you accuse me of delusion, I can offer up the following proof. As soon as I had assembled the new bike and successfully carried out a test ride, the old bike exploded. When riding the new bike I'd enjoyed the crispness of shifting, a lack of squeaks and a headset that didn't judder every time the brakes were pulled. So I decided to have a slight fettle with the old bike and see if it could be improved. It was sat in the garage in a right sulk so I took it in to the warm house and sat it on a towel. It was looking a bit rough and I thought a refresh of cables would cheer it up. I eased off the handlebar tape and carefully, lovingly removed the cables from the right-hand shifter. I gently oiled the shifter and gave it a little test to see if things had improved and it wouldn't work, no clicks, no shifts, nothing. I haven't a clue what I did wrong, in fact, I didn't do anything wrong at all, this was the old bike being vindictive. Pound for pound there is nothing more expensive on a Campagnolo geared bike than the shifters. This single action had cost me over £150 as they can only be purchased in twos.

Because I don't have a job anymore drastic action was required and continuing the theme of mechanical ineptitude I decided to take it apart and see if I could fix it. Seeing as the shifter was now beyond repair, I turned my attention to the rest of the bike. A cursory attempt to fix the headset judder resulted in the rounding off of one of the Allen key bolts and a stem that is now a permanent fixture of the bike. I broke a gear cable stop trying to remove it. Typically, the bike has non-standard stops and I cannot find replacements anywhere.

You see, the bike had it in for me. It resented the fact that a younger colt had now entered the stable and was making me pay for it. I've learnt a valuable lesson here. In hindsight, I should have lavished attention upon the old bike and used *"pass-me-downs"* to outfit the new. I should have explained to it that the new bike was joining the fleet as an apprentice, to learn and properly earn its wings. Next time I'll not be so insensitive because at the moment the old bike is making me pay.

Next, we come onto over-ambition. This is all down to a single ride, the Greenwich Meridian, that has been an ambition of mine ever since my friend Bill mentioned it in the pub. He described a cycling challenge that as far as I am aware has not been attempted before. Knowing my luck this means that I will only be rider number 59,876 to complete it including Percy McCutherbert the one-legged Penny Farthing rider who did it in 1849. The route has required a huge amount of planning as it is well over three hundred miles long and includes a nice little trip through the centre of London.

This comes with its logistical challenges including the avoidance of one-way streets, flyovers, Jeremy Clarkson and bendy buses. I've spent the whole week glued to street-view trying to work out the best way through the maze. All other spare time has been spent desperately trying to augment my fitness as I want to get the route done in three days of hard riding.

As you can probably tell, I end the week not feeling like an author at all. The current emotion is that everything appears to be collapsing around me as I take on projects that are way out of my league. It feels a lot like it used to when I was working in IT, maybe I can delegate this ride to another? I wonder who's going to get the blame in the post-implementation review?

Greenwich Meridian

For those of you who were as bored and inattentive as I was in geography lessons, here's a quick recap. The Greenwich (or Prime) Meridian is the line of zero longitude from which other lines of longitude are measured. It runs from the north to south poles and luckily for me spends a short period striding boldly through England. I'd always thought it would make a great cycle route. Much more ambitious than a simple coast to coast as it heads right through the centre of London because it was derived from the position of the Royal Observatory at Greenwich.

Helen and the kids were roped into this plan and we decided to stage an attempt during half term, me riding the bike, the family looking on sympathetically from the camper van. On Saturday we drove to Newhaven and stayed on what can only politely be described as "the worst campsite ever". It was so bad that we did the washing up in their sink and then took everything back to the van for a good going over with anti-bacterial surface wipes. Drinking water was dispensed from blue hoses that I am convinced were connected straight to the gutters and we made the mistake of plugging our fridge into the mains, which tripped the entire site's electricity supply.

So, I was pretty happy to leave the place at 7 am on my bike for a short trip over to Peacehaven. As has become customary, I couldn't find the Meridian monument at the clifftop. It took a couple of miles of riding up and down the dodgy cliff path to eventually locate it and take a picture. I then pedalled north following a route that stuck as close as possible to the true line of zero degrees, only deviating for motorways or lack of roads. Within five miles my careful planning of the previous week had unravelled. Using Google Earth I had found a small tarmac road that followed the line out of Peacehaven, this looked rideable and even had cars on it, so it went into the plan. The problem is that Google had imaged this road in summer, I was riding it in winter when it was raining. Cyclocross riders would have got off and walked. The track would be well labelled as *"having a little bit of the Somme about it"* and after I'd finally negotiated the last crater and made it to tarmac road the shiny new road bike was beautifully decorated in brown. Luckily the next fifty miles up to London passed without incident and as I summited the North Downs at Titsey I met a set of roadies having a go at timing themselves up Titsey Hill, a classic and steep hill climb. My cheery "Hello" was met with looks of hatred mixed with bits of lung, they weren't very talkative for some reason so I left them to it and went on to do battle with the centre of London.

My urban route planning was spot on up to the Greenwich foot tunnel and I enjoyed hacking through the suburbs, shouting at cars and inventing new obscene finger gestures for the drivers who thought Sunday was a good day to "door" a passing cyclist. I now have the utmost respect for those riders who do this every day through the rush hour as I found it challenging enough on a quiet weekend. The worst offenders appeared to be the buses whose drivers have been fitted with a special set of contact lenses that render cyclists invisible. I lost count of the number of times they calmly attempted to kill me, the only strategy for survival is to assume that without exception they mean you harm.

I even had a tussle with a mountain biker. A "dude" pulled up next to me on a full-suspension rig at a set of lights at the bottom of the hill. He did not return my "Hello" at all but shot off at speed on green. Sadly his legs and gears failed him and I casually span past halfway up the hill with a further doff of the helmet. This went on for miles, he'd catch me at the lights, stare straight ahead, sprint on green then enter lactic threshold as I'd amble past and practice my sardonic yet brotherly smile. To be honest I felt bad for him as I was pretty shagged out and not really trying, his problem was that he was genuinely unfit and had forgotten to lock out his 160mm forks. Eventually, I got to a traffic light and sat there on my own, he'd jumped it and I mourned his cheery banter.

The plan was to cross the river at the Greenwich Foot Tunnel, but like the vast majority of British infrastructure, it was broken and so I had to take a diversion through the Rotherhithe road tunnel. I don't recommend this for cyclists, quite simply because it does not contain any oxygen. The next few miles were equally fraught as I dashed from cycle path to street to bridge to street to path to shopping mall, to back out of shopping mall to street to try and get past the A13 and on to Walthamstow. In short, I made it. Nearly thirty miles of really hectic London riding without a rest. I was completely shagged out. At around about 3 pm I dragged my sorry self onto a campsite in Hertford with 105 miles in the legs. I then had to wash the bike in near sub-zero conditions at which point Helen took a photo that we still refer to as *"that picture where Dave looks simultaneously malevolent and half-dead"*. The picture ages me somewhere around three hundred and fifty years. It does convey the utter shagged-outed-ness that I was feeling at this point. Normally I look like one of Take That. The damage of the ride and cold water was evident.

The next day I got up even earlier and left the campsite with the dawn chorus in full swing. This ride was another epic of 120 miles up to Boston. It benefitted from a characteristic that the day before was sadly lacking. Flatness. The route headed north over the fens and once past Royston was flatter than an M4 hedgehog. I've never ridden flatness like it. I come from Wiltshire and even the flat bits have hills. My legs were pretty wasted after the day before but even the weakest of efforts saw the GPS declaring my speed as 18mph. So you'd think the day was set to be pretty easy, well it was until I tangled with the A14.

I cannot for the life of me think what moment of madness caused me to plot a three-mile section on the A14, a dual carriageway. However, the "utterly utter" madness was in carrying on down the slip road into the maelstrom, just to see if it would get better later on. I had entered the fifth level of Dante's Cycling Hell. Lorries thundered past blasting their horns, cars came within inches of me at eighty miles an hour their drivers glued to their iPhones. I grovelled my way along the hard shoulder furiously scanning for bushes in a vain attempt to hide from the traffic.

I was saved by a B road. A short diversion led me back on route and into country lanes. The rest of the ride breezed across the fens without major incident. I spotted a few windmills, nearly rode into some huge ditches and wondered where all of the cars had gone. It was my longest day in the saddle this year, the mileage for the day stopped the clock at 122.

Day three was a mere sprint of fifty miles up to Cleethorpes. The roads went sharply upwards after twenty miles. This was a bit of a shock after nearly ninety miles of flat but variety is the spice of life and thus I enjoyed a bit of a tussle with gravity. The ride finished similarly to the start. Thirty minutes of riding up and down the promenade looking for the Meridian marker. Eventually, I found it and claimed the Greenwich Meridian as *"ridden"*.

Now, the pedants amongst you will be saying *"Hang on a minute Dave, there's still a little more land to go to truly finish the job, what about the bit to the east of Hull?"*. Well, I spent some time looking at this section and it suffers from two issues; it's pointless, and it's grim. The ride to get to these final few miles is a huge diversion and includes a traverse of Grimsby and then Hull. My view is that the spirit of the ride is a straight line North sticking as close to the Meridian as possible. If there was a Humber ferry, I'd have hopped on it and ridden the final few miles. But for now, the Meridian ride ends at Cleethorpes.

Peak District

You know that saying *"The best-laid schemes o' mice an' men Gang aft agley"*. Purists will applaud the original, not the anglicisation. To begin I'd like to ask since when has a mouse ever made a plan other than to shag, find some cheese, or get eaten by something? But with that ponderous question out of the way, I think it is fair to say that the schemes of this week have certainly "Gang aft" for me. I'd planned to spend days sorting out the writing that I have done so far. It needs to be edited in a manner that flows, makes sense to the reader and more importantly engages them. One of the greatest pieces of writing advice I was ever given came from Dan Joyce, editor of the CTC magazine. He sent me a commission with a paragraph along the lines of *"please don't write one of those 'I turned left at the junction and then rode down to the cafe' articles, you need to bring the reader into the ride"*.

At the moment most of my writing reads as if I turned left at a junction and went to a cafe, so it needs some "riffs" (to steal another phrase from Dan). All was not lost as I did get up to all sorts of other useful stuff that is related to cycling and some of it will even make it into the book.

I drove to Kent and took over 600 photos of cyclists taking part in the Hell of the Ashdown sportive. This has nothing to do with a lycra fetish and everything to do with the fact that they were riding in an area that is covered by one of my routes. The plan was that these photos would be awesome and save me having to return and stage some shots. Sadly of the 600, five can be classed as "ok" which is why I am taking steps to sort my photography out with the aid of a professional.

Seeing as I had worked the weekend, I gave myself Monday off to go mountain biking. That's as long as the term *"mountain biking"* encompasses *"riding a demo full suspension bike that I can't afford round Afan, returning home than buying it"*. I've had the *"it's the last bike ever Helen"* conversation. Her eyes glazed over and like a bored barrister, she pointed to the evidence in the garage. This episode takes me back to buying my first ever mountain bike from Mitchell's Cycles in Swindon. It was sold to me by Mr Mitchell himself and in his broad Irish accent he declared *"It's the only bike you'll ever need"*. I should sue him for misrepresentation. *"M'lud I refer the defendant to the significant holes in the plaintiff's bank account and the fifteen bicycles that have passed through his doorway since"*.

Tuesday was spent documenting the Meridian ride I did last week. The route needed a severe amount of tweaking to take out the many diversions and dual carriageways that I'd encountered on the way. This then left Wednesday for planning. I'd agreed to meet my friend Andy the next day and attempt a huge ride in the Peak District. You'd be surprised how much time goes into route planning. However, I can't escape the fact that the majority of the effort was spent gathering the paraphernalia required for a couple of days riding, stuffing it into bags, becoming unsure that it was packed, emptying the bag all over the floor again and then repacking it having discovered that said item was in a sock.

The next day I was riding with Andy, one of northern disposition. We set out to do the classic Tour of the Peak route. For those not familiar with it, draw a line that is one hundred miles long and inclined at 45 degrees from horizontal, that is probably a fair indication of the route profile. My poor choice of campsite dictated that we begin by climbing Winnats Pass. If you draw another line that is inclined at about 85 degrees from horizontal and is a mile long then you've crudely but effectively created an artists impression of the climb.

The fact that the temperature was hovering around freezing didn't help. At the top, we scooped up and untangled each other's lungs, reinserted them and toddled on to the next gradient-based challenge.

Thirty miles of this led to a cafe, Andy cracked first and within minutes Power Bars and Hi-5 were replaced with cappuccino and ginger cake. The cappuccino was suggested by Andy, he may have lost some "northern" credibility by straying from the hallowed tea. It was the right decision, those milky coffees carried us on for another 30 miles over just about every major climb in the region.

At 60 miles we parted company, Andy deserves a medal for riding this far, his first proper road ride of the year. I'd have made excuses at the cafe about a knee or something and sloped off home hours earlier. I needed to finish the whole route and had another forty miles to go. It was tempting to follow Andy back to his car, but he had reassured me that the climb to the Cat and Fiddle was "steady". Typical northern understatement. I chewed my handlebars, top tube, gear levers, stem and even the front wheel for a bit as I ascended over 1200 feet to some godforsaken pub at the top of a windswept moor with the wind sweeping right into my face at ever-increasing speed. I was bloody freezing, shagged out and the sun was doing its best to get to Australia as quickly as it could. Finally, the GPS proclaimed that my altitude was 1600 feet and I thought to myself that it must be all downhill from here.

Well, it wasn't. The Cat and Fiddle had got its height and it was determined to hang on to it. Now and then a little was given away only to be snatched back by some nadgery little incline waving two fingers at me. I made it back to the van after 100 miles and 13,185 feet of climbing, I've only ever done one ride harder than that in my life and that was in the Alps in the summer after months of training. Reviewing the route, I spotted at least two possible shortcuts that I had ridden past, I'm going to ask Andy if I've now qualified to be northern.

The next day Andy and I returned to the Peaks route to take some photographs. There were fleeting instances where we almost looked as if we knew what we were doing as we stood and discussed F-stops, depth of field and made rectangle shapes with our hands. It wasn't the best day for coming up with cover shots though, as the mist had descended and it was bloody freezing. For some unknown reason, my legs were elected as the pair that had to ride up and down each hill segment only to be told by Andy that we hadn't got the shot. He had some secret agenda going on. We were trying to exhibit the steepness of one particularly nasty corner on the Strines. Andy made me stand on it to get the focus right, then asked me to "step back a bit", then "step back a bit more". I was falling for the old comedy photography trick that usually ends with the subject falling into a pond. In my case, the pond was absent so I simply slipped on some spilt diesel and fell into the road. Coincidentally, Andy took his best shot of the day.

Plans

Almost one-fifth of the way into this project and I'm still riding the bike and attempting to write lucidly about the experience. To be honest I'd always wondered whether I would have cracked by now and skulked back to my old job with enquiries about "consulting". I was offered a little bit of wedge by another company to talk bollocks about IT to them, but I've held fast and wasted my time reading cycling magazines instead. You may remember that I acquired a huge volume of cycling magazines. This week I've been ploughing through them, gleaning all sorts of useful snippets of research and inspiration. This has not been the easiest task and my record is 75 magazines in one sitting. You'd have thought that sitting on your arse in a shed flicking through magazines would be about as taxing as reading a Katie Price novel, but you'd be wrong.

After 30 or so magazines I'd developed a weird form of RSI, my shoulder and left hand were both hurting from the repetitive strain of flicking through the pages. To overcome this, I tried a new technique of licking the index finger on the right hand and using a deft cross flick to switch pages. This worked 60% of the time, the other 40% simply deposited phlegm onto the page. So I tried lying on the floor instead, but this gave me a tummy ache and I was scared of the woodlice lurking near the skirting board.

This author lark is filled with hidden pitfalls. When you become a fireman or a nuclear scientist there are manuals and training courses that ease you into the profession. Where the hell would I find a mentor or guidebook that would inform me that attempting to become a writer comes with the risk of catching a strain injury from piles of magazines.

Anyway, enough of my moaning, let me do some for Helen by proxy. I've been thinking about the impact of my career change upon the household and Helen in particular. It would be tempting to imagine that I've turned her life upside down with the irresponsibility of leaving a good job and the chaos and insecurity that comes with this decision. However, I realised that not much has changed really because she is married to a cyclist, and being married to a cyclist is an absolute bloody nightmare. Let's take the house as a starter for ten. It's hard to find a room where cycling has not had a major impact. Starting with the kitchen, or more specifically the sink we had installed in the utility room to help with washing up and vegetable preparation.

Oh dear, it's full of cycling crap. Then we have the dining area that we spent ages sorting out, including knocking down walls and reflooring, it too is full of cycling crap. Moving on, we have the garage, whoops, lots of cycling crap. Then there is the spare room, TWO bikes, one on the turbo trainer and one on the wall (for the record, it's Helen's bike on the wall).

You'd think the bedroom would be a sanctuary devoid of cycling paraphernalia, think again, my bedside table is heavily burdened with books, a large percentage of them cycling related. Finally, we come to the shed. We built this as a playroom for young and old alike, the idea was that it was somewhere that anyone of us could go to escape the routine of day to day existence and murder some aliens on a games console (or murder a perfectly good tune on Dave's electric guitar). Currently, the shed is out of service, not due to any technical fault, but entirely due to it being filled with cycling magazines.

I don't care what anyone says, I know that other cycling homes are the same, because I've been in them. It's one of those pastimes that creeps into every area of the house like ivy and no matter how much trimming you do, it finds a way back in. This then got me wondering about other households, for example; what does a gynaecologist's garage look like? Would it be possible to live with a steam engine enthusiast? Does a campanologist fret for days about their doorbell chime being out of tune.

But coming back to the original point, you can see that I've spent years preparing Helen for this career move and I'm sure that she would agree that whilst there has been a slight increase in the volume of scuddy cycling shorts, it's pretty much business as usual in the Barter household as far as cycling tat is concerned.

Let's move on to a bit of necessary profanity. Previously I wittered on about the lack of flair and panache within a lot of my writing to date. So this week I applied myself properly to the task and to coin a phrase I used to use a lot at work, I've come up with a decent amount of *"fluffy wank"*. Don't bother googling *"fluffy wank"* it's not Australian for sellotape. *"Fluffy wank"* is that stuff that you don't need to make something work, but it looks a damn sight better when it's added to the mix. In my old days working in IT *"fluffy wank"* was churned out by our web designers when they took a break from lattes and chanting obscure Tibetan mantras. I need some of this stuff for the book and have spent a fair few hours writing depressingly few sentences. But I'm starting to get somewhere with it.

The IT professional in me could not be suppressed and I've even managed to create a process for writing some "fluffy wank". I wasn't sure whether to be elated or extremely depressed after developing a series of mind maps in support. This is a dangerous game. Mind maps will morph into full process charts, which in turn will require implementation plans and then quality plans and GANTT charts. Soon, if I'm not careful, I'll re-enter that wonderful world of technology projects where the actual doing of stuff will be eclipsed by the time and effort of planning to do it and realising that this time spent planning has meant that the doing can't be done now and more planning is required to work out how to do what you were going to do anyway in a shorter period but with the same amount of planning and control.

Cold

In 1898 HG Wells wrote the "War of the Worlds" and in that book, he made a subtle prediction that has proved correct across the centuries. The prediction was not that some spindly-legged aliens would take over town centres and dominate us all. So we can let Peter Crouch live as he offers no threat. The key postulation was that the common cold leads to downfall. I won't hesitate to agree with Herbert George, who showed great insight, but I'm not convinced that he'd applied "downfall" to the relevant user group. As far as I am aware we have yet to fend off any extraterrestrial master races by sneezing on them, maybe coughs and snuffles act as such a deterrent that they've all stayed away. Sophisticated alien spectroscopes have scanned our galaxy, identified earth-based snot and posted a bloody great "Biohazard..keep out" notice on the dark side of the moon.

But, the common cold has led to my sporting downfall on several occasions and this week in a cruel twist of fate the two sports I take part in were united by the disease. I was invited to dinner with a group of scuba diving friends. I've made a few bubbles in my time and we were going to discuss the feasibility of a few diving trips later this year. The diver's number one enemy is the common cold. To put it bluntly, it can kill you, going to depth with blocked up sinuses is an extremely bad idea and so as soon as you get a cold, you can't go diving.

Therefore, I was mildly surprised to find that dinner with the divers was punctuated with a soundtrack of sniffs, nasal grunts, throat clearances and coughs. The bloody divers all had colds.

Cycling and colds do not mix well either. It's not quite as extreme as scuba diving and I have yet to hear of a cyclist who has died as a direct result of a trip out on the bike with a head cold. However, it's never a good idea to cycle with the sniffles. Firstly, they have a bad habit of morphing into highly resilient, chest battering flu attacks and secondly every single piece of apparel you own soon becomes covered in snot. There is a distinct art to clearing one's nose when cycling and I can claim to be at the top of my game in terms of discrete nasal emptying. However, a cold puts paid to these hard-won skills as each snort releases a champagne supernova of the stuff all over your nice clean lycra. You end up looking like you've survived a stampede of snails.

I was sat there listening to the cacophony of illness wondering whether etiquette allowed me to get up, declare them "unclean" and leave. But being a polite, mild-mannered person I "grinned and bear" ed it. And caught the cold.

"What the hell has this got to do with writing the book?", I hear you cry. Well, quite a lot actually as writing a cycling book requires a large amount of riding to be undertaken, and as I have patiently explained above, colds are not conducive to large amounts of riding. I'd planned a huge great loop in Wales taking in several large climbs, and on Tuesday I set out to do it with the cold brewing. You all know how it feels at that point when you are well aware that you've caught a cold, but it hasn't yet got the guts to come out and show its true colours.

As I drove along the M4 and over the bridge I had misgivings. I had a bit of a headache, slight snuffles and soreness in the throat area. I pressed on regardless. I felt OK'ish as I straddled the bike but fifteen miles into the ride it was clear that whilst the engine had plenty of fuel it wasn't performing at all efficiently. I felt each turn of the pedal and my head seemed to be three times too large for my helmet but I wasn't prepared to abandon, the drive had been too long for that.

Fortunately, the ride I had planned was a belter. My woes were worn away as the road marched up into the Brecon Beacons, pain erased by views coupled with the tranquillity of a quiet mid-week bike ride. I stopped to eat something at the bottom of a huge great climb (The Bwlch) and heard a voice say "Hello". I looked from left to right searching for its owner, but they weren't there, it was only when I looked down that I spotted the guy on a handbike down at my feet.

He'd been paralysed seven years previously whilst out mountain biking and had lost the use of his lower body. Yet there he was on a bike, at the bottom of a major climb about to climb over 1100 feet using only his arms. We chatted for quite a while about his racing ambitions, he planned to travel to France, Spain and other countries to race with other handbike riders.

Eventually, we parted company and I headed off up the climb. It was going to take him a while to do it and he had shooed me on in front of him. I didn't say anything, but he'd proved to be the perfect antidote to my cold. There was me fretting away about doing a bike ride with a stuffed up nose when this guy only has one-third of his body available to him. He was out there on his own and had planned a pretty hefty loop unsupported. After that encounter my whole respiratory system obeyed orders and I just got on with the ride, (actually I was nervous that he'd come hooning past me with a cheery wave).

The cold gave me another day of respite and during that rest day, I'd pushed the word count significantly, until Thursday when I finally succumbed to its clutches. The nasty little germs headed south into my lungs. Old Herbert George would have been looking down on me with a wry smile as, like one of his fictional tripods, I keeled over and became completely ineffective. I tried my hardest to write, plan routes, think, research anything to move the projects forward but ended up defeated. I watched half an episode of Bargain Hunt.

The only thing I have to show for Thursday is some comfort food, homemade gnocchi in tomato sauce. Bollocks to the cycling book, I'm going to become the next Gordon Ramsey. I can swear as well as he can, my face is pretty cratered and I think Gary Rhodes is a twat.

After hours of self-pity, I reached for whatever remedies I could find in a wretched attempt to alleviate the suffering. I came up with three in ascending order of effectiveness; a lemon, an out of date box of Lemsip, a bottle of Talisker whiskey. After a few decent measures of remedy number three, I no longer cared about the cold or anything else, to be frank.

As the week headed for its end, I arose from my pit of despair and gave myself a right good kick up the arse. I sat down at the computer and planned a monster week of riding and writing. Finally, to make myself feel a little better I gathered a few statistics on progress to date:

- Total words written, all projects: 39,000
- Total photographs taken: 950
- Hours spent riding: 129.6
- Miles ridden: 1752
- Feet climbed: 121,639
- Number of punctures: 5
- Bikes purchased: 2
- Total income to date: £0

The last two key performance indicators are of some concern. The businessman on my right shoulder would like to hold a board meeting to discuss the balance sheet. But the entrepreneur on the left is shouting him down with words like "investment", "future return" and "get Helen to work more hours". I bet you didn't know that HG Wells was into cycling? He even wrote a short novel entitled "The Wheels of Chance", it's based around the character Mr Hoopdriver who is full of "Mitt-esque fantasies" and has shaky riding skills. Hmmm, I'm worried that Herbert George predictions go further than the potential impact of the common cold.

Wales

I wish to inform you of an observation that has origin in my tat filled attic. I was up there ferreting about in the mass of discarded toys, mobile phone chargers, book filled suitcases and dodging the odd bat. My task was to find some notes for a cycling article that I had written many years previously but I was quickly distracted by a folder entitled *"Continued Fractions"*. I opened this up and was presented with a sixty-page paper neatly handwritten by some mathematician who was attempting to bring clarity to a subject that is both obscure and complex. I won't go into detail, simply because after page three, I was completely lost. Huge great equations and words like *"incongruity"*, *"lemma"* and *"euclidean"* had me reaching for the kid's *"Hungry Caterpillar"* book just to reset my brain back to a mental level that I could cope with.

I put the folder down and then picked it up again wondering what on earth it was doing in my attic, then I noticed the author, it was me, I wrote it as my university thesis. I sat down on a rafter and stared at it for a long time. How on earth had I understood such an obscure subject? How had I found the time to write all of that? How had I managed to make my handwriting legible? Who on earth was the twenty-two-year-old who hammered that lot out, because it certainly doesn't feel as if it could have been me. I've spent years tinkering with all sorts of things, from mapping websites to desktop arcade machines to unfinished Airfix models that are still lurking in drawers somewhere. I'm notoriously bad at sitting down and focusing upon something for months until it's finished.

However, if I'm going to succeed in my writing projects I need to change my outlook. I've got to make sure that I attend lectures and listen to the tutors (riding the bike is the analogy here). I need to complete my research and properly document all of my sources. I must conclude and present my arguments clearly and effectively. I need to become that pimply-faced youth of twenty years and become very focused upon my "thesis".

Why has it taken me twelve weeks to come up with that revelation? The truth is that it hasn't. In finding that thesis I've gained more inspiration to do this thing as well as I can. This authoring lark does have its ups and downs and I do suffer from the occasional bout of self-doubt (if you define occasional as weekdays that don't begin with "H"). The thesis gave me a little boost, biologically I'm just about the same person that wrote that paper. Dentists, doctors and "stimulants" have taken a few bits out over the years. But if he did it, then I can. And so I started the week with a renewed vigour.

A whole series of new routes were planned including a couple of Welsh epics. Sunday's weather forecast can be summarised along the lines of *"This week would be an extremely opportune moment for cyclists to spin round Wales every day"*. And so the van was packed, the family abandoned and off I toddled focused upon my book writing research and objectives.

Well, when I say "focused" I suppose I ought to come clean with the fact that in addition to the road cycling paraphernalia, the van also contained two mountain bikes and Malcolm. Additionally, the van may have stopped at the Afan Argoed Mountain Bike Centre and Malcolm and I might have sneaked off for three hours around its trails.

I've justified this as business entertainment. Malcolm has lube running through his veins, bathes in Muc Off and slices pizzas with chainrings. As a fanatical cyclist and next-door neighbour, his services will be required in the future, so let's just file the Afan diversion as schmoozing and move on to the rest of the week's cycling.

The sun came out and with it my legs. I rode for ninety miles up and down many many hills in the Gower region. Cars were flashing me as the sunlight glared off my pale skin, but it felt so good to synthesize some vitamin D for the first time this year. During the ride, I came across a signpost that had me puzzled. It was advertising "Dog Holidays". Dog holidays? Whatever happened to kennels and how on earth do Dog Holidays work? I can just imagine Rover and Mitzi getting up before breakfast to throw a couple of towels over a sun lounger, spending lunch lying in the sun demanding cold Margaritas and then heading off for an evening's worth of Dad dancing to eighties music whilst off their heads on cocktails. I can't contemplate how anyone would pay good money to send their dog on a holiday.

Then I realised the genius of the enterprise. I bet the company owner has a fabulous brochure or website or video showing soft-focus images of labradors cavorting in daisy spangled meadows. The literature will promise that Bowser will spend a week being pampered, petted and well-fed all for a very reasonable (yet not inconsiderable) sum. The owners will be hooked, Bowser will be dropped off and left in the hands of smiling carers who can't conceal their delight at having Bowser as a temporary companion.

As soon as the car is down the drive. Bowser will be taken up the hill and shoved in a shed with the other "holidaying" dogs. He'll sup on Tesco's finest for a week until his owners return to collect him. A quick dust over and he is handed back. How the hell can Bowser grass them up? He can "woof" all he likes, they'll just think he was raving over the mini-bar (for which they will have been billed separately).

I regretted booking into a campsite at the top of a steep mile-long hill and the end of the ride nearly featured walking. Consolation was found in the views from the van and that rare adult treat. A whole packet of chocolate Angel Delight to myself.

The next day I drove to Pembrokeshire, diligently following my directions to a campsite that I had booked previously over the phone. The owner had informed me with great enthusiasm that the site would cater to my every need. I informed her that I had a motorhome, needed electricity and hard standing to park on. "Yes, yes, yes" she retorted, "We have all of that, it'll be fine".

I drove past this site three times until I finally spotted the sign and it was then that I realised I'd been talking to a world champion embellisher. The campsite was her garden. My van wouldn't have made the turn through her gate and into the mythical motorhome Valhalla. I rang the doorbell out of courtesy, but there was no answer, so I sodded off to a much more salubrious site complete with shower, flushing toilets and a Welsh landlady whose accent caused me some trouble. "Would it be ok if I stayed until 5 pm on Friday" I tentatively enquired? "Pobbleycym llanfarglythwingoggerith" she replied which I took to mean "Yes".

Photography

When writing anything remotely interesting the author must avoid all manner of cliches. This is particularly true in the world of cycling which is full of them, such as; "legs screaming", "lung-busting" or even the dreaded "I was on the limit as I...". I'm sure that pedants will now manage to find each of these in my writing somewhere, but while they are ferreting away, let's look at one of the all-time greatest cliches ever.

"A picture is worth a thousand words"

At face value, it seems pretty damned obvious, instead of reading a page full of tedious meanderings, simply glance at a diagram or photo and you've understood the concept. But some common sense needs to be applied as this, like all cliches, can be taken to the extreme. For instance, examining the novel "Moby Dick" written by Herman Melville, a book I've attempted to read following a recommendation, but ended up defeated by the early lack of whale action. Moby Dick's word count is an impressive 214,681 words, I've read about three hundred of them. But if we apply the cliche, Herman could have saved himself a whole lot of time and wrist ache with 215 photographs or illustrations.

I'd probably have made it to the end if Moby Dick had been delivered as a photo essay. The book would have begun with a picture of a bloke with a "Call me Ishmael" speech bubble. Next, we'd have all sorts of ships sailing all over the place with a mean-looking captain standing on the deck. Finally a dramatic shot of a whale, a rope and a startled captain heading to the bottom of the sea. Now you see how dangerous cliches are. I've taken a classic piece of literature that must be read, absorbed and considered, then reduced it to a pamphlet that can be read on the loo.

However, whilst I may not be the greatest fan of Herman Melville, I do have a sneaking admiration for the cliche. It's missing something for me though, I'd like to re-write it as; "*A picture gives life to a thousand words*"

The right image will draw the reader into the text, cementing it within their imagination and urging them to read further to "contextualise" its meaning. This is particularly important when writing about cycling and is vital to my project and therein lies the problem. I'm a bit shit at photography.

So after vowing for a long time to do something about it, this week I took action. I spent a day with a professional photographer reviewing the basics and learning some of the subtleties of cycling photography. Seb Rogers has spent many years in the business and is particularly well known for his mountain bike photography. I'd booked a day's tuition with him and he'd asked that I bring along a model to ride the bike up and down the road whilst we practised snapping. Kate Moss was busy so I fell back to Andy the Derbyshire whippet. He drove down the day before and we went out on a "recovery ride" which seemed to consist of riding for 30 miles at 20mph, having a cup of tea, then doing the same again.

Slightly tired, we met Seb in the Cheddar area and he went through some of the basics with me. One of them was the importance of dressing the rider correctly and he warned against the use of garish road club kits. I made a mental note to remove every single photo of me in Swindon Road Club blue and orange from the project. We'll come back to the dressing point later.

Seb very patiently sorted out my poor technique and provided pointers towards better site location and composition. Simple ideas were a revelation. There's me thinking photography is all ISO settings, focal lengths, shutter speeds and seriously expensive lenses. Seb refocused me onto *"the picture"*.

During the day he showed me compositional techniques that turn what was a flat road with a cyclist on it into a blur of action and excitement. He sorted out how I hold the camera and my panning technique. He also got me working outside of the auto modes of the camera, choosing my points of focus and making my own decisions. The day was a real revelation and I left with a head full of ideas along with a determination to come up with decent photos for the book.

Let's return to the dressing of the rider. Andy had ticked most of the required boxes for a cycling model/bitch. He wasn't covered head to foot in logos and his leggings and top were neutral enough to look good on film. However, Seb and I, for all of the right reasons, did not inspect Andy's arse region closely. This proved to be the undoing of what was probably the best shot of the day. It turns out that Andy's leggings had taken on a degree of transparency. As any keen cyclist will know, most of us eschew underwear when wearing lycra as it tends to rub. Seb had me working on a corner where we composed a dramatic picture of Andy sweeping round it at high speed, or *"the arse shot"* as Seb described it.

Sadly the combination of the light, Andy's tight lycra and its transparency led to the arse shot moving from light-hearted banter to reality. We did not spot this in the camera's viewfinder. But a quick review on the computer back at base showed that I had captured a perfect cycling moon. Andy has sworn to never help me again if I publish the shot in its full glory. [*Postscript: it's in the book, Andy does not speak to me anymore*]

Moving on from photography, I've been spending a lot of time researching Tommy Godwin for secret project number two (whoops, I've just given it away). As I've previously mentioned, Tommy holds the record for the longest distance ridden in a single year, a staggering 75,065 miles.

Using newspaper clippings and other sources I have managed to pull together a full picture of his year. This includes a spreadsheet that shows the mileage he rode each day. Being an ex-techie type, I have taken this further and loaded all of this information into a database. Some coding wizardry has connected this database to Twitter and I've set it up such that a daily tweet is sent to followers informing them of the mileage Tommy rode that day and his cumulative total for the year. Andy "The Arse" contributed another feature that gives an idea of the distance involved by postulating two towns that Tommy could have ridden between to achieve this distance. Seek out @yearrecord to follow the "Year Record" Twitter account. There was method in creating it that may well be exposed later in this book if I can remember.

Another highlight of the week has been the simple pleasure of letter writing. Much of my research has involved talking to an older generation of cyclists. Many of them are tech-savvy and communicate by email, but others are only reachable by post. During the last five years working in IT, I cannot remember writing to anyone via the Royal Mail. This week I sent ten letters, properly composed and formatted and signed with an ink pen at the bottom.

I am clearly getting old as I took real pleasure in weighing up the stack of hand-addressed envelopes, carefully sticking stamps upon them and ambling over to the post box to send them on their way. I found it interesting that a paper letter made me think so much harder about the message and its construction. My emails are dashed off with little thought, riddled with grammatical errors and spelling mistakes. The letters were formal, coherent and structured harking back to an age where communication had rules.

At school, I was taught how to structure and layout a letter. This made me realise that my kids are not given this advice today with email or social media. My old age is showing when I find myself harking back to the days of pen and ink. But apparently, I'm not old enough. I've been rejected from the Fellowship of Cycling Old Timers for being too young. At forty-four, I'm deemed a mere whippersnapper and have another six years to wait until they will let me in. At the age of twenty-one, you are told you have the key to the door and can do anything. Well, you can't. And I've got a long wait before I can feast upon their hallowed quarterly magazine.

Writing Style

According to the fossil record man never encountered a Tyrannosaurus Rex, some sort of David Icke type event wiped them out before we had a chance to say "Hello". I believe this is a very fortunate occurrence as the T-Rex would have posed a huge threat to mankind, mainly due to its spindly arms. There's an ancient man merrily hunting and gathering when up pops a T-Rex in front of them. The fight/flee impulse would have died in an instant as the caveman doubled up in laughter at the disproportionate dinosaur in front of him. It would have been like eating popping candy as the caveman giggled his way down the T-Rex gullet, still chortling at the arms.

Keen cyclists such as I, who work in offices are similarly proportioned. Below the waist, we are a mass of muscle, sinew, veins and rugged-looking knobbly bits. But as the eye travels further upwards it all starts to go to pot until we reach the willowy arms. All these arms ever really do is hold handlebars, type insults into internet forums and struggle to unwrap an energy bar. A cyclist's arms are next to useless for manual labour, as I discovered this week.

It's the Easter holiday. Fine for those being resurrected or getting married at the taxpayers' expense, but not so good for working parents. Helen is the only wage earner in our house so I bravely elected to stay home and look after the kids. Being blessed with teenagers entails physically prizing them off electronic consumer goods whilst chuntering on about how I didn't have a TV in my day and had to entertain myself with a stick. Therefore, it became clear that

I would not get a huge amount of bookwork done this week and so I turned my eye to several household tasks that had been neglected.

Task number one was the tree in our front garden. My father-in-law Barry or "Hatchet Baz" as he is known in arboreal circles, had recently deposited most of a tree on our drive. Barry cannot go past any piece of vertical wood without considering it as fuel. He keeps a chainsaw in his car's glove compartment and where most people would use it for road rage, Barry sets about any tree showing a momentary sign of weakness. His lumberlust was partially sated when he moved to a house without a fire, but as soon as we installed a wood burner in ours, Barry was back on the rampage.

My son Jake had arisen early at 11 am so the two of us decided to undertake a bit of father-son bonding and turn the dismembered tree into logs. Jake's job was "stacking" and I picked the short straw of cutting and splitting. My T-Rex arms gave out after approximately five minutes of using the axe and so I retreated to power tools. Wielding the chainsaw proved equally tiring and it took the two of us several hours to create a proper pile of firewood. At which point Hatchet Baz turned up with another tree. The imbalanced cyclist's physique was stressed further as the relentless cutting and chopping continued. I'm not sure I approved of Jake's smug tone of body as he lay in the wheelbarrow by the log pile awaiting another delivery.

Any sensible cyclist would have realised their limitations and decided against any further upper body stressing for the week. Remember, this is me and the word sensible was in that sentence. The very next day I decided to lay the foundations for the next generation bike shed. There is a distinct lack of floor space in our house due to bikes and so the decision was taken that a new shed was in order. I recruited the kids for help and they both immediately took on supervisory roles. I used my T-Rex arms to shift over a tonne of sand down the garden and flail about with heavy slabs. The result is a bit like me, not pretty but functional. However, my entire upper body was now devoid of Adenosine Triphosphate which meant that the evening's mountain bike ride had to be done no-handed. I'm considering a unicycle for these situations in the future.

There's been little progress on the writing front. But in a way, I am glad of the break. I don't mind stating that I've been struggling a bit with the tone and voice of my writing, what sort of style should I use for my books. There are several options available currently in use by other writers out there on the marketplace:

Mountaineering book style: "*As I summited the hill, missing three of my limbs and most vital organs, I bathed in the majesty and solitude of my surroundings by ignoring the lines of traffic either side of me. I was on empty having only eaten a raisin in the past three weeks but managed to keep going after sucking the nutrients from a daisy. I thought of those before me who had tried and failed, friends who had perished of old age, driven back by the "fuck that for a game of soldiers" mentality. Somehow after thinking of my daughter, drought in Africa, the magnitude of bankers bonuses and Kerry Katona, I managed to write a paragraph that at first glance is meant to take you into the mind of the climber, but in reality, is designed to make me look great*".

Mid-twentieth century cycle touring guide style: "*As I merrily crested the hill, having put in a sterling effort to see off the stiff climb, I reached for my neckerchief and dabbed my brow to remove a small pool of perspiration that had made its home above my forehead. "By Jove" we were on an adventure! Myself, my two wheeled companion and a knapsack of cheese, onion and milk to help us along the way. What joy! what elation to be had in this Britain that surrounds a man and his bike. I pulled up at my toe straps, gaily rang my bell and whistled "Jerusalem" as I advanced upon the road*".

How my daughter would write it: "*Well, I was like riding, you know when, like oh my god there was this hill, and it was like steep and stuff and so, oh my god it was like soooooo hard innit. Shudup! You wasn't there, like I was, and oh my god, lol! we were like all over the place. So I like facebooked Tanya at the top, she txtd Kyrone (but he don't like her really) and he like msn'd back that he'd lol at us, like it was bare funny*"

You can see, it's a difficult job to find the right tone, however, I'm not losing sleep over it as I still have a long way to go with the project and I think it is one of those things that will slowly fall into place.

Speaking of "*long ways*" this week delivered a relatively stable weather forecast. Which provided a great opportunity to head north. I struggle to contain my excitement about this. Scotland is my favourite place on earth. You can keep your temperate regions, stuff your arid deserts and shut up about the lack of rain or snow.

Scotland is like a very dodgy nightclub with two surly bouncers on the door. On your way in they warn you that something bad might happen, it could rain for weeks, you might be eaten by insects, you could inadvertently eat a year's calories in a chip shop. But still, you enter because no experience in the nightclub is ever the same. It's a wild place, man has tried to tame it and failed as the landscape growls menacingly down at the roads that traverse it. Riding a bike in Scotland is like taking a beating from your father with love the overriding emotion that is there to diffuse the pain. I always look forward to my thrashing.

Scotland

Us sporting types are strangely obsessed with doing things that are "est". Without these things, we have nothing at all to brag about in the pub or over the internet. An achievement needs an "est" attached to it if it is going to have any kind of bragging validity. "Last night I caught a fish in Dexter's Lake" will only really raise an eyebrow in the Sahara. However, "Last night I caught the biggest fish in Dexter's Lake" is going to attract attention.

"Are you sure? How do you know it was the biggest? Mick reckoned he had a ten-pound tench from there a few months back, was it that one? Have you got any proof? Show us the photos...."

Adding an "est" to any kind of achievement will either earn praise, stimulate debate or lead to outright derision. And it is no different in cycling. Mention the hardest road race to a cyclist and they'll come back with one that trumps it. A gramme can always be shaved off the lightest bike and don't even attempt to go near the fittest female cyclist debate.

Therefore I'm out to cause controversy in the book I'm writing by claiming to have conquered TWO "est"s in a single ride this week, the hardest and highest road climb in Great Britain. I might even elude to a third, with me becoming the shaggest out rider ever at the top of it, although I suspect there is some serious competition for this coveted spot.

In my view, the hardest cycling climb in Great Britain is the Bealach-na-Ba or Pass of the Cattle as it is known in English. It's the hardest for the following reasons; It starts at sea level. It finishes nearly 2000 feet later, no other public road goes this high. There is not much horizontal distance between the start and finish. It has a splendidly long section of 20% gradient. Lots of other books and internet things say it is.

This climb needed to be ticked for the book and so I tearfully left my family at the end of a week's holiday and went back to work in the depths of northwest Scotland. Usually, it rains when you are on holiday and as soon as you go back to work the sun comes out. I had a wry giggle at this as I pulled on a set of waterproofs and headed out of Kinlochlewe with the rain trickling down the back of my neck.

The ride started with a long climb towards Achnasheen, but for some reason, it seemed easy. I was on fire, riding at nearly 15mph up the gradient, it must have been the Spanish burgers I ate the night before? This continued to Achnasheen where the road did a U-turn towards Loch Carron and here I learned the truth. The wind was blowing at nearly 20mph into my face. I'd been flattered by a tailwind which subsequently flattened me as I turned and faced directly into it.

A dead stag by the roadside looked up at me sympathetically as it witnessed my struggle. I had a macabre sort of conversation with it as I ate an energy bar but I suspect it had other things on its mind.

The battle between the wind and me always falls in the wind's favour. It's not a fair fight, to be honest, as the only resistance I have to put up is ten weedy stones of weight and a couple of spindly legs. This combination does pretty well when having a stab at gravity, but it doesn't really augment the frictional force at the wheel/road interface much and so I suffer. To be precise I suffered for over thirty miles and the wind played its trump card after five of them.

For some inexplicable reason, the tempo of a few random gusts reminded me of the Wham song "Last Christmas". This then became lodged in my head as a particularly malignant earworm and led to a battle on two fronts. A physical fight with the wind, and a mental one to displace George Michael's moanings with something less annoying. What's worse is that I only know the following lines:

"Last Christmas I gave you my heart,

The very next day, you gave it away,
This year la la la la la la,
To give it to someone special"

I haven't a clue what the "la la la la la" bit is which made it even more painful as this couplet went round and round my head. Not only was I stuck with this annoying tune, I didn't even bloody well know the words. And so the trio of George Michael, the wind and the rain did all they could to sap my energy before I arrived at the bottom of the climb.

I stopped to take some pictures as a car with a strange-looking bike on it pulled up and disgorged a rider. It took me a while to work out that the bike had tri-bars on it. The tall gangly rider chucked leg over this machine, got into an aero position and shot off up the climb. His family gave him a few minutes then drove off after him in support. I immediately got the hump over this. Firstly, he'd cheated driving to the climb, I'd sweated out forty miles before I got to it, and secondly, he looked a right twat and was giving us cyclists a bad name.

I gave him an extra five minutes head start to prevent any kind of macho ding-donging on the climb. Looking up this monster, the last thing that I needed was a race to the top. The climb description shall be saved for the book. But you will be pleased to know that I made it and summited thirty seconds after the cheating time triallist. This just goes to prove that George Michael is much more effective than tri-bars on large Scottish road climbs. He gives you a four and a half minute advantage and only makes you feel a twat.

After the Bealach it was off to the Isle of Skye for some more riding and writing. This was a long drive in the motorhome and I arrived mid-afternoon with not enough time to complete the ride. Instead, I put on some red socks, donned my rucksack, packed an apple and headed off for a quick walk into the hills. I knew of a path that led to the base of Sgurr nan-Gillean, a particularly fearsome Cuillin mountain, and I planned to go and look up at it. I had no intention of climbing it whatsoever, as I knew it was very high and very hard it has a rock climbing grade.

Toddling along the path I met another red sock festooned walker,

Mike. He was on his way to the top having failed at a previous attempt due to adverse weather. We had perfect sunshine and no wind. The conditions could not have been better and as we got higher we met other walkers coming down. I asked them what it was like at the top and without exception, they all said "*It's fine mate, not that bad at all*".

I should have realised that these weren't walkers, they were serial mountaineers or just plain hard Scottish types who are made of girders. Mike worked on me a bit further and suddenly the summit bid was on and I committed to completing the route with him. Things gradually got steeper and harder as we got higher, but so far I was within my comfort zone and confident that I could make it to the top. That was until we met our first English bloke on his way down. He looked a bit sweaty and we asked him how it was upon the ridge. "*Fuck me it was scary, I fucking shat myself up there mate. There's a couple of places where I thought 'Oh my God, Jesus Christ*", was his succinct reply.

I started to give Mike a speech about going cycling the next day and saving my legs etc...He just pointed upwards and so that's what we did. The exposure was bearable most of the way to the top as we followed a shallow ridgeline. However, 100 metres from the summit it all disintegrated into a high level exposed rock climb. The harsh gabbro rock opened up a small cut on my finger and I bled all over the place as we climbed higher. And I mean "climbed". It turns out that the English bloke was right as far as I was concerned and eventually Mike and I perched on the summit admiring the view. Well, Mike was, I was clinging to the minuscule amount of rock available and wondering how the hell I was going to get down.

The problem was that in my haste to get it all over with I had not taken the time to remember the way up. This had consequences when we were surrounded by 1000 foot drops on all sides. Gingerly we began to make our way down until I spotted a dabbing of blood on the rock. Salvation! Like Hansel and Gretel following a crumb trail, I made my way down the climb by following my discarded blood.

Five hours after setting off the two of us clutched pints in the Sligachan Inn and bathed in the achievement. Mike had ticked off another Munro, and I was just happy to be alive. Although it turns out that my legs were not. The previous day's "hardest" climb and a lack of walking muscle memory meant that my legs began to seize. The next day things were much worse, they simply did not want to walk at all, and I had a seventy-mile bike ride to complete. Attempting to walk made me look as if I was trying to impersonate a duck, but I had to do the ride as the weather was perfect and opportunities such as these do not often arise.

Strangely, the bike muscles appeared to work fine. Which must have looked odd at my cafe stop as I gracefully pedalled to a halt then waddled in some weird sort of ostrich parody to the counter. I was immensely glad of this as the ride around Skye was perfect in every way; weather, scenery, empty roads, hills, valleys, sea views and a curious hare that watched me pass quizzically rather than running away.

This theme continued in the Scottish borders where I found roads and hills that seem to be off the motoring map yet designed for road cyclists. The weather remained on my side for the remainder of the week and I left Scotland with another three chapters in the bag. Driving home I regained radio reception on the M6 and was informed that whilst I was indulging in my Scottish odyssey others were being forced to camp out on the streets of London in deference to the monarchy. As I admired the lorry drivers on either side of me who were controlling their vehicles by mobile phone I reflected on progress to date. Great British Bike Rides is back on track after a very productive week. The trip has inspired me even further to do all I can to cement the joys of British cycling into as many minds as I possibly can. This has nothing to do with avoiding a proper job whatsoever.

One of them days

Didja' ever
Didja' ever get
Didja' ever get one
Didja' ever get one of them
Didja' ever get one of them days, boy
Didja' ever get one of them days
When nothin' is right from mornin' till night
Didja' ever get one of them days
Didja' ever get one of them days

My ability to remember and recall facts is by no means Olympian. It hardly even ranks at pre-school sports day as evidenced by a recent sound thrashing I took at Trivial Pursuit. So when I state that I think Elvis sang the above-mentioned lyrics I will undoubtedly have made a mistake. But I don't care, because they are very apt for the week I have just had. Although I would like to inform Elvis that I had not one, but two of "them days", oh, and it should have been "those days" Elvis, but I'll let that pass.

The first of "them days" occurred on Wednesday when I set out to do a route in the Cotswolds. This had been designed by Malcolm the Elder who used to be my Club Captain in the Swindon Road Club. Malcolm has now been promoted to the heady heights of President, but in his lowly Captain days, he was responsible for planning the weekly Sunday club run.

Malcolm has a particular talent for finding roads that do not exist and some roads that should not exist. He is a walking Ordnance Survey map and knows every nook, cranny and pothole of southwest England. If any of our club rides ventured off course onto uncharted lanes the cry would arise that we had "done a Malcolm" and a hasty retreat would be beaten.

Therefore, I knew that the Cotswolds ride Malcolm had designed for me would be full of adventure and away from humanity. I set off from Fairford on a beautifully sunny day, awash with a mixture of gleeful anticipation and grim foreboding. However, within five minutes I had "one of them days". Quite simply, I wasn't working very well.

It's hard to put into words the problem I was having, it wasn't profound tiredness, it wasn't a cold or flu or stomach bug. It was almost as if the engine room was suffering from a bout of apathy. I wasn't going particularly slow, but I couldn't go fast. I didn't feel terrible, but then again I didn't feel good either. Eating, drinking, changing gear, whistling all failed to alleviate the symptoms so I had to resign myself to having "one of those days" and plodded on.

This has consequences for the book. As not only was I not riding very well, I wasn't describing it into the voice recorder in a professional manner either. Replaying my comments that evening made me wonder whether Jeremy Paxman had hacked into it and overridden my route descriptions. This went on for 85 miles and to be honest I had spent most of them looking forward to getting back into the car and driving home.

The only moment of respite occurred when I happened upon a little old lady riding an electric mobility scooter. I drafted her for a few miles to rest before summoning up the energy to overtake and mouth a cheery "Hello".

Having had "one of them days" I didn't really do Malcolm's ride justice. This is a shame as it was a real "lane fest" and I hardly saw a car all day. I've put off writing it up until I am in a better mode.

I resolved to not have "one of them days" the day after and sat down to do a little bit of computer programming. This was driven by laziness as I've worked out that the book needs some graphics and that

I could auto-generate the graphics from some data I have. This is always a good idea where I am concerned as the only thing I can draw is an Oyster Catcher.

This stems from junior school where my teacher asked us to draw our favourite animal. Even at the tender age of eight, I knew I was crap at art so I scurried through an animal book looking for something easy. I had to skip the worm as I couldn't embellish it enough to warrant favourite status. But the Oyster Catcher looked dead simple. Black, white with a long orange beak and not much else. So I drew it and handed it in, a puzzled teacher filed it next to the lions, tigers, dogs, cats and proper animals.

Back to the plot. I sat down in front of my computer and proceeded to give it instructions to draw nice looking things on the screen. This should have been easy as I've spent twenty years in IT and computers are my mates. But, I "had one of them days". Everything that I tried, failed. The computer resolutely refused to display any graphics, instead, it spat out messages like:

"Invalid reference to an unallocated pointer"
"Syntax error at line 67 unexpected "fuck off" in for loop"

No problem, I thought initially and fired up the internet. However, it was having *"one of them days"* as it was chock full of people asking how to deal with error messages like "Invalid reference to an unallocated pointer" and pictures of tumbleweed. It took over twelve hours of work to get my data into the computer and I finally called it a day at 10 pm. I'll return to this particular problem next week when hopefully I will have nothing in common with Elvis.

I needed a boost on Friday, luckily it came. I spent a lot of time on book design and templating. I think I've cracked it and with a little help from others, I should soon be in a position to start constructing it properly. At the moment it is spread across several software packages. Once the template is done, the book can begin to come to life properly and I may even show it to some publishers.

I also persuaded Malcolm the neighbour to help me. Based upon this week's experiences I think I can safely say that Malcolms are without doubt incredibly useful. If you need anything done scout around for a Malcolm and you'll quickly find one willing to help. The second Malcolm agreed to come out and do some photography with me. Which gave me a chance to put all of the advice Seb Rogers had given me into practice.

I met Malcolm at Hackpen Hill, he lycra'd up and was complete with a properly clean bike. I was holding the camera and shouting instructions. We'd set out to get some good shots of a cyclist and the Hackpen White Horse within the same frame. Malcolm obeyed orders and rode up and down and I snapped. The results are fifty times better than anything I've ever taken before, wholly down to Seb's advice on composition and camera settings. I'm a million years off being a professional photographer but I think that a number of the pictures of Malcolm will make it into the book.

Self Employed

In October last year, my intentions to leave a proper job and follow the path of self-employment were broadcast to friends, family and work colleagues alike. I must confess that there were not many naysayers. Yes, there was some bored resignation, a few "tuts" and a decent sprinkling of "good riddance", but in the main, most people seemed to think that working for yourself is pretty much an ideal scenario. Especially when it involves your passion and is entirely unrelated to XML. Well, it's week nineteen now and I've given some time to reflect on the working life of the self-employed home worker. I've realised that the office-bound have never had it so good. To illustrate this fact I'll take you through a typical working day.

The alarm goes off at 7 am and we all congregate in the kitchen for breakfast, well when I say "we all", three of us do whilst a fourth family member lies in bed and groans. This is the family member who has the enviable talent to be able to sleep at any given moment, in any given situation, for huge lengths of time. The rest of us are borderline insomniacs. We eat breakfast whilst shouting up the stairs until a mass of hair and wrong-way-round school uniform appears at the bottom.

I calmly read the paper whilst the others frantically search for work passes, phones, homework, shoes, keys, PE kit and Shergar. I'd help, but the most effective way of finding anything is to ask my wife, and she is the one looking for the stuff in the first place. Asking her would possibly create some dangerous recursive reaction that physicists would find difficult to explain. So I usually provide my stock line of

"Where did you see it last?" and go back to the headlines.

Suddenly, they're gone. I'm alone in my dressing gown covered in toast. There's nobody at the school gate ready to berate me if I'm late. There's no factory clock or office manager or security guard to report me for tardy timekeeping. Just me and some toast. The first difficult task of the day is to motivate me to get on and do some work, oh..and get dressed and shave and stuff, it is so tempting to simply park myself in front of the computer dressed only in pants. Would you feel dirty if you knew I'd typed this nude? Eventually, I make it to my little office and stare down at the desk. It's dusty, disorganised and covered in crap. Office workers have cleaners and clear desk policies to ensure that each working day they arrive at a pristine workspace ready to rock. Me, I have to sort out the mess from the day before myself. This provides a nice thirty-minute distraction as I shuffle paper, reorganise my stationary, put my entire cycling literature collection back on the shelves and desperately search for the "to do" list.

And here's another area where we differ. When I was at work I had managers and colleagues and charts and plans and calendars and all sorts of other stuff that meant when I arrived at work I knew what to do. If I didn't, there was someone there to tell me. Prioritising tasks in the office was simple, all you had to do was to listen. People would be shouting at you from all directions, across the office, down the phone, by text, via increasingly impatient email or by proxy using a carefully crafted "grass" to drop you in the crap. All you had to do was sum the volume of moaning on each task and address them in order of loudness.

I now have to do this prioritisation myself and the list is often something like:

- write 5000 words lucidly and in a grammatically correct fashion
- carefully lay out a chapter
- construct striking graphics that fit with the theme
- diligently research a geographical or historic feature
- write an awesome code routine

- plan a cycling route
- update website

The following items are never on the "to do" list:

- browse internet cycling forums
- stare inanely at social media
- look at body parts in the mirror and wonder how they grew that way
- read cycling magazines trying to avoid the adverts
- stroll to the bike shop, purchase cycling components

After I have completed all of the second list I stare forlornly at the first wishing I could delegate it. And there's another facet of office life I miss, delegation. It used to make me smile when my boss advised me that the key to success was delegation. If this is followed through, the lowest echelon in any company would do 100% of all work with tiers of managers above them furiously delegating down the tree. Which is how it works for me as all tasks without exception are delegated my way.

Eventually, I pick the easiest option from the list and get on with it. This lasts about ten minutes before I remember something of interest in the fridge. So work is parked yet again in favour of snack construction and being away from the office I can eat whatever I want without any kind of derision.

I've had marmite on toast with scrambled egg, garlic sausage apple and salad cream sandwich and, an amazing delicacy, fruit yoghurt with jaffa cakes crumbled in. All of these are wrong, each one would have resulted in a week's worth of piss-taking were I working in an office. But working at home means I can eat what I want and whenever I want, which has an obvious downside, an obscene calorific intake.

Somewhere near midday, the postman arrives with a sack full of bills. I then get to spend an afternoon, as many freelancers do, hiding behind the sofa hoping that the bills won't find me. In the old days when I worked in an office, bills were not such a huge problem as they were covered by my salary. All I had to do was turn up each day and argue a lot. Now the bills find their way into my savings account. Each hurts that little bit more than it used to as it eats into my future holiday and bicycle component whimsy.

It's at this point that I need someone to moan at. But the house does not have a watercooler, and even if it did, I would be the only one standing there. There is no doubt that working from home comes with the significant disadvantage that the only company you have is your own. Which is a problem if you're a miserable bugger like me.

To make it worse, most corporates frown upon social networking such as Facebook, Twitter or anything that isn't directly generating shareholder value. People who work in proper offices are not to be trusted. Therefore, I can only chat online with my super-geeky mates who have hacked their way around the ban. This is a problem as all they want to discuss is function prototyping or episodes of The Big Bang Theory, they have no time for my various woes.

And so another afternoon will pass with me talking to myself or the radio. I flit around the various tasks that need to be done and restrain myself from revisiting the fridge just in case there is something that I haven't eaten. If the sun's out, I'll go for a ride.

Going for a ride instead of working sounds like a perfect existence. However, it is not as simple as that. Going for a ride is procrastination, whatever I was doing or was about to do will now not be done and I'll have to do it later. My office colleagues are typically done with work at 6 pm and therefore free to watch the One Show without any guilt at all. My wasted hours messing about on the bike force me to work an evening shift, which means Eastenders and Coronation Street are mysteries to me.

There is also a whole myriad of other benefits that I miss out on as a home worker; The annual appraisal, now I have to call myself an idiot once a year instead of having someone else do it for me. Human resource policies, I have nobody there telling me that I am valued whilst handing out more money to other people. Car park spaces, I have one and am unable to moan constantly about the lack of it. Pension, actually, that is not strictly true, I have plenty of other places to put money where I will never see it again

You'll understand that being self-employed has its pitfalls. Your daytime social life is compromised, your TV viewing habits are restricted and you'll eat all manner of strange concoctions that Greggs will never purvey. You'll go cycling when you should be working and there's nobody there to sue if you feel a little bit left out in the workplace. So while you are all sheltered in your air-conditioned office, receiving praise and direction from your manager, eating proper sandwiches and looking forward to an evening with Peggy Mitchell. Think of me sitting in my pants suffering for my art.

Numbers

Normally when the government write to me it is a polite but firm request for money, which is subsequently used to kettle students or buy lodges for ducks. Therefore, I was mildly surprised to receive a letter from them expressing concern that I was getting old and suggesting that I get myself down to the doctor's pronto for a check-up. They'd even made an appointment for me to hasten the process. The letter attempted to reassure me that this was normal for men of my age, just to make sure I asked around.

"Ah yes, the old 'cough and drop' check", one of my friends replied. I was immediately filled with terror. I'd managed to get to my ripe old age without ever experiencing a doctor's hand rummaging around below the waist, despite spending a year at university round the corner from St Barts medical school. As a cyclist, I have experienced many and varied forms of pain/humiliation but the testicles have been largely absent from these experiences, due to the cold.

I fretted about this for days and then expanded my panic further by considering the prostate. As we get older, we males become more susceptible to prostate cancer, so I imagined that I'd undergo some form of test. Which would possibly involve latex gloves and lubricant. To be frank I had no idea what would await me in the doctor's surgery. So on Tuesday, I went for a long pre-humiliation bike ride followed by an hour's worth of scrubbing and trimming in the shower. I spent far too long on underwear selection (for a man) and nervously made my way to the appointment.

Terror was utterly compounded when my name was called out by a young lady in a nurse's uniform who firmly gestured towards the outpatients' room. I stammered my way through a short questionnaire as she filled me in on the procedure WHILST PUTTING ON LATEX GLOVES. My heart rate must have been somewhere in the 200 beats per minute as I projected forward to a near future where a young nurse wondered why she was examining a tailor's dummy.

Then I heard the magic words; "All we're doing today Mr Barter is blood pressure, weight, height, heart rate and cholesterol"

And within seconds an armband was strapped to my puny bicep and pumped up so hard it hurt. Some little machine next to it spat out my blood pressure and heart rate, 66 beats per minute. Now, any normal bloke would have been dead relieved at this point. He'd escaped naked humiliation and his heart rate was under 70bpm which is pretty good. But you forget I'm a keen and sometimes competitive cyclist. The last ECG I had measured my resting rate as 52, but the stress of blond nurses combined with the lunchtime bike ride had pushed it up into the 60s. "It should be 52", I queried, "Can I have another go? I need to calm down a little". "No, 66 is fine for a man your age" was her retort and no matter of pleading could get her to change her mind. She shut me up by stuffing a needle into my arm and stealing a few cc's of my blood, which I'm convinced go straight into the DNA database. I'm fully expecting to be convicted of a Saturday night urination against a wall that happened in Bristol in 1987. I'll plead diminished responsibility and call the Fleece and Firkin as a witness citing their premise brewed beers.

This obsession with numbers related to cycling has continued into the week. I've sat and stared long and hard at blank pieces of paper to figure out how to describe the difficulty of climbs. Well, when I say "blank pieces of paper", I mean my Apple Mac. You'd have thought that the best way to describe a climb would be to simply state its height and length and leave the rest up to the reader to figure out. However, I come from an industry where we constantly strive to "add value", which put simply means we make things much more complicated than they are to charge lots of money for them.

So, I've been sitting there trying to "add value" to the descriptions of the climbs that are going into the book. I've toyed with a few off-the-wall options which will probably end up discarded, such as:

- "the shagged out index" - a rating between 1 and 10 of how tired you will be on completion. A score of 1 is given if you can sing "I'm shagged out" like the bloke from the Go Compare advert, 10 applies if you don't have the oxygen to say it.
- a diagram showing the number of helium balloons that would be required to lift you from bottom to top were you of average weight and height (bit of a problem these days as average weight appears to be hovering around the twenty stone mark)
- a count of the number of Higgs Bosun particles required to break the gravitational force that you will need to overcome to summit the climb - this one would have been a flyer but the Large Hadron Collider has not found the Higgs Bosun yet. (STOP PRESS: It has now)

Seriously, the diagrams are hard. I'm spending loads of time fiddling about with Adobe Illustrator to try and make the book look nice. I'm not sure if this is what we writers are supposed to do? I'm pretty certain that Barbara Cartland dictated all of her novels prostrated on a pink sofa whilst fondling poodles. I bet she never had to do battle with the complex gradient tool or decide which CMYK to pick from the colour swatch.

In fact, in terms of cycling adventures, May has been a bit of a write off for me and when I look at my timesheets for the month they provide the following information; Researching cycling - 6%. Cycling - 6%. Writing about cycling - 6%. Dicking about with Adobe Illustrator - 10%. Organising wife's secret 40th birthday party - 72%.

As you can see, there is a clear message for any aspiring authors in those figures. If you are going to leave a decent job to write a book, whatever you do, do not attempt it in the year your wife is forty. The secret birthday party project was doomed from the start. I painstakingly contacted all of my wife's friends and family and swore them to utter secrecy. This was immediately undone when one of them texted her to ask what was happening on the 14th of May. I think Helen replied "My secret birthday party".

I then had to counter the text with further distractional subterfuge involving sending her to a health farm for the day and pretending that this was the treat. Meanwhile, the proper party was arranged at my house, which came with its own issues as I had limited places to hide all of the food and beer. The neighbours have been very restrained and didn't tuck into the wine and champagne hiding out in their garages (well I don't think they did but it seemed rude to count it on the day). The kids were not too impressed with snuggling up to sausages for a few nights and the rat in the shed is now fed up with Doritos.

Hours have been spent running around supermarkets fretting about bread rolls, dithering in butchers about the number of sausages and pissing myself laughing at ancient photos of Helen supplied by my mother-in-law. One of the photos made me laugh longer than others, it was Helen looking as miserable as Anne Widdicombe's beauty therapist as she finished the London to Brighton bike ride riding next to me.

Rest assured I am not laughing at the fact that Helen completed London to Brighton with a broken wrist. Oh no, you should see my bike! That thing must have cost less than £100. It has cantilever brakes and the wheels are attached with nuts. I had flat pedals, a pannier, a huge lock attached to the frame and reflectors all over the place. There is some sort of weird dangly thing hanging off the handlebars which looks suspiciously like a bum bag. What was I thinking? The rear mech on my current bike costs more than the sum total of that lot and as for that purple helmet, let's forget and move on.

Another Book

If you have kept up with my progress so far you must be congratulated. Your weary eyes may have traversed over many thousands of words worth of inane, self-indulgent dialogue without really having a clue what on earth I am trying to do. However, fear not you are not alone I'm not one hundred per cent sure myself. So let's have a quick summary of the current works in progress.

Book number one - a celebration of road cycling within the UK. This is what I set out to achieve in the first place. It involves a large amount of cycling followed by vain attempts to illustrate it graphically and metaphorically. This is the book I will wave at the Grandchildren when they ask me "What did you do in the Great Recession of 2011 Granddad?". They will then strike any remaining hopes of a large inheritance from their minds and go back to Facebooking their hamster.

Book number two - a factual account of the "Year Record", a cycling feat undertaken between 1911-1939 whereby riders would compete to ride the greatest number of miles in a single year. I plan to embellish this in my particular style to put it into a modern context, or to quote the great Spike Milligan, "I'm going to jazz it up a bit"

Both of these literary attempts are non-fiction, which means that they must be factually correct to reduce the risk of me being sued by a disgruntled relative or Milton Keynes. This takes up a significant portion of my day as a single paragraph can contain a large number of facts that I think are correct. But think is not good enough and I have to verify them with reputable sources. Given that the internet is composed of approximately 90% pornography with the other 10% comprising of 140 character long messages describing the author's lunch, it can hardly be deemed reputable. "I found it on Google your honour", carries about as much weight as "It's OK, Harold Camping is convinced it is correct" in the modern court of law.

This issue is particularly pertinent to book number two which I'm hoping will become an iconic piece of cycling history, similar to my Swindon Road Club Hill Climb victory of 2006. And believe me, I have a lot of fact-checking to do from a sparse landscape of material given the record attempts petered out after 1939.

Therefore I can now add "Amateur Detective" to my current job description as I chase and verify facts across a large number of diverse sources that range from old cycling magazines to simple hearsay that exists on the internet. This week I made a huge breakthrough.

Over the past five years, I have painstakingly sought detail as to the daily mileages ridden by Tommy Godwin, who took the year record for good in 1939. Using clippings from a wide variety of magazines I have created a spreadsheet of mileages and used averages to fill in the gaps. This led to a Twitter account (@yearrecord) that reports Tommy's mileage each day.

However, I had heard a rumour that he kept a diary, as did many cyclists, of his daily mileage. This is common practice, I do it and am quite anal about recording every ride I do, its length, duration, height, the bike used etc… Tommy's diaries would unlock project number two for me, as I could properly verify each day and compare them with my incomplete records. I would also be able to superimpose his ride upon historical records and work out how far he rode on the day war was declared or when the 1939 weather was at its worst.

So this week, I found them and the owner has kindly lent them to me to complete my research in this area. Finding them was worthy of an Arthur Conan Doyle story and I will cryptically state that there was a Professor Moriarty in my quest for their discovery.

Opening the diaries for the first time was an incredibly moving experience. Tommy Godwin has been my cycling hero since I first discovered him in 2005. To see his heroic mileages written in ink brought the whole record to life. In places the handwriting was sketchy, and so it should be having ridden over 200 miles on a winter's day in the snow.

As you can imagine this was a real lift for me and driving up to Leeds with the diaries in the car felt like I was piloting a Securicor van loaded with a million quid in used notes en-route to a bank.

"Hang on Dave! why were you going to Leeds, you don't work there anymore", is what the inquisitive reader would have blurted out were there an inquisitive reader to do the blurting. Well, coincidentally an ex-work colleague is friends with a film producer. I dropped him an off-the-cuff note about the year record and whether there would be any interest. He fixed up a meeting for me in Leeds to see if there was any *"mileage"* in the idea.

Walking past my old head office dressed in "civvies" was a strange experience. I somehow felt guilty and naughty at the same time. I had an almost irrepressible urge to skip past security and run riot through the building in my jeans and cowboy boots whilst shouting " Free yourselves now! Come and join me in a world of whimsy and pipe dream, there's more to life than EBITDA". But then I saw the lights on at 7 pm and thought of the colleagues finishing reports or hacking at spreadsheets spurned on by less sympathetic partners.

We met in the pub. Sufficiently lubricated, I talked utter bollocks for ten minutes and sat back expecting a "Very interesting Dave but I've got a train to catch" retort. The complete opposite response had me on the floor. It appears that we have the genesis of a potentially interesting documentary and so not only am I going to appear on the Sunday Times bestseller list, I'll be treading the red carpet and rubbing shoulders with Tom Cruise in no time at all. Well, he'll be rubbing his shoulder against my elbow but you get the picture. I woke up the next day with a little bit of a hangover. And seeing as I am the boss, I deemed the morning to be dedicated to "rest and recovery" in the form of a mountain bike ride. After a Little Chef Olympic Breakfast, I dragged the bike out of the car at the Gisburn Forest centre all set for 12 miles of singletrack to clear the mind and reset the liver a little.

I was not alone. A large group were preparing to leave ahead of me, nearly twenty teenagers and an instructor who was showing them how to use the brakes. This did not bode well for my plans. I egotistically projected a future where I tootled along technical singletrack at "break nothing" speed held up by a group of beginners. No sweat meant no hangover cure, I threw on my gear and chased after them determined to pass before the trails narrowed to a single lane.

I caught the group just before the forest trails. You'd think I would have politely passed them with a cheery wave at a pace that accorded them no threat. But, no, I did the thing I've always hated, the "Elite rider on the left" syndrome. I simply hammered past the group as fast as I could causing all sorts of wobbles, shouts and possibly even some browning of the inside of the trousers. I nearly shouted "Film star coming through, please make way", but was too focused on getting past to spare the breath. To be honest my behaviour was pretty indefensible. I selfishly strove for clear trails ahead and left all thoughts of patience in the car. Luckily there is a deity that keeps an eye out for these sorts of occurrences and is ready to step in and apply redress where needed.

Said deity ensured that I completely overcooked the first corner and slid off the trail. My chain skipped off its chainrings and decided to twist itself through ninety degrees. I compounded the twist by continuing to pedal thus twisting the chain further and rendering the bike completely inoperable. Minutes of frantic fettling solved nothing and I stood at the side of the trail as the group carefully passed me with polite "Hellos" and enquiries as to whether they could help.

After they'd gone I sat forlornly on my arse, cursing my impetuous nature, bad behaviour and Sram, the makers of the chain. Eventually, I resolved to remove it completely and push the bike back to the car. Using a special tool I took out a link of the chain and it fell to the floor intact, straight and in "good as new" condition. The deity had rescinded my detention and let me off with a warning. Five minutes later the bike and I were back on the trails, after ten minutes I caught the group again, sat behind them patiently and waited until a wide climb before carefully making my way past.

Riding through the trees I contemplated the other meeting I had attended earlier in the week. This one was with a publisher. When you set out to write a book for the first time you have no idea of how well it will be received. Will anyone want to buy it? Has it been done before? Are you capable of doing it well? Can it be marketed?

This was my first attempt to find out. I'll be candid about the meeting as it is still early days, but I think it is fair to say that the road cycling book has potential and the feedback I received was incredibly positive. It must be good as he bought me a sandwich in the pub and he wouldn't have done that unless he was confident that the investment would be returned from future book sale profits. This was a huge boost for my confidence, as I must now confess that I have previous form.

Many years ago I decided (along with the rest of the population of the UK) that writing children's books must be pretty straightforward. I sat down and authored my first tome, a short story entitled "We turned our Dad into a Panda". I'd conceived a whole series of stories under the banner of "Consequences", a set of tales that taught children that their actions can lead to consequences, told in a light-hearted sort of way. I was utterly convinced that this was a winner, if some ginger princess can sell stories about helicopters then I could make double with cleverly constructed stories that meant something.

I hammered the story out and sent it off to approximately thirty publishing houses and literary agents. I was inundated with five replies, three polite rejections and two acknowledgements that were never followed up. There ended my fiction writing career.

Insurance

There's an old cycling adage which goes something like; "*Before you set out to ride a series of long hard routes it is important to smash your knee repeatedly against a rock until it bleeds*". Ok, I lied. There is no such saying, but can somebody please explain to me exactly why I insist on following it to the letter? This week I threw everything I own into the van and headed off up to Scotland again. The plan was to complete the Scottish section of the book within a single trip. This required a significant amount of road riding but inexplicably my mountain bike and all of the associated gubbins sneaked into the van as well.

My first stop was Glentrool, however, the sat-nav was in league with the mountain bike and directed the van to pass tantalisingly close to the Dalbeattie mountain bike trails. Like a failed alcoholic passing an off-license, I stopped for a cheeky blast around the trails. What could go wrong? I'd brought my knee pads and the trail was graded red, well within my capabilities.

The car park at Dalbeattie was empty and in a schoolboy-esque display of impatience, I was out of the van and riding within fifteen minutes of arrival. Any true mountain biker knows that this is ridiculous. At least forty five minutes of faffing are required before a mountain bike can be properly mounted. Kit needs to be found, turned inside-out, have the mud shaken off it, packed, and then unpacked when it is realised that the spanner needed to adjust the saddle is at the bottom of the bag. Shock pressures, tyre pressures, gears, brakes, cleat tension and saddle height must be messed about with for at least thirty minutes until they are returned to the settings as measured on arrival. Then every other biker in the car park must be questioned endlessly as to the trail conditions, length, grading, height gain and tyre requirements.

I threw all of this to the wind and rode off up the trail. A sign labelled "skills loop" beckoned me over and a further sign announced that the next section was "black" grade and entirely unsuitable for Daves. Being a sensible sort of fellow coupled with the fact that I had forgotten to put my knee pads on, I rode down it. Well, that's if you define "rode" as rolled the front wheel onto some rocks, shat myself, stopped, failed to unclip from pedals and then fell sideways onto said rocks.

At this point, I decided to take an irrational dislike to Mr Pavlov. Sod his dogs and their stimulus/response learning, I was going to forget the pain and go round for another go. Sadly the rocks were not prepared to play the same game and as I rolled over the lip they shouted "boo", I crossed myself, fell off and damaged the knees further. Lying on the ground I cursed my luck versus mountain biking ability and thought back to the other trials this week has presented me with.

Firstly, there was my van insurance company. It was time for renewal and they had sent me the usual letter asking me for four times the premium of last year just in case I forgot to shop around a little. So I phoned them for a little chat and they miraculously halved the quote by unticking the box labelled "Lazy idiot with too much money". The operator asked me if any of my circumstances were different from last year and then I made the second greatest error of the week. I told them that I was now self-employed and working as an author. The lady immediately put me on hold.

I then spent five minutes listening to a computer called Enya singing about "Sail Away" or something. Eventually, the insurance lady returned and sheepishly informed me that they would not insure my van. I asked her why? She told me that it was due to my change in employment. At this point, I lost it.

"So young lady", I patronised her, "you are telling me that when I was an IT

Director working 60 hours plus most weeks, driving hundreds of miles whilst ranting into a hands-free mobile phone you were happy to insure me. But now that I live the life of Riley, casually flitting from town to town at my own pace and driving much slower now I'm footing the bill, that I'm a higher risk?"
"It's not me it's the underwriters." she responded, "I'll give them another call".

Before I could stop her, she switched the computer singing lady back on and I spent many more minutes on hold. The response was no different, IT Directors *"yes"*, self-employed writers *"sod off"*. A five-minute call to renew a policy had now morphed into half a day's worth of information gathering and messing about on insurance websites. It turns out that Equity Star are not the only company that discriminates against authors and the search was elongated further as I attempted to find a company that understood that we don't spend all day smoking opium, quaffing hemlock and answering every question with *"forsooth"*.

After the van insurance issue, I had to buy food for the trip. What could possibly go wrong there? Simply go to Sainsbury's, pile beer, doughnuts, Mars bars and beef burgers into a trolley then pay for it. Sorted. Well, there is now a significant complication that I have to deal with. You may recall that I recently went for a health check. On the day all of my scores were acceptable for a man of my age, but I was to wait for my cholesterol reading as this takes a while to process. Recently I received a letter from the doctor with some bad news, my readings are higher than average.

I nearly phoned them back for a long rant as to how this was impossible as I have a toast rack for a chest and cycle over two hundred miles a week. But then I thought about it. The large volume of exercise has caused me to fall into the *"I can eat and drink whatever I like trap"* and the trap gets wider at the end of each cycle ride. I get home and binge eat whatever I can find, biscuits, cakes, cheese, ice cream, crisps and half the contents of the refrigerator. I never pass up the offer of something unhealthy as I can always *"cycle it off"* tomorrow and usually I do.

But some of this crap must still be hanging around even after a two-hour interval session. So I've resolved to turn over a new leaf and cut all of the crap from my diet. This has added hours to my pre-trip shopping as every single item I would have taken is graded "fat bastard". Modern food labelling has been incredibly helpful in denying me access to anything that tastes remotely nice. All I have packed are grapes, fish fingers and lettuce. I'm not convinced that this will sustain a working cyclist, but I'm determined to get top marks at the next visit to the doctors.

Then I had to deal with my route planning. Well, I didn't because a workman went "hammer drill happy" in Old Town Swindon and cut off our power for an entire morning. I immediately lost all of the routes I was working on and was unable to console myself with an episode of Bargain Hunt or a game on the Wii. I abandoned the house and went shopping instead, but that was out of the question as the shops were all broken as well. Traffic was chaos with the traffic lights shut down and I hate to think why the woman was standing outside of the local massage parlour having a fag. What electrical thing does she need to continue her trade?

Another half a day lost and to be frank I'm amazed that I made it up here at all. Scotland was pleased to see me as it sent out a welcome committee of approximately three hundred million midges. For once I was ready for them and had covered all exposed flesh in a variety of repellants, but midge number 10334467 remained undeterred. In a heroic act of selfless courage, she flew up my shorts and entered the underpants zone. With no regard for her own safety, she bravely bit me in the "nether" region. This is after said region had remained unwashed after many hours of driving and mountain biking. I doubt she made it back out, but she can die knowing that her legacy lives on in the discomfort I am currently suffering.

Tired and almost defeated I set out from Glentrool Holiday park for ride number one of this series. The rain and wind held off as did the traffic. It was eighty miles of pure self-indulgence as I raved into the voice recorder about the roads, scenery and situation. Sat here typing this, all of the week's trials are forgotten. It's amazing how a bike ride can do this, it seems to reset the soul to the default position of "Well pleased with being alive".

Selfies

Try and take a photograph of yourself that looks good. That's right, you can't. No matter how hard you try one of the following will occur; You'll suddenly gain fifty chins as you shift your head as far back as you can. You'll take a photo up your nose. Your forced smile will make you look like you're pooing. Some idiot will hold two fingers behind your head. You'll realise that your twenties went a long time ago and you'll delete the photo.

I know this because of social media and the photos a number of my friends use as their profile pictures. You see, I took them and this is why my friends use these pictures, they weren't selfies, they're action shots. Now I'm about to insult all of these good people via implication, so strap yourself in and grab a cup of coffee. But before any of them get the major league hump, let's be clear that I am one hundred per cent guilty of the crime myself.

Consider this. As you progress beyond your thirtieth birthday the mirror gives up on the lying and responds with the plain truth. You really are a saggy old bugger and the halcyon days of trendy haircuts and cheeky instant pull smiles are gone. The person you imagine yourself to be is not staring back at you, it's some repulsive stranger instead who has spinach on their teeth and an inordinate number of lines pointing to their eyes.

You can live with that until asked to provide a photo that sums you up in a single image such as a social networking site profile picture. You take a quick picture on your iPhone, but it's in league with the mirror and a dated, worn, hairless old head gurns from the screen. Now you are in a quandary, old rivals, ex-girlfriends and even uglier old mates are going to see this picture and in desperation, you flick through the photo collection looking for the "action shot". This is a photo that shows you doing something young, like getting huge air on a snowboard, skiing like a professional, climbing a really hard rock problem, riding a bike with finesse or simply hiding behind a glass of beer.

Take a glance at my profile picture (edit: you can't I deleted Facebook years ago), what a surprise! it's me riding a mountain bike looking like I can almost do it. It was taken about five years ago and most people I've ridden with will argue that it is the wrong way up. But here is my point. You CANNOT take these pictures yourself.

It is impossibly hard to place a camera on a tripod in the alps, set the timer to the precise moment that you get air, walk up the hill, mount the snowboard, ride down the slope, get the air at the precise moment and position that ensures sharp focus. Imagine the same with the rock climb. How the hell will you set the camera, create some sophisticated self-belay system, leg it up the rock and remote release the shutter whilst still hanging onto the cliff face. Can't be done. And then there is the beer shot. You are either going to have a little bit of camera holding arm in shot, or a pub full of faces behind you pissing themselves at the idiot trying to self portrait the quaffing of a pint of Stella.

Anyone who is still speaking to me will ask aloud "But you haven't mentioned the bike Dave?". Well, there is a reason for that. I've spent the week attempting the impossible, creating quality self-portraits of myself riding my bike for the book and it's unbelievably hard. If I'm to complete the Scottish section on this trip, it needs to have photos. And a book on cycling without photos of cyclists may receive the odd negative review (although I do know of one that has done well with just pictures of roads).

The first attempt was a ride through Glentrool. I decided to use the camera's self-timer which can be set to wait for thirty seconds and then take a series of four shots. Brilliant. Taking photos should be easy simply park the camera by the side of the road, press the button, ride back down, turn around and pull a winning smile. In my case, it delivered a beautiful image of a solitary rear wheel leaving the shot. Fair enough I rode too quickly. So on the next shot, I took my time a little and captured myself far too far away to be of any use. And so began an odyssey of pressing the shutter riding around the place getting it wrong and almost getting run down by a car in the process. Even when I got the positioning right, other things would go wrong, including a shot that does look like I am having a cycling poo.

It's not just about camera positioning either as I managed to overexpose my shots as well. Everything was right apart from the camera settings creating a photo that is now only suitable for an episode of Doctor Who.

Sometimes it's not even my fault, you do everything right and something encroaches upon the frame that you weren't expecting. The *"car picture"* was particularly ironic as the driver was a photographer who stopped for a long chat about his book, a montage of Scottish landscapes. Thankfully he agreed to take the shot for me by hand and did a damn fine job of it as well.

Suffice to say, cycling self-portraits are blinking hard, but I'm beginning to get the hang of it now. These won't be two-page spreads within the book but they will serve to illustrate the rides and hopefully allow the reader to believe that I did ride some of them. I'm aided by a magnificent piece of kit. The Canon S95 compact camera. It's about as near to a DSLR in a fag packet as you can get, has a fantastic lens and more importantly has lots and lots of tweakable settings that help you get stuff right.

For example, bracketing. Which in layman's terms means taking loads of photos of the same thing with different settings so hopefully one of them will be right. Seb Rogers, who taught me the basics of action photography, will be turning in his bed (he's not dead) if he ever reads that. He'd tell me to get it right in the first place and not mess about with multiple exposures. But he's not the impatient, knackered idiot who has just ridden 75 miles uphill and desperately needs the photo before he can go back to his van. Seb recommended the camera to me as suitable for one who is slightly serious about taking good action pictures but work-shy enough to forgo carrying any sort of load.

The compact camera has saved me big time on this trip and three rides in I'm feeling confident that I'm going to arrive back home with the Scottish section just about bagged.

It's been a long week on the road and I am sorely missing my family. Life on the bike and in the van is often devoid of conversation for extended periods forcing me to chat with anything that will listen. I now thank the sat-nav at every spoken direction, converse with radio presenters and talk to myself incessantly. Shop visits are particularly stressful as I natter away to the nice lady at the till whilst she silently wishes I would sod off and stop wittering on about cycling and the weather.

I'd phone the speaking clock for a quick chat if I could but I'm not even sure if it exists anymore? Which would be a shame as I look back with fond memories of my Dad phoning it every time I got a watch for my birthday. In a bid to ensure that said timepiece was correctly synchronised. I suspect he still knows the number, you can take the Dad out of the RAF but you can't take the RAF out of the Dad, or something like that.

I met a very friendly fellow as I sat on a bench overlooking Loch Riddon and the Isle of Bute. I had the sensation of going all light and glanced to my left to see a *"man of weight"* lowering itself onto the seat. He was grasping a packet of Embassy Number Ones and I detected the smell of Eighty Shilling as well. *"I'll be needing some information on that"*, he softly demanded and pointed to my lightweight titanium steed. Slightly bemused, I informed him that it was a bicycle and that I had used it to propel myself to this point without the use of fossil fuels or Big Macs. *"Aye, I ken that, young laddie, but as you'll agree I cud dae wi shedding a poooound or tae"*, is what I think came back in response. Pushing my luck I told him that I'd looked similar about a year ago until I'd purchased the bike and that my wife had forced me into it after moaning that I was twice the man she'd married. It was touch and go, but eventually, he beamed back at me and we talked for a few minutes more.

The conversation was animated as I spouted on and on about cycling, its benefits, where it takes you and how it had certainly changed my life. I saw a strange emotion in his eyes, almost a longing.

He was over 60, obese, a smoker and being tugged around Scotland in the back seat of his offspring's car. I felt as if there was a small spark in there that wanted to do something about it but it would never grow into a flame. He said he'd look out for my book, I hope he is still around to see it published.

Van Life

I'm fed up with living in this van. There, I've said it. If you'd asked me a year ago *"Dave how about decamping to Scotland in your van for three weeks and cycling round the place?"* I'd have salted, ketchuped and sandwiched your hand before devouring the whole thing raw in moments. That's because I'm the sort of person who only really thinks in positives. I find it hard to consider that anything can actually go wrong and often throw myself into tasks without due consideration.

This worked well when I was younger as my friends had a permanent crash test dummy for any mad escapade that presented itself to them. Consequently, I wrecked clothes in muddy bogs ("Dave, see if you can get across there, it looks ok"), broke my arm falling off fences ("Dave walk along that fence while we kick footballs at you, it should be ok"), nearly died riding a car bonnet down a steep hill backwards ("Dave, hop on that car bonnet and we'll give you a push, it doesn't look that steep") and almost drowned coasteering ("Dave, jump into this watery gully there's no risk of a freak wave").

Therefore, heading up to Scotland I was of a positive mindset and visualised myself cycling easily through picturesque glens during the day and then relaxing in a deckchair watching the sun go down with a whiskey in the evenings. However, I failed to consider the following, midges, the elderly, Dutch and German tourists. Let's take each in turn.

Remember the midges a few pages back? Let's reinforce what utter bastards the little devils can be. Their search and destroy mechanisms are so unbelievably well-honed that I've yet to find a part of Scotland where they can't find me. I believe that at the border a troop of midges are personally assigned to you along with a mission to make sure that any time you spend outdoors stood still is as uncomfortable as it can be. I've been bitten on beaches, remote roadsides, mountain tops, valley bottoms, lakesides and even in a bus shelter.

The only place you are safe is in a town centre, and that's because every single person in suburban Scotland smokes. This is true, the only way to get served in an Inverness cafe is to pop round the side door and ask the waitress to put down her fag for a moment and make you some coffee. So, the quiet evenings sat outside the van enjoying the countryside are out. I'm stuck inside it all evening along with my minging cycling clothes and post-ride flatulence.

Next, we consider the elderly and those of Dutch and German descent. These are my only companions because this is outside of the holiday season and they are the only people resident within Scottish campsites. This would be fine if they didn't have a "distinct" odour and could talk about something else apart from the weather. The foreigners can cite language difficulties as an excuse and to be fair it's a fairly safe way of striking up a conversation. But the old people can't hide behind that one. They are quite simply lacking in any kind of originality whatsoever. I'm tempted to remind them that they are letting Eric Morecombe, Spike Milligan, Bob Monkhouse and Hattie Jaques down in a spectacular fashion. But I think they would blame it on the recent rain and the possibility of hail at the weekend.

As for the smell. It has to be all of them because every time I get into a campsite shower there is a lingering aroma of Imperial Leather mixed with mothballs and sausages. I'm pretty sure the Dutch and Germans contribute to this in some fashion as, without exception, every shower I've used up here has been slightly rank. It's going to be such a luxury to go home and use one that is above tepid in temperature and does not need a button to be pressed every 15 seconds. Also, I can't wait to get away from all of the stupid patronising signs that litter campsites these days. For example: "Please leave the shower as you would like to find it". Where on earth am I going to get naked women and champagne in the middle of nowhere at 10 pm?

It would be unfair to focus on the lowlights though as there have been plenty of highs. Let's take the wildlife for starters. Scotland has plenty of proper wildlife and it's not scared of showing itself. Back home in Wiltshire, we get all worked up about spotting a deer mainly because it is a refreshing change from our cows and sheep which all look the same. Scotland has loads of sheep as well, but theirs have character. They have horns and come in different sizes and more importantly, they fight each other. Our sheep hang about in fields looking nervous, but up here there are proper gangs of chav sheep, hanging around looking for a rumble. On a walk, I came across this bunch who got bored and decided to have a proper fight. This included head butts with a running start that made an impressive "bang" and didn't seem to phase the combatants at all. Further up the road some of their out-of-order but hornless mates decided to prevent a fire engine from reaching a true emergency.

I've also spotted stags, mink, stoats, goats, hairy cows, huge cows, horned cows, fat cows (Inverness town centre), too many birds to mention and this chicken who insisted on hanging around my van when I camped near Lochinver. I sussed out that she was on the scrounge for food and I know I'll go to hell for this, but couldn't resist a little experiment in feathery cannibalism. The result? well, they're right bastards those chickens, they'll eat anything.

I should also mention bike riding. Scotland is the best place in the world to ride a bicycle. Any cyclist who begs to differ would soon witness a grown man place a finger into each ear and recite "Na na na na na na" ad-infinitum until they went away. I'm sure there are more spectacular places to ride, with better climates, nicer roads, more salubrious campsites and fewer Germans. But that is not the point.

The best way to exhibit this is via an analogy that only my generation will truly appreciate. Having to choose between riding in Scotland or anywhere else in the world is like being Gregory in "Gregory's Girl". Clare Grogan represents Scottish cycling and Dee Hepburn the rest of the world. On first impression, you'd want to go with Dee, blond, leggy, intelligent etc...but waiting in the wings is our little Clare and what she has is "character". In Girl Top Trumps Dee would probably come out the winner, but I and most other men would be gutted if we lost our Clare card. We'd find it hard to explain why (of course that was if our wives/girlfriends/partners didn't exist etc..). Scottish cycling is exactly the same. It has a certain character that does not exist anywhere else. A weirdly attractive smile, a certain tilt of the head a quirky haircut that keeps dragging the eye back for a second look. Oh, and hardly any cars apart from old/Dutch/German people driving their caravans about the place.

So it's with considerable excitement and considerable regret I make my way home. I've been away from the family for far too long and miss them like mad. Hopefully, the locks won't be changed after the Clare Grogan admission and I'll still be allowed in the house. Then I have a marathon effort to do justice to this place in words and pictures. I'm comfortable with the former but think the latter may need a final visit with a proper camera and a more photogenic model.

Diagrams

If you were to review my CV the following things would strike you; I've worked with Leslie Crowther and in the past twenty years I've only ever had three jobs, including this one. Working with Leslie Crowther may be a slight exaggeration. Many years ago I was charged with leading a project to develop a public *"self-service"* fax machine to be located within Post Office Counters. It's one of the most interesting projects I've ever undertaken as this machine was to have a direct interface with the British public which in turn presented its own set of challenges. An industrial designer undertook the vast majority of the design which we reviewed with several postmasters. They all looked at the drawings and then asked *"What about the fluids?"*. We scratched our heads a lot and stared back at them for a while before asking *"What fluids?"*. *"Listen, lads, what you learn about working in a Post Office is that the general public will bring and spill almost every liquid known to man over its surfaces. Coke, squash, puke, piss, nitro-glycerine the lot. You need to design a method of wicking away the fluids"*.

Our industrial designer then spent days fretting over tubes, gullies, seals and runaways to channel the piss away from the integrated fax machine and onto the floor where it belonged. Anyhow, eventually we finished the design and manufactured a staggering four units for a test launch in a carefully selected set of Post Office locations (we studied geographical incontinence data for weeks to make these decisions). Our marketeers searched high and low for a figurehead to launch the latest hi-tech innovation bursting from Royal Mail Research and

Development all fingers pointed towards Leslie Crowther.

For those that are not aware, Leslie Crowther was a TV presenter whose CV included; Crackerjack, The Price is Right, Stars in their Eyes and even The Black and White Minstrel Show. He was the man to educate the British public about the benefits of transmitting paper documents over the wire whilst staring at pensioners queuing for their bingo money. Alternatively, for a modest fee, he was prepared to say nice things about anything that smelt of piss.

On reflection, my name dropping is in division four when compared to others I've encountered. They can reel off Bill Gates, Tim Berners-Lee, royalty, Lord mayors and dictators. Whilst I'm stuck with alcoholic TV presenters, Emu and I once played in a band with a bloke who works with Andy Partridge from XTC.

Putting Leslie aside, let's look at the other point, only three jobs. This means that I have resigned twice and when you resign sometimes your colleagues will club together and buy you a little leaving present. I'm never sure whether the message conveyed by these is *"Good Luck"* or *"Good riddance"*. On leaving my first job I was presented with a GPS wrapped in my P45, if I was paranoid I could have read this as *"Dave, please use this to leave the premises and navigate yourself as far away as feasibly possible"*. The second set of colleagues generously gave me a gorgeous Cross fountain pen. Could the message have been *"Dave, step away from the keyboard, go back to basics and learn how to write properly"*. However, regardless of the motives for their gifting, I could not carry out my current job without these important recording devices, so let's take each in turn.

Most people think of a GPS as a device for telling you where you are, and they'd be correct, it is pretty good at that. That is as long as you a happy with turning to the wife and kids with *"It's OK we're at 51.709711,-1.781931 I know where this is"*. That is a little flippant as these days they have maps and arrows that display a dirty great *"You are here"* on the screen. But for me the GPS is a critical recording device as it not only tells me where I am, it tells me where I've been.

Having done this for twenty-six weeks, I must doff my cap to the authors who have gone before me in the lo-tech days. Their process would have gone something like this:

- ride along a bit, almost get killed by a charabanc, see something pretty
- stop, remove pen and notebook from saddle bag
- tear out the soggy page, retire to phone box out of the rain
- remove Ordnance survey map from saddle bag
- remove compass from saddle bag
- take bearings from hill to the left and church with a steeple on the right
- triangulate bearings on the map to identify the current location
- notice that there is no phone box at the calculated location
- leave phone box, re-take compass bearings away from ferrous objects
- re-calculate location
- open notebook, scribble notes concerning "something pretty"
- stare at the blank page
- retrieve inkwell from the saddlebag, insert a pen into the inkwell, draw in ink
- scribble notes into notebook avoiding multiple areas of splodged blue ink
- replace all items into the saddlebag
- ride onwards
- return, pick up pen, notebook, map, compass and inkwell
- replace all items into the saddlebag
- fasten saddlebag straps
- ride onwards
- return home
- laboriously transcribe soggy notes onto Basildon Bond whilst struggling with multiple Ordnance Survey sheets

You get the picture. In the old days of paper and pen it must have been laborious in comparison to the way I do it:

- ride along a bit, almost get killed by BMW, see something pretty
- wipe the rain from GPS, note the current distance

- pull voice recorder from jersey pocket, speak distance, repeat the word "um" five times until inspiration strikes, speak description trying to avoid the word "alpine"
- replace voice recorder, nod at bemused pedestrian ride onwards
- return home
- download the track ridden from GPS into mapping package, hold head in hands when noting the calculated average speed
- play voice recorder, relate distances to the electronic track displayed on the screen and easily transcribe locations with descriptions into a word processor

As you can see I've got it dead-easy and when my book is published older authors will turn to me and give me the *"You had it easy lad, in my day...etc..."* speech. To make things even easier for myself, I've spent significant time this week building a computer program to read the GPS logs and automatically generate route description graphics for the book. I attempted this in week eighteen but to be honest, rushed it. So this week I've spent some "quality time" putting aside all other tasks and concentrating on tool making. This is how man evolved and it is how I'm hoping to evolve in this job as a cycling author by using as many tools as possible to increase productivity.

You're expecting a tale of woe, disaster, late evenings and frustration aren't you. Well, sadly you'll have to read previous chapters for that as this one has gone pretty damned well. I have a piece of working software, it's analysing rides and creating diagrams and will soon be doing all sorts of other jiggery-pokery.

This may seem trivial to the untrained eye, but take it from a ham-fisted IT veteran that this is a major step forward for me. (Any IT experts reading this, please no comments just nods of appreciation, we need to keep the complexity myth rolling. I'm sure it may be easy for you, but if you state this publicly we may have problems with future client estimates.)

So, I've blathered on about the GPS, but what about the pen? Strangely the pen has become an integral part of the arsenal of techniques I use to convince myself that progress is being made.

Further up the page I blatantly "dissed" the old school pen and paper way of doing things. Yet here I am with a moleskin journal and a fountain pen, scribbling in it every day about the things I have done and the ideas I've had.

I simply can't find a better way of doing this. There are loads of bits of software that allow you to mind map, document ideas, write to-do lists, keep a diary, scribble down notes, store names and addresses and doodle diagrams. But they all suffer from the following problems:

- there isn't anything that does all of that in one place
- they have instruction manuals that need to be read (I'm a male last time I looked)
- they can disappear in a puff of nothing during a power cut
- you can't use them on the loo

And so I resort to the tried and tested world of pen and paper. At the end of every day, I write a little note reassuring myself that I did something useful. Sometimes I even cross off items from a never-ending "To Do" list and occasionally there will be a little "*" which indicates that I've had a moment of genius. Most of these starred ideas don't seem so clever a few days later, but it is satisfying to flick through the journal and see that in the past 6 months I've done stuff and thought of the odd mad idea. This alone keeps me sane, the illusion of having made progress and something physical to back it up.

A Mountain Biker Ruined?

This week's weather forecast foretold a brief parting of the clouds and some potentially clement weather to the west of Great Britain. This coincided nicely with my plan to tidy up the Welsh section of the book with some riding smattered with photography. I rounded up the majority of my cycling paraphernalia, gathered some light reading material, cleared Co-op's shelves of Pot Noodles and in no time at all was paying the exorbitant entrance fee on the west side of the Severn Bridge.

Two rides were planned, both should probably be rebadged as climbs given the ascent required to complete them. On Tuesday I fought my way around the first, which included an unplanned diversion to a Welsh Post Office to satisfy a major Coca-cola craving. That evening I collapsed into the van and tried to do some writing. I failed, completely and utterly shattered I reached for some reading material to divert me from the lactic acid burns coursing through my muscles.

The nearest thing to hand was a mountain bike magazine. I opened it, turned to the lead article and within minutes my face was covered in phlegm. That last bit was a metaphor. You see the author of the article was having a right old rant about mountain biking. It started with a bit of a dig at those who don't ride as much as they should, quoting stupid domestic issues that get in the way such as dealing with the responsibilities of procreation and earning enough to stay alive. I yawned my way through this as the author vitriolically [not sure that's a word Dave. Ed.] spat his opinion 6 inches from my face..and was almost prepared to let it go as a poor bit of mountain biking Clarksonising [not sure about that one either Dave. Ed]. But then I read a sentence that proposed the following; every road riding mountain biker is a mountain biker ruined.

This caught my attention. Am I a mountain biker ruined? I think anyone looking at me riding a mountain bike would coin that phrase regardless of the deviation into road riding. But seriously, does road riding ruin mountain bikers? Has it taken me away from the joys of riding off-road and the challenges that present themselves?

And so I began to list all of the aspects of mountain biking that I loved and tried to work out whether these could apply to road riding. The list would have been physical, but the only paper I had to hand was the previous day's newspaper and I'd attempted the sudoku. Every single area of whitespace had numbers scrawled in blue biro. The sudoku had three great big blue lines through it, a tear and the phrase "Oh fucking hell!!" scraped across it. Luckily, I can just about remember the list which went something like this:

- sense of adventure, going places other people don't
- technical challenge
- being out there in the scenery
- coming home with a good story to tell
- communing with nature
- spending money I can't afford on things that make no rational sense but are lovely
- companionship and banter

That's not a bad list to start with and at face value, it looks like Mr "Metaphorical Spitter" was right and road riding would never live up to this set of values. But then I thought back to Tuesday's ride and something didn't feel right. As I parted the curtains of fatigue and looked back at it, his hypothesis began to disassemble itself right in front of my face.

Grab yourself an Ordnance Survey map and navigate to grid reference SO 25442 10514. This is the top of a classic Welsh road cycling climb known as "The Tumble". It's a B road and many a sportive have continued down it ignoring the turn off to the left. And that's because no sensible event organiser would ever take a thousand riders down that road. It's tiny and yellow and has DASHES on either side. The Ordnance Survey key tells you that this means *"Desperately small road, probably knackered don't go here you might meet a fierce tractor"*.

But I couldn't resist it. My sense of ruined-but-was-once-a-mountain biker dragged me down that road and to be perfectly frank the experience was as good as any mountain bike descent I've ever survived. It was steep as hell, it wound all over the place, the surface was dodgy which required real-time decision making on line choice and it was littered with hazards including potholes, a farmer, a lost tourist in a VW and a very dark section in trees designed to thwart those wearing sunglasses. Any sensible cyclist would have stopped, ridden back up and taken the proper route down from the mountain. I did completely the opposite, I sped up, swerved around as much as I could and held on for dear life for the rest. At the bottom I slammed on the brakes, narrowly avoided colliding with traffic on the A4042, leant back and laughed.

This is exactly what I do and how I feel when mountain biking. I love looking at maps and wondering what would happen if I rode down that bridleway? Usually, the answer is a sleepless night due to an overdose of stinging nettles, but sometimes I find a hidden gem. And now I'm doing the same thing on the road. Granted the bike is a bit different and the clothes look a little tighter on me, but I look a mess in whatever I wear so you're not going to get me on that.

Ok, adventure and technical challenge ticked off. In my case both apply to both disciplines, we'll move on to scenery. There's no question that the right mountain bike ride takes you right into the heart of some of the most beautiful parts of our green and pleasant land. I've ridden up mountains, through valleys, in more woods than a serial dogger, over, along and through many water features and on one occasion, that we will keep quiet about, a tower block. But to be fair, the road riding list is almost the same (putting aside the tower block), it's just that the aspect is different. On the mountain bike, you are in it, sometimes fighting it but often looking out, with the road bike you're an outsider looking in.

Another aspect of road bike riding is in scenery volume. Illustrated by Tuesday's ride. On the mountain bike, I'd have been able to do about forty miles of the loop off-road, taking in two of the mountains and a bit of the farmland as well. On the road bike, I covered 90 miles, saw the Brecons, mountains, valleys, farmland, hills, more hills, even bloody more hills, some sod off great big hills I wasn't expecting and an amazing little road that wound between two striking great mounds of green. With mountain biking, you can sip the scenery but physical ability prevents getting completely pissed on it. Road biking's like drinking lager, you can take bloody great quaffs of scenery in a single ride. Nine pints is possible if you're up for a big session but you're going to feel rough the next day.

Right, it's a one-all-draw on scenery. Can stories or encounters with nature tip the balance either way? Frankly, no. Again, I refer you to Tuesday's ride. I stated above that my mission included photography, which given that it is a solo mission, means pictures of me. This in turn meant a little subterfuge to steer my eventual reader away from the fact that many of the pictures are me. To that end, I purchased a red cycling top and planned to take photos without a helmet (we'll discuss that another time) using different glasses. The red top was size medium, bought in haste and not properly tried on. Sadly I now size small.

Us ruined-mountain-biking cyclists put stuff in the rear pockets of our cycling top. So you can guess what happened when I loaded the already too big red top with a sandwich, tools, tube, phone and camera. It sagged, a lot. The stupid thing went nearly down to my knees and of course, I discovered this just as I was about to set off. The only answer was to don a gilet (a bad move on a really hot day) and use it to stuff the excess baggage up the back. From the rear, I looked like an upside-down Diana Dors in a wonderbra, and I rode like her, constantly having to stuff my wayward back breasts back up into their container.

Stories done, we move onto nature, or more specifically animals. On Tuesday's ride, I had another revelation, in the past six months, I've become a connoisseur of sheep. They're everywhere, it's not just Wales, they're all over the country and riding on the road brings you into contact with many and varied varieties. I've seen so many that I've found myself critiquing them, marking them out of ten for size, shape, wool style and hygiene, headgear and bleat. I even talk to some of them, this may be a sort of madness that afflicts those riding long mileages, but often you get a weird sheep stare that warrants a retort. It's usually something along the lines of "Who are you staring at mint sauce?". Completely lacking in finesse or originality but strangely satisfying knowing that the fence prevents any retaliatory action from the sheep. Road biking brings you as close to nature as mountain biking does, with the bonus of a fence as a safety net.

I can quickly skip over spending money as my wife will affirm. I waste money in equal measure across my entire fleet of bicycles. No steed receives special measure, each is equally spoiled.

Let's finish then on companionship. I've met many good friends through riding off-road there's no question of that. Out on rides, we tend to hoon down something, stop have a chat, hoon down something else, fall off, laugh at each other and occasionally repair to the pub where the falling over and laughing continues. The road experience is a different one, these days I meet people as they're just tapping along. They'll catch me up or I'll catch up with them. We'll chat about the route, the day, the weather, our bikes whatever we're riding. In fact, on Tuesday I met a guy called "Mike" on The Tumble. I passed him as I'm made of helium whilst he is water-based. I could have ridden apace to the top and snarkily waved as he struggled behind. But instead, I waited and we rode over the top together.

On reflection, this was the best part of the day as we discussed our riding, our plans and why we were out doing it in the first place. Mike is training for a sportive, bloody good luck to him, I hope he has a great day out. I enjoyed connecting with another cyclist for a brief few minutes and it wouldn't have happened if I was a ruined mountain biker. Because I am not.

You see what I am is a mountain biker who's taken all they love about the sport and applied it to the road. And I honestly feel that in my case it fits. Mr "Metaphorical Spitter" may have set out to decry my dabblings with the tarmac, but what he has done is reaffirm them.

Somewhere in all this bollocks I write, I whinged on about finding a "voice" for the book. Mr "Metaphorical Spitter" has helped me towards that voice and I'm now energised with a new passion to remove the dryness, boredom, unfriendliness and lack of adventure so often implied by riding on the road.

Even better than that is that I've found my perfect customer. My friend Alex, takes the piss out of me, a lot. Alex has me down as a cycling crossdresser who's now moved to the full sex change. He's a die-hard mountain biker but has had the odd dabble himself (bi-curious we call it). Alex recently wrote in jest that he'd not buy my book because it is focused on the road. He's a bloody liar though as the true reason is that, coming from Yorkshire, his wallet has been passed down the family unopened for generations. Like a vintage wine, they're too scared to open it in case the contents turn foul. If I can get Alex to buy my book I've succeeded on two fronts. I've extracted money from a northerner, but more importantly, I've convinced a child of the baggies that their thrills can also be had on the road.

Lists

There's an issue with fathers, you inherit things from them. Many's the time I've glanced sympathetically at my son Jake who's quietly oblivious to some of the genes that I've sneaked into his system. At the age of forty, he will glance down at the paunch hanging over his belt and be straight on the phone demanding an explanation. But it seems it's not only physical attributes that are passed down the line, certain behaviours are transmitted as well.

Take my Dad, a retired RAF pilot who served a long and distinguished career doing silly things in the sky. Hardly anyone believes me when I tell them that he used to tow fake missiles past ships for naval target practise or that he landed his Hercules on pallets after some stupid idiot in a Vulcan had blown up the runway at Port Stanley. However, it wasn't all kippers smoked for breakfast and handlebar moustaches. A side effect of a career in the RAF is lists. I'm convinced that RAF basic training consists of nothing but list-making. Dad was obsessed with them.

From an early age, I was exposed to Dad's lists. Every pub visit needed his pen and a packet of Rothmans. He'd enquire as to our required beverage (always coke) write it three times on his packet of Rothmans and toddle off to the bar. Our house was littered with things detailing gardening tasks, shopping items, the names of his children and reasons to be cheerful. The crescendo was reached when he moved from fast jets to propeller based Hercules. Our downstairs loo had its walls festooned in lists of aeroplane technical terms. He'd sit there with his Rothmans revising away for his Hercules exam. I must have been the only twelve year old who knew the sequence of cross feeds from wing based aviation fuel tanks.

My brother and I occasionally sabotaged them. One day Dad wrote the following:

- Wash car
- Weed runner beans
- Phone David's teacher about the shaving foam incident
- Set watch to the speaking clock

Mark then added:

- Purchase crack
- Smack bitch about a bit
- Get some bling

Highly amusing but Dad was not phased and it was discovered later with the following amendment:

- Hide list

There's me taking the Mickey and inciting my younger brother to force Dad into a life of crack when the truth is that I've become mildly obsessed with them myself. This week of book writing has dissolved into a melee of list-making to solve a complex set of logistics. Firstly, I rode the route of the Dunwich Dynamo. Preparing for it required a whole series of lists, here's a list of the lists I had to make:

- bike preparation tasks
- food purchases required
- directions to train station
- items to be packed in the car
- items to be carried on the bike
- waypoints for ride route

- things to test for working order before departure
- directions to ride start
- things I should be doing around the house instead of bike riding

Each list spawned more issues and more lists threatening to bury my desk. I arrived at the event start completely exhausted from the effort of cataloguing all the things I had to do in preparation. Things took a turn for the worse as the week progressed. School broke up on Wednesday and I'm in charge of the kids for a week. A few centuries back the Factory Acts made good progress in limiting UK child labour. I've torn all of that up and my kids are spending the week at work. We're off on a mini road trip to fill in some of the book's photographic gaps, mainly the Greenwich Meridian. [Postscript: the ride didn't make it into the book].

I rode this in February. I just about had the time to survive on the bike and photographs fell by the wayside. Therefore, what better way to get them taken than spend a few days of family bonding with me on the bike and Jake and Holly behind the lens. And what better way to prepare than more lists:

- accommodation - what a nightmare this has been, trying to find rooms for one adult and two children. Are hotel owners secretly trying to help with the government deficit by deliberately overcharging so that they can pay more tax?
- photo locations - I thought I'd be clever and program the car sat-nav with these. I spent ages working out their locations in one co-ordinate system, only to find that the sat-nav supported another
- things to entertain the kids with - so far I've come up with fishing at Newhaven and a visit to a llama farm, probably need a bit more thought here?
- things I should be doing around the house instead of sodding off with the kids

Before departure I held a masterclass in cycling photography with Jake and Holly, this consisted of me giving them the camera and telling them to go outside and take a few pictures. I went as far as showing them the on/off button, but they're kids and don't need instruction manuals, they have a habit of figuring stuff out for themselves. Finally, let's end on the most frightening list of all, this is the master list of items that I need to finish before the book is complete. It looks something like this:

- ride all over England
- write about riding all over England
- take photographs of riding all over England
- turn the loose notes about riding all over Scotland and Wales into proper writing
- complete layout designs using Adobe CS5
- create graphics to support layout design in Adobe CS5
- pull the whole thing together into a book
- proofread it
- sell a single copy to my Mum
- update CV pretending I spent the previous year caring for a sick relative

It's still a daunting list and I'm always on the lookout for ways to improve my productivity. The use of children as low-cost labour has inspired me though and I am hoping that it will pay dividends very shortly.

Greenwich Meridian Returns

"Never work with children or animals", so spake William Claude Dukenfield and I would agree with half of that statement. At the moment I'm not a big fan of animals given that one of them has decided that my lawn is far too flat. So he has constructed lots of little tumuli all over it to give it a bit more character. I've tried every single humane mole deterrent there is, he loves the lot of them. I've even tried an inhumane approach, hovering over his little hole with my son's baseball bat waiting for him to pop up. But he's a hardy little bugger and took my wooden kisses to be a sign of affection.

This mole has tarnished me as I now have no desire whatsoever to work with animals only an increased appetite for eating them. As for children, William Claude (or WC Fields to friends) was completely wrong as I've been working with my kids and reckon I've hit a goldmine.

Jake (13), Holly (12) and I spent this week taking photos of the Greenwich Meridian ride I undertook in February. Or, being a bit more specific, we contravened every single health and safety rule imaginable to get the shots in the can. You see, taking photos on any English road is always going to be fraught with danger, they are primarily used by motorists who are late for something. A professional photographer would have handed in their resignation after being buzzed for the thousandth time, but when Dad says *"Stand there with the camera, you'll be fine"* the innocent trust of childhood kicks in, truly believing that he will protect you from the nasty cars.

We kicked off at Peacehaven, more specifically the monument that marks the beginning of the Greenwich Meridian on UK soil. Jake and Holly faffed about with cameras whilst I lycra'd up and sucked in my stomach. The first photo went well, I rode towards the camera and promptly fell off the bike. Jake proved that he has no future in the media by laughing, instead of capturing the moment and uploading it to social media. A quick dusting off and the photo session continued with the two of them choosing their angles and messing about with polarizing filters and apertures. The results were brilliant. About thirty pictures later Holly pointed left and said "Hang on Dad, that's the sea isn't it" and very quickly I discovered one of the differences between working with children and professional photographers as they both dived into it.

The next day we moved north and attempted our first "hill session". Taking photos of cyclists on hills is bloody hard. It is incredibly difficult to give a proper sense of steepness, especially in the UK where our hills tend to be short, sharp and surrounded by annoying interferences such as trees and hedges. Our first attempt wasn't doing it for me as the zoom foreshortened the road and the kids were finding it hard to focus on the cyclist. Also, the light was variable with the sun fading behind an ever-thickening cloud.

We scratched our heads for a while until a candidate shot was spotted. Looking down the leafy avenue we espied a patch of light. We conferred and decided to use the light for a bit of drama, the idea being that the contrast in light/dark road would accentuate the hill. How many Dads have conversations like that with their kids? I nearly cried a little as the "grownupness" of our dialogue struck me. Normally conversation between us goes something like this:

Me - "Holly, can you please tidy your room"
Holly - makes a noise like compressed air being forced between two wet sea lions having a cuddle

Flushed with our success on the hill we sped into the centre of London. Our objective was a shot that includes me, my bike and the Greenwich Observatory. In hindsight, a better plan would have been to look at the calendar and avoid the weekend. I hadn't realised that every Saturday Italians commute from Rome to London for a nice days perambulation around Greenwich Park. They don't perambulate around the park. What they do is take photos of each other with the Greenwich Observatory sign in the background. I am convinced that it means something rude in Italian, as hordes of them lined up to get that special shot.

Holly and I stood for nearly twenty minutes whilst parties of Italians pushed their way past. They lined up Granddad and snapped away, then lined up Grandma, then Auntie Corleone closely followed by Giuseppe, Annamaria and little Roberto. We'd take a step forward, but they weren't done. They hadn't got Grandma, Roberto and not Annamaria, or Auntie looking serious followed by Auntie coyly lifting her left leg. It was a nightmare, I nearly said something along the lines of "Please please please, can we just take one shot of the bike going past the sign then the place is yours". But we were too polite. Well, I was, Holly gave them a very long hard twelve-year-old stare that had "fuck off" written all over it. All in all a very successful few days. The kids worked hard to take the shots I was after and we had some great Dad/son/daughter bonding to boot.

Up North

If I had to list my faults I'd struggle to fit them all onto a single sheet of A4. However, there is one that would be notable by its absence, forgetfulness. It's not that I don't forget things, it's the fact that I would forget that I am forgetful and therefore forget to add it to the list. This caught up with me as I was driving north on the M5 this week. I was feeling smug in the knowledge that this trip had been planned with military precision. I went through the list of items that I usually leave behind; tea, route maps, duvet, spanners, common sense. But all were present and correct stowed neatly in the van cupboards.

I was about to lean back in my seat and enjoy the views of texting Audi drivers slipstreaming lorries when I realised I'd left my laptop power supply at home. This might seem of no consequence to many, but to me it was critical. The week's routes were still on the laptop and needed transferring to the GPS. I had loads of writing planned and I use the laptop to back up any photos taken. I added more pain to my stress as forgetfulness twisted the knife further, had the laptop been on charge, how long would I have on battery power? Then I looked at the distance travelled, 75 miles, too far to turn back now.

I fretted my way up to the Wirral for the first stop of the trip. A meeting with Dave Smith who had an item of interest. Tommy Godwin's bike. I'm still on a mission to research the lives of the year record riders. I've done pretty well with Tommy and found loads of useful information but his bike has avoided me for years. A chance discussion with one of his family led me on a trail that ended with

Dave. Walking up his garden path I knew I was in luck as he sat, spanner in hand, drinking tea in a shed stuffed full of bikes.

We chatted for ages about bikes, hills, races, cycling personalities and all sorts of other two-wheeled guff. Put any two cyclists together and this will always happen. Two cyclists meeting react into sparky conversation like sodium hitting water. It's a wonder we ever manage to ride our bikes in between all of the story swapping. Eventually, we got round to Tommy's bike, which was hanging in the corner of Dave's shed. It matched my research well, a 1939 Raleigh RRA, 42" wheelbase, Brooks saddle and Sturmey Archer 4 speed hub. I asked Dave if I could take a few photos, he gave me the bike instead.

Dave wanted me to make use of it. He was keen that I complete the research to tie it properly back to Tommy, but even keener that I use it to recreate a week of the record as I have planned. Dave's a proper cyclist, he knows that bikes aren't meant to be hidden away in sheds, they're either to be ridden or admired or both. He saw that I'd make use of it and without any caveat gave it away. I'll be forever grateful to him as it will aid me significantly in my research and I'm committed to passing it on when I have finished, either to a museum or to one who shares a similar passion to me.

I left Dave and broke the news to Helen that we needed to find room for another bike. Her immediate reaction was "Where?" and I suspect that the bedroom may soon have the door replaced with a turnstile to prevent me from taking it in there.

Onwards to Cheshire and a meeting with Andy who had agreed to join me for my next ride. He'd taken a little diversion via PC World and arrived with a laptop power supply which was gratefully received. We sat and drank tea for an age but as the excuses dissipated it was time for the ride. Andy's cycling had been sidelined by DIY but the pace started briskly and my voice recorder notes were a little more breathless than the norm.

This continued until Mow Cop. Gravity was a little kinder to me here and I shot to the top of this legendary climb and waited for Andy to arrive for some pictures. As I lined up the shot I sat down on a wall without checking the arse landing zone. I felt a burning sensation and jumped back up. A large stinging nettle sprang from my behind and the burning sensation changed to a series of sharp forks being stuffed repeatedly into my shorts.

Andy laughed at my predicament as I hopped around the road fondling my arse. This resulted in me requiring *"a few more climbing shots to get the angles right"*. It might have made him smile, but I rode the Mow Cop ramp once, and he was forced to do it four times. For the record, the first shot was fine.

With the ride done I ferreted through the van fridge in search of an appetising dinner. But the forgetfulness reared its ugly head again with a solitary apple providing slim pickings. The nearest shop was a three-mile walk away, hunger drove me forwards and I took to the lanes by foot. Halfway into the walk, I encountered a well-dressed lady on a massive horse. She had the full set of gubbins on from top to tail, all of it well polished and pristine. I waved a cheery *"Hello"* and she nodded back. Her horse joined in by letting off a ginormous equine fart followed by a grin and a little *"neigh"*. A bicycle would never let you down like that.

With Cheshire ticked off, it was on to Llangollen for another feast of hills. Fifteen of them to be precise. The weathermen were trying to put me off with predictions of rain, thunderstorms, wind and showers of frogs. I'm sure that happened somewhere, but I was accompanied by the sun. The ride was sublime as large sections of it were carried out on closed roads. Not the Tour de France type of closed, the "it's fecked and needs repair" type closed.

My visit must have coincided with a Welsh festival of tarmac (Tarmacy dar boyo?) as a least ten miles of my route were shut for repair. At first, I was resigned to following diversions, but in the end, decided to plug on and speak nicely to the workers. This was the right decision as there were only about five of them, all leaning on spades taking the piss out of each other. I formed a welcome distraction and they took the piss out of me instead whilst waving me through the cratered roads. One came up with the following; *"I've used to have a bike mate, then I married her"*. I took huge offence at his degradation of bicycles and pedalled aloofly away.

Cornwall

"The duck sucked the muck"

To the vast majority of the British population, that phrase would be nonsense. An ornithologist might conjecture that this is possible were a duck looking for a tasty morsel in a particularly repellent pond. But the Barter siblings would all point directly at their father whilst smirking at his calendar. The reason is that Dad used to catalogue every night that we spent sleeping in a tent in neat print on our kitchen calendar. Being a man of the RAF this had to be done using a three-letter acronym. Dad thought long and hard about this and came up with DUC, SUC and MUC.

If you can crack the code before I tell you, you'll realise just how long ago this was. I'll give you a clue, "D" stands for Dave, "S" for Sally and "M" for Mark. Now you have to get the "UC". Give up? It stands for "Under Canvas". As a result, our calendar was covered in DUCs, SUCs and MUCs and on occasion a full house of DUC/SUC/MUC. Being children, we would snigger away at this and chant *"The duck sucked the muck"* to ourselves.

My Dad set an impressive benchmark for nights under canvas (CUC in his case). He told me that he'd managed a full year and his Dad had given him a pipe (or something like that) as a reward. Cogs whirred in my mind and I enquired as to whether we had a similar reward scheme. It turned out we did and in my youth, I notched up an impressive 730+ DUCs gaining a rucksack as a result. Most of the

DUCs were in our back garden which probably still has the two yellow patches in the grass (one was the tent, the other was pure laziness).

I increased my DUC count by one during a planned trip to the West Country. Cornwall and Exmoor were on the agenda and most of the roads there were designed for wheelbarrows rather than motorhomes. So, I shoved the tent in the car along with a dusty sleeping bag, a gas stove, roll mat and my coffee pot. Then I drove into the depths of Cornwall and rode my bike around for nearly seventy miles.

I'd forgotten how hard Cornwall is for cyclists. There is not an inch of flat and all inclines go properly up without any fannying around. I reckon I only used three of the ten gears available to me at the back of the bike and the big ring at the front went into a major sulk after being left out for fifty miles. Cornwall also has properly closed roads. None of those mincey little signs with a bit of resurfacing going on. Oh no, Cornwall closes its roads with hulking great boulders and clay.

I arrived back at the car properly knackered (after a steep climb to get to it of course) and drove off in search of a campsite. A few miles up the road I stumbled upon a holiday park and a tent sign. I should have known better, but fatigue drove me forwards to the reception and a living Miss Marple who manned it.

"I'd like to book a pitch for the night please" - I politely enquired
"£14.99" - she replied over her reading glasses
"It's just a small tent"
"£14.99"
"I don't need electricity or water on the pitch"
"£14.99"

She drove a hard bargain, I tried every angle to get the price down but she had been programmed to respond with "£14.99" to every plea. I considered asking if she had a daughter just to see what the response would have been, but even I have to draw the line somewhere. £14.99 poorer I drove to my pitch, or "the side of another steep hill" as she should have described it. I rushed back to reception, but she'd locked up for the day. She and my £14.99 were off to Asda. I was stuck on the slope.

I made the best I could of the experience, by pitching the tent and driving to Mevagissey where I spent the evening queuing for fish and chips followed by hiding from seagulls and fat tourists. The night in the tent was awful. I awoke curled up at the bottom of it with dead arms and legs. All cycling pain was forgotten replaced with tent induced bruises, hernias and blood-filled feet. I ate a sulky breakfast and left, somehow dropping my voice recorder in the process. This will cause much puzzlement to whoever finds it when they wonder what on earth the breathless bloke was up to.

"<puff><puff> four point five miles <wheeze>country lane<puff>poorly surfaced, steep<rustle><rustle><sound of not switched off voice recorder in pocket>"

I realised I'd lost it nearly forty miles from the campsite and phoned Miss Marple back to see if she'd found it. But she wasn't taking my calls so I diverted into Launceston to buy a new one for the planned Exmoor ride. What a mission of optimism this proved to be, attempting to purchase a solid-state voice recorder in deepest Cornwall.

"Hello, do you sell digital voice recorders?"
"Oi don't think we do my lover, but I sell e' a pasty?"

After a fruitless hour in the town centre, I left with a pasty and directions to Argos who knew I was coming as they were having a voice recorder sale. At Exmoor, I booked a room in a pub. This came with a bath, telly, flat floor and all of my favourite drinks in a bar below. Tempting as it was to cut loose, I only had the one due to Thursday's ride looking even harder than the Cornish epic. I was up bright and early for a cooked breakfast then jumped on the bike and headed off into Exmoor which was covered in sun.

It wasn't only the sun that made an appearance, the hills did as well. Exmoor had heard about Cornwall and got all competitive. The hills were as steep as the Cornish ones but elongated a tad. Dunkery Beacon was the first objective, it climbs 1,200 feet in 2.4 miles with a mile-long section of 17% gradient. I used to like climbing until Dunkery Beacon. Now I'm going to retrain as a time trialist and stick to flat roads that are ten miles long. Dunkery Beacon flogged my legs up and is still flogging them as I type this now. Believe me, I had to give myself a right good talking to before I was able to ride back down and take photos. Descending the other side I met a cyclist putting on his gear. "Did you make it?" he inquired. That for me sums up the Beacon, it's not a case of how long it will take you to climb, it's whether you will manage to climb it at all.

The rest of the ride was equally hard, long steep climbs mixed with absolutely no flat bits at all. Even the cows decided to have a go. All I was trying to do was take a nice little picture, but the hairy bugger was having none of it. "Not on my manor" he mooed at me in cow language. I attempted to pedal away at speed, but speed morphed into amble due to the hill. I was saved by a particularly succulent piece of heather that distracted him from his intention to munch upon my legs. I finished the ride exhausted and drove back home to Swindon. Another long week on the road.

Down South

As an avid newspaper reader, I'm regularly faced with a list of things that will shorten my life if they pass my lips. Cycling magazines are just as bad, they make every attempt to steer me away from the things I love if I'm to maintain my performance on the bike. Recently my doctor colluded as well and posted me with a list of foods that I am now only allowed to smell or face the consequences of death by cholesterol. It's all very well their ganging up on nice food but you'd expect them to warn you of other health risks as well, for example, punk rock.

How often have you sat in the armchair flipped open Cycling weekly and turned to the feature labelled "Why Cyclists Shouldn't Attend Punk Rock Gigs When Training"? The answer is "never" because they have no imagination and only ever preach the obvious. Well, as a public service to all of my spinny legged brethren (and sistren) I'm here to inform you that punk rock gigs are places where cyclists don't want to be for reasons entirely unrelated to pogoing.

This week I attended a punk rock gig. GBH to be more specific. The last time I'd watched them play live the United Kingdom had its first-ever national Glow-worm day (give in? 1985). Trotting down to The Furnace I was filled with the anticipation of meeting a few old friends, sharing a few old stories and drinking a few old pints of watery ale. All of this happened and the band didn't disappoint, apart from Jock Blyth whose legendary Mohican was now replaced with a bald patch.

I returned home unscathed, or so I thought. A few days later I'd developed a cold. "How on earth can this be blamed on a punk rock gig?" I hear you ask. Well, there is no other explanation, it has to be down to the spitting. I wish that in 1976 somebody had invented a camera that tracked airborne spittle. This camera could have been placed in punk rock concert venues and the spittle spectrum produced would prove to be very interesting indeed.

Like the earth's magnetic field, the spittle spectrum would flip over a period of time. In the 70's and 80's the spectrum would show the majority of the phlegm leaving the audience and following a trajectory directly onto the band. In the 90's and noughties the spectrum would thin, with only the odd stray globule appearing. But in our current decade, an interesting phenomenon would be observed, the spectrum would turn through ninety degrees and be visible in the vicinity of the bar.

Scientists would have scratched their heads for years over this, but to me the explanation is clear. Punk rock is dead and the only attendees at such gigs are old. Being old, we're all a little deaf and a tad more dribbly than we ever used to be. We're not used to all of this loud music anymore and we don't have the energy to pogo. So we all hang around at the bar and shout at each other from a range of two inches because the music's too loud and we can't hear each other speak. This is what generates the spittle, shouted conversation and wider gaps in the teeth. I must have been covered in the stuff as old friends bawled into my face about their pensions. To be fair, I shouted back about cycling. They would leave and another old friend would take their place.

There's the old myth about Marc Almond, but I would like to have had my left ear analysed as it contained fifteen different types of male phlegm. At least one of the samples would show traces of nasopharyngitis.

Fantastic, a cold. Just what I needed with two big rides to complete this week and an insane cyclocross race the week after. It made itself known on Tuesday, a hectic day of route planning, preparation and much loose-end-tying. What's worse is that it is one of those weird colds that appears to be polite. Instead of barging into my head and lungs, ripping them to shreds and throwing half of them out of my nose, it has politely crept up and made me feel "headish". Something is in there, but I'm not sure what.

There's been the odd sneeze, a bit of sensation in the lungs, but this cold backs off as soon as I start to moan. I'm wondering if the last virus left some lung wall graffiti along the lines of:

"Dear next cold in residence. Don't go too mental on this one mate, he resorts to whiskey much quicker than other hosts and doesn't believe in that Night Nurse nonsense. If you have at him early he'll hit the Scotch malt and you'll lose to the hangover. I'd play it cool for a while, a few stabs here and there should keep him on the orange juice which we know doesn't work".

You can guess what happened next, instead of sitting it out as a sensible bloke, I went cycling. Surrey was venue number one, the route conveniently went past my ex-business partner's house so I blagged a parking space. My battered car next to his Bentley, there's a message there, he's still working for the business and I'm not. Hurricane Irene was nowhere to be seen as I tootled off into London and minced around Richmond Park as all good roadies do. A few more miles and I was out of London heading into the Surrey hills.

At this point, the cold was nowhere to be seen. Things were looking good as long as I kept my heart rate down and my breathing nice and regular. London motorists were well behaved as well. I had plenty of room, passing speeds were low and even had an "After you, no you, no you, oh go on then, thank you!" exchange with a lorry driver at a busy junction. The bad experiences of the previous motorists began to fade until British Telecom let the motorists down.

It had to be BT didn't it? Everyone who has ever dealt with them in some way has been let down. Broadband failures, phone line disconnections, email non-delivery. Even their adverts subtly conveyed their art of letting you down. Maureen Lipman's screen grandson gained only an "ology", thus becoming a living metaphor for BT.

It was a BT van that forced me off the roundabout. I was going straight over, he decided I wasn't and executed a deft swing of the van that cut off my intended path. BT's strapline used to be "It's good to talk". Not in our case. He shouted about hand signals so in response I made some for him. I don't think they are in the highway code and they tried to make them illegal in Scotland.

No damage done I tapped along to Box Hill making a mental note to "take it real easy in case the cold decides to have a go". Box Hill is quite well known in the cycling world, it will be even more well known next year when the Olympic cycling road race goes up it ten times. I was planning on once and a steady once at that, which would have happened if I wasn't made of male.

Two corners into the climb I spotted some lycra ahead. He was about a hundred yards up the road and an exploratory push on the pedals showed he could be caught. I was calmly sneaking up on him at a manageable pace until he glanced over his shoulder and realised he'd become prey. His excess of Y chromosomes ensured that he pedalled harder as well, and so the chase began.

Ignoring the cold, the remaining fifty-five miles and any sense of decency I upped cadence and went on the attack. He tried as well, but weight and months of training fell in my favour. The gap began to close. I caught him before the final bend where he saw sense and began to slow. Stupidly I passed him at a reasonably high speed. I saved a few breaths to emit a nonchalant "Hi" then continued in my predicament. Passing him at this speed meant I had to carry on. It's desperately poor form to chase and then give up. If you catch at full gas the rule book says you pass and continue at full gas without looking back.

So that's what I did. The rest of the climb was completed at competition pace, a fantastic remedy for a brewing cold. Suffice to say that the rest of the ride wasn't. The remaining route was sneaked round at a CTC cadence. Five miles from the end I was musing on the lack of closed roads. The last set of rides had been peppered with them, but today appeared to be remarkably closed road free. One mile later predictability came to the fore.

The rest of the week was lost in a flurry of map fettling and another cold and weather forecast defying ride. All signs pointed towards a very wet Friday, but I've got a rigid schedule so threw caution to the wind with a very early start in Rutland. The journey there was uneventful apart from my encounter with the world's most dexterous woman.

I was doing 70mph on the A43 (in a car) when a black Audi passed, piloted by a young lady. She was steering by friction alone using the little finger of her left hand, the other fingers were holding a compact mirror. Her right hand was fully occupied by the lipstick. This wasn't the smoothest bit of road either, but from what I could see the lipstick was being applied uniformly. Insanity. It was nice to end the week on a high note as the forecast rain morphed into sunshine and light winds. I had a lovely 65 miles putting aside the wasp who flew into my helmet and stung me. Let's qualify that this was my cycling helmet and you'll be relieved to know that I followed the correct procedure:

- shout "bollocks" loudly (bollocks is OK by the way, I heard it on Radio 4 this morning in a John Humphries interview with a historian)
- undo helmet strap, throw helmet into the verge
- unclip, dismount and run around with hands in the air shouting "He stung me, he stung me!
- stamp repeatedly on wasp
- watch wasp fly away (stamping on wasps with road cleats on is entirely ineffective)
- retrieve helmet from the ditch
- remount, cycle onwards
- return to ditch for sunglasses

Revelations

Writing a regular blog is a funny old game. It may seem simple; survive the week, sit back and reflect upon it and then hammer away into a word processor followed by the push of the "Publish" button. I see it differently though. To me, it is a commitment with a weekly deadline, designed to discipline me into writing something vaguely amusing that bears some resemblance to the facts as they happened. This is not as easy as it sounds. Even budding authors suffer from repetition and I often get to Friday thinking, *"What on earth am I going to write about given that all I've done is cycle a bit and record the salient details into a computer?"*.

Consequently, I scratch around the week looking for tangential elements that I hope will appeal. Sometimes it works, sometimes it doesn't. This week is proving to be another one of the tricky ones. It followed a formula that's been running for months:

- pack the van and forget stuff
- ride hard bikes routes and suffer
- meet lunatics on campsites
- break bits of bicycle
- have "issues" with motorists

A nice little google tool called analytics tells me that I am a long way from being a famous and well-respected blogger. Some recent market research that I carried out indicates that my readers are probably currently lying in bed reading this on a tablet wondering just what the bloody idiot has been up to next. Well, the answer is that the "bloody idiot" has been thinking he's been thinking quite a lot and I'd like to share some of the results with you and have a little chat.

I've been cogitating around "the book", my big project to enrich the lives of road cyclists with the joys of the highways in Great Britain. There's a danger it could be a little bit boring. I know this because I've spent time reading a lot of the books that have gone before. That's a lie. I've flicked through a load of these books but never sat down and read them. All they do is describe leafy lanes and witter on about escaping from traffic. After page 40 I'm willing the author to say something interesting even if it's completely unrelated to the route they want me to ride.

There's another problem, I find it very hard to write and detach myself from the words on the page. In English, this means I'll never be a journalist, a proper historian or a copywriter. I'm only really productive when writing from the viewpoint of Dave. This is a problem when you are an arrogant, opinionated little twerp with a warped sense of humour and slight inferiority complex. There's been a fair few moments of head in hands recently as I've tried my hardest to bend to a discipline that I'm just not programmed to action. I've been tempted to give up and write the last nine months off as "a learning experience". And then I found this:

"You've probably read "In Search Of Robert Millar", "Flying Scotsman" and loads of other cycling books. Well, there's a new one due out next year, and reading this chap's blog on its progress, it should be a cracker."

It's from the front page of the Barrow Central Wheelers cycling club website. I have to confess I've never heard of them. I'll probably be reminded that I know one of their members but my amnesia in the matter will be genuine.

The person that I don't know who wrote it has inspired me forwards more than they can ever know. Because they've made me realise that any book I try to force out is going to be crap. It's got to be written by me and in my voice or not be written at all. My sister will have her hand in the air and be shouting, "Dave I told you this in February." Yes Sally, you did. Sometimes I can be a little bit slow on the uptake, take it from me seven months is good going. Now, there's no guarantee that writing in my style will eradicate the potential for crap. But hopefully, I can sell a copy to the Barrow Central Wheelers with "no refunds" written on the back in bold.

This single (yet bleedingly obvious) revelation has been a huge weight off my shoulders. It has an impact, in that, I will be drawing a thick black line through nearly forty thousand words and writing "could do better" in the margin. But it frees me to be a little more personal and creative in the description of routes.

For example:

"The next few miles consists of delightful smooth tarmacked lanes that lead up to a stiff climb to a church"

Can now be replaced with:

"Mate, eat all your energy bars now before you blow out of your arse on the climb and expire at the top. No worries if you do as there's a graveyard to hand, it might be worth warning the vicar".

More so, I can weave my experiences into the routes and try to bring them alive, a sort of "idiot not abroad" type of experience.

The final huge advantage stems from the issue of photography. There are over forty routes in this book in forty different locations and I had naively assumed that I'd be able to locate and cajole forty different riders to help illustrate the rides. Nine months into the project it is clear that this was ridiculously optimistic given that there are probably less than forty people in the UK prepared to suffer my company for more than an hour.

I've got shit loads of photos of me looking shagged out and fed up with it all at the top of remote hills. These would be incongruous against text that was not describing my journey around the routes. The photos must fit with the words and visa-versa, using my new writing strategy they will. So there ends another statement from the Ministry of the Bleeding Obvious. This book and the others I am working on will be selfishly focused on my journey and my experiences. Because if they ain't, I can't write them.

Cycling activity has been a virtual *"war of the roses"* having taken place in Lancashire and then Yorkshire. Yorkshire won the battle hands down with 4,000 feet more climbing than Lancashire and ferocious westerly winds. Riding over Ovenden Moor was probably the scariest experience of the year as I had gale force winds on one side of the road and spinning wind farms on the other. A complete lack of recent pies meant that I was in clear danger of being plucked from the tarmac and neatly shredded in the turbines. I can now see why the fat lads maintain the lager/doughnut/kebab strategy, on top of Yorkshire hills it makes a lot of sense.

The Matrix

It's been another long week of toil in the saddle and whilst my arse has been rubbing away at the plastic I've been wondering whether any non-cyclists reading understands just exactly what I go through on a long ride. I've got a very clear idea seeing as I've done over forty of them now to write this bleeding book. But my thoughts were crystallised on Tuesday as I rode the last few miles of a humungous great loop in Yorkshire. This ride had followed a tried and tested formula designed to push me well beyond the sane. It started with an unfeasibly steep and long climb, continued with many more of them and then ended with the steepest and longest of the ride which I wasn't expecting. As I pedalled back to the van, the road behind me littered with emotions, I realised that these long rides tend to follow a similar pattern. Subsequently, I've been working on a theory that many other cyclists suffer a similar experience to mine which I've attempted to capture in the matrix below:

	Miles Travelled				
	10	30	60	90	100
Things that ache	Arse	Knees	Bottom of feet	Arms and ears	Everything
Things you crave	Your youth	Marmite on toast	Sunday roast	Public transport	Mummy
Songs in your head	Agadoo - Black Lace	Onwards Christian Soldiers - Traditional	Go Compare Advert	Alice - Sisters of Mercy	Winner Takes it All - Abba
Your rationality	Alice Roberts	Jeremy Paxman	Bruce Forsyth	John Prescott	Katie Price
Food and water available	Plenty	Plenty	Plenty	Moisture under saddle	None

It's highly scientific and exhibits the physical and mental state of the cyclist during key mileage points within the ride. I'm highly confident in its accuracy and have road-tested it throughout 2011. As a control, I believe all motorists would agree that none of the columns applies during any of their regular commutes or holiday journeys for the distances stated. Taking each line in turn I will attempt to explain my findings and therefore bring the non-cyclist into my world. Cyclists, time for a cup of tea during these paragraphs as the emotions and physical manifestations will be all too familiar

Things That Ache

This line presents the physical manifestation of pain during the ride. It begins with "arse" which is logical as very few bicycles come equipped with sofas. Placing your arse on something hard for any period is going to hurt, moving it about rhythmically will hurt more and bumping it up and down only goes to increase the suffering. The pain is noticeable up until 30 miles when the knees kick in and start to shout louder than the arse. They have a fair old crack of the whip up until 60 miles when a new and unexpected ache enters the forum, the bottom of your feet. Think about it, the main point of contact for the majority of the force cyclists produce is the ball of the foot. After 60 miles this area has pressed down on the pedal approximately quite a large number of times.

Moving up to 90 miles we have arms then everything, but hang on, ears? How on earth can cycling cause ears to ache? Well in my case it does because I wear sunglasses and I can't explain why, but after 90 miles they make my ears hurt. Maybe they prevent the ears from flapping about in the wind? Maybe they're too heavy for my lightweight ears? Maybe they just don't fit properly?

Things that you crave

Surely all of the entries in this line are self-explanatory. To qualify the first entry, I usually feel pretty good in the first ten miles spinning along feeling a bit Eddy Merckx. I yearn to be able to have a brief chat with a seventeen-year-old me who is about to dispense with the bike in favour of beer and cigarettes. I'd tell him that if he'd invested properly in his legs then, mine wouldn't start to hurt so much in a few miles time. Thing is, he'd have flicked the v's and wandered off down The Mallard for a pint.

Songs in your head

The titles listed here actually happened during the 95 mile Yorkshire epic. For some reason, the first earworm is always a repetitive piece of pop nonsense that plagued the airwaves for months. I've had Wigfield, St. Winifreds School Choir, Chas and Dave, but this week it was Black Lace. I fight hard to remove it for miles often resorting to whistling the intro to "Sweet Child of Mine" (it's impossible by the way, try it), but to no avail until at 30 miles I remember Patrick Humphries. Patrick stood next to me in the school assembly. Yes, stood. I went to a proper hard Cornish junior school in Padstow and we stood for the duration of assembly. Many weeks there would be a fainter, but it changed nothing. We stood and sang hymns that Mr Penner had loving handwritten onto a large piece of paper. "Onward Christian Soldiers" was a regular at assembly and Patrick loved it. Problem was that he had a voice like a fisherman gargling slurry. He was much bigger than me so I was never able to offer constructive feedback. I suffered for his art and let him imprint this tone-deaf rendition on my mind ready to oust Black Lace after 30 miles of bike riding.

It would take something seriously repetitive and annoying to push Patrick into the background and what better than a piece of classic opera ruined by an insurance advert. Things are not going well after 60 miles of this lot in your ear (maybe the songs explain the ache?). It's time for a real downer piece as every bit of me feels sorry for myself. Many of you won't have heard of the Sisters of Mercy, keep it that way. A number of us spent the eighties waving our hands around mysteriously whilst wearing eye make-up. The sombre mood continues into the ninety miles. "Winner takes it all" was a song I associate with the death of my first pet, Sooty the guinea pig. When I hear it I'm reminded of grief, suffering and hurt which is about right with one hundred miles in the legs.

Your Rationality

Here, I have attempted to exhibit the cyclist's rationality over distance by comparing it to well-known celebrities.

- Alice Roberts, perfectly sane, good looking, bright, intelligent but hold on, what's with the red hair?
- Jeremy Paxman, sane enough for mainstream television but the occasional rabid bark or irrational line of questioning
- Bruce Forsyth, getting on a bit but can still be lucid for short periods, prone to making strange body shapes and emits frequent gibbers
- John Prescott, probably best not to approach, the wrong line of enquiry could result in a swift left hook
- Katie Price, all sense of the real world has left the body, in fact, not much of the body is real body anymore

Food and water Available

Suffice to say that it takes about 60 miles for me to remember that I'm hungry and need a drink. At that point, I'll eat everything and a few miles later wonder where it has all gone? On Tuesday I passed a house with a sign advertising "Homemade jam". I'd done over eighty miles and had nothing left in the jersey pocket. It was so tempting to pull over, sneak a jar away and go all Winnie the Pooh on it.

Cover Shoot

How many great ideas have been hatched in pubs? I would postulate "bloody loads". Pubs are entirely conducive to idea hatching as they contain a variety of liquids designed to free the mind of conventional thought and spur the thinker forward to the moment of genius. I believe that the first successful ascent of Everest was planned in a pub (OK pedants it was a hotel, but it had a bar). The Duck and Drake Inn harboured Guy Fawkes and his mates as they brainstormed ideas for obliterating the Houses of Parliament. And let's not forget Heston Blumenthal who came up with the genius idea of charging the public a mortgage for a plateful of nothing in the Fat Duck at Bray.

Therefore it will not surprise you that I came up with a moment of genius in the Pack Horse, Louth over a pint of lager. The fact that I had a moment of genius will probably surprise you, but the pub and pint of lager will simply be business as usual. It was here that I sketched out a design for the cover of my book. This issue had been nagging at me for months as book covers are critical to their success on the shelf. There's loads of marketing-type-speak out there to guide you, but simplistically, it's got to be bold, fit the content and stand out from the crowd.

Seeing as I own every cycling book in the world, it is quite straightforward to work out what has been done before, and I'm fairly confident that my idea is new. The major problem is the picture. I need a photograph as the basis of the design, that summarises the contents and inspires the reader to pick it up and have a little nose inside. It's a crucial photograph and to be quite frank I don't think I'm capable of taking it. So this week I shone a picture of a VW camper van onto the bottom of a cloud in the Mendips. Seb Rogers duly emerged from his professional photographer's "Sebcave", dived into the Sebmobile and drove up to the Peaks clutching a poorly constructed book cover commission. The idea also needed a rider who was riding a good looking bike and was wearing a cycling jersey of a certain design. They need to look good climbing and descending and be able to understand and action clear instructions from the photographer.

Almost everything in that previous paragraph ruled me out of the equation. I'd bought the jersey but it was too big for me. I won't even go into the rest as it just hurts. So I recruited Andy to the cause as he lives down the road from our chosen site, fitted the jersey and has a proper road bike with gears and stuff that work.

The three of us met in the car park above Mam Tor. It was pissing it down, the skies were "John Major" grey and my car thermometer read somewhere around about 4 degrees. I took a quick nervous inventory of my clothes; cycling shorts, cycling jersey, lightweight waterproof, jeans and a T-shirt. Seb had done this before and I noted that his inventory differed slightly from mine by including; woolly hat, gloves, a full set of waterproofs, dingy and distress flares.

At 10 am conditions were getting close to biblical. Winds were trending towards gale force, thick rain fought hard with hail to batter the earth and all manner of cloud formations whizzed across the sky as they deposited stuff upon the ground. The three of us walked down Winnats Pass for a quick reccie but Andy was beaten back by the hail. Seb and I picked the first location then dived back into the car before we were stoned to death.

I was already ready to go home and we hadn't even started but Seb remained calm. He'd seen that the weather was moving and experience told him that we would get our shots. We sat it out for a while until the sun popped out from nowhere forcing Andy to kit up and get on his bike.

Seb had chosen the steepest point of Winnats Pass for the first location. He climbed up the side of the pass whilst I removed coke cans and piles of hail from the road. Andy was ordered onto his bike and told to ride up the climb, again and again, and again. At one point Seb said *"Andy, can you go faster?"*, to which Andy nodded and then rode down to me muttering *"Dave, tell him it's a 20% gradient !"*. But he got on with it, sprinting out each interval and adjusting the angle of his elbows on demand.

I had a little chuckle to myself when Seb asked Andy to look a little more cheerful. It was blowing a gale as a headwind, lower than 4 degrees centigrade and a ludicrously steep climb. Not laughing material, especially when you come from the north where a smile begins and ends at the eyebrow. The weather continued to oscillate between sunshine and armageddon. At one point the three of us were hunched down by the side of the road like garden gnomes in an attempt to hide from the hail.

Shortly afterwards I began to shiver and was curtly sent back to the car by the other two to get warm. A good decision as I'd been standing around doing not much in completely inadequate clothing. The day continued in a similar theme, sunshine punctuated by horror including a brief spell of thunder and lightning. Andy and Seb were unphased, they worked incredibly well together to get my shot and at around about 3 pm I reckon they nailed it.

We'd moved location to Mam Nick, Seb had found a spot that met my criteria and also led into a gorgeous slab of Edale that would set the scene perfectly. Initially, we were shooting in clouds until the sun broke through and lit the landscape ahead of us. Greens, yellows, browns, roads, skies and a rider looking right on the bike. I've not seen the full-size picture yet, but Seb and I are confident that we've got it. We flipping better have, as I doubt I'll be able to convince Andy to wear a silly jersey and ride hill intervals in the hail again!

Driving home I knew I'd made the right decision to use a professional. I'd have turned around and gone home in weather like that, but Seb's experience told him that we'd get the shots and more so that the dramatic weather would serve to light the scene exactly to my needs. Next time though, like a teenager going to a party, I'll ask the question "What will you be wearing today?".

It's not all been glamour and photoshoots though. The rest of the week has been a flurry of planning, planning and more planning.

Sadly, none of this planning has been done in the pub. I've sweated over maps, bed and breakfast guides and cycle touring websites to come up with the ultimate Lands End to John O'Groats route (*Spoiler: It did not make it into the book*).

This has been on the agenda right from the start of this project. I've ridden the route before and found it had "niggles". Some bits were too urban, some bits a tad boring and a few epic riding opportunities were wasted. Therefore, I've designed a route that answers all three. It avoids towns, passes interesting landmarks and does some Scottish stuff that could almost be classed as wilderness.

I asked for a volunteer to ride it, but all eyes went to the floor and so it's down to me to head off into the weather and do battle with the route. Lands End/John O'Groats in October, only an idiot would attempt that? Yes, an idiot will attempt it as I set off on Monday, unsupported.

I've done a similar trip before in Ireland. Riding with minimal gear and using B&B's instead of campsites. The approach has its risks and issues. There's only room for one set of kit which requires a unique ability to wash and dry your clothes using shower gel and available towels. Evening wear has to be paired down to a t-shirt, boat shoes and trackie bottoms. There's also the terrible gamble of which bike spares to take and what to leave behind, knowing that the discarded kit will become essential items as soon as you're miles from a bike shop.

I like to travel as light as possible to enjoy the road as if on a Sunday run. The Van Nicholas blew a bottom bracket this week and has been retired to the stable lame. It's a Campagnolo bottom bracket and they are made of gold encrusted with diamonds, so we'll need to sell the house before it can be replaced. The trusted Omega has whinnied its way out from the hay and is champing at the bit to get ridden. Different bike, changeable weather, new route, eccentric B&B owners and a lingering sinus infection. Hopefully, you can understand my nerves at setting out.

Working Holiday

This year I have been very fortunate in combining family holidays with work. This might not have been so successful when I worked in IT. I doubt that Helen, Jake and Holly would have enjoyed sunning themselves in a data centre server room. Whilst the temperature would have been higher than any other destination we've visited previously, flashing LEDs hold a limited fascination and the hum of cooling fans gains tedium similar to most of the board meetings I was forced to attend.

I guess I could have broken it up with a session where we vehemently blamed each other for a major system failure followed by a brief interlude where we nodded in agreement at company strategy presentations whilst secretly thinking "How did this idiot ever get on the stage in front of me? And why has he just pretended that he cares about us whilst looking at his watch?". However, my current job as a cycling dosser pretending to write a book does have certain holiday based fringe benefits. Essentially I can con the family into thinking they are on vacation whilst I extract free labour from them in the name of "fun".

This last week has been spent zooming around Scotland in the motorhome. Partly due to me having cycled up here in the first place and needing a lift home. I managed to guilt Helen into packing the van full of treats, kids and warm clothes followed by a long drive to pick up her wounded warrior lying spent by the side of the road. I skillfully sold the idea of a holiday whereby the family would develop their photography skills in various scenic Scottish locations. Coincidentally these locations would be places that I had failed to photograph and uncannily they would be taking pictures of a cyclist fighting desperately to complete the content for his book. That'll be me then.

Our quest began in Torridon, halfway up the Bealach Na Ba. The last time I was here it shagged it down with rain and I was shagged out. All of this shagging prevented me from taking any meaningful shots so I persuaded Helen that we needed to get as high up the pass as possible to nail some decent piccies. She agreed as long as I drove the van, there are a multitude of warning signs at the bottom that advise motorists to walk. I got it about a third of the way up before crapping myself and insisting we walk the rest. Later a Scottish omnibus descended from the top and put my driving skills to shame.

This was Helen's first foray into cycling photography, she took to it pretty well. It was all of ten minutes between *"Which button do I press?"* to *"Please ride that again, without the stupid gurn and try to keep your hands off the brakes"*. The kids disappeared with my spare camera promising to take some moody scenic shots. I've since deleted the selfies.

Our session was rudely interrupted by a mad walker. She strode purposefully up the road and enquired as to "How long we would be taking photos?". I hadn't realised that the Bealach was metered and that only a fixed period was available for the taking of landscapes. We fobbed her off with "twenty minutes" and watched her march off up the hill muttering to herself about "yellows, blues and scenery".

Next, we hit Skye and drove most of the way around the island in search of an open campsite. The trusty Sligahan site was closed and we decided not to break the "Don't shit in the motorhome" rule. Eventually, we found a croft next to a loch that had expanded out into camping. We paid, asked for pub directions, parked up, admired the view, then trooped up the road in search of food. After half a mile conversation ceased drowned out by rain. We'd broken Scottish rule number 43 subsection a).

"No matter how clear the skies, how low the wind and how dry the roads you shalt always carry a coat as it will probably rain"

Hiding out in a bus shelter Helen confessed that she'd done the "man thing" of nodding as directions were supplied but failing to take any of them in. We sent Jake out on a scouting mission up a small lane. He returned wet with no sightings of ale. Hunger drove us out into the drizzle. The first pub we found had stopped doing food. The landlord of pub number two was so fat that there was no question of a lack of pies in the vicinity. Suspiciously they were out of steaks and burgers. Given that his wife was a similar size I did not doubt as to where the red meat had made its home. To make things worse he matched me pint for pint from behind the bar and then had another to ensure he kept the lead.

Helen made me work it all off the next day though as I rode up and down the Skye hills to ensure that she got the shot. Another long drive after Skye to Aviemore and a planned rest day from photography. We'd promised the kids a day doing "their sort of stuff" and nervously pushed open the door of Tourist Information for a perusal of their "stuff to do leaflets". Jake immediately pounced on a terrifying full-colour shot of a bloke haring down a fast-flowing river with only a car tyre for company.

"Dad, I'd like to go river tubing please"

I was tempted to pretend that my phone had no signal, but Jake is a tenacious little beggar and I knew he'd find a payphone. I gave Helen a resigned glance and dialled the number on the leaflet.

…Please don't answer, please don't answer, please don't…
"Hello, Stupidlydangerousoutdoorwatersports, can I help you".
"Ermm, yes, you don't do river tubing do you?"
"Yes sir we do"
"Oh shit"
"But sadly we finished a few weeks ago"

Jake was a bit confused when the news that we couldn't go river tubing was accompanied by two adults dancing around the Tourist office punching the air. We let them go on the Treezone high wire forest course instead, who very sensibly did not require adult supervision for the over 12s. We consoled Jake further by introducing him to the fine Scottish tradition that is Irn Bru. Though he betrayed his middle-class credentials by taking it from a glass laden with ice. Luckily the cafe did not have umbrellas or olives.

We curtailed the rest day due to a complete lack of rain and drove up into the hills to knock off a few evening shots. It all went a bit wrong for me here as a complicated piece of book continuity planning meant that the photos must be taken in summer-ish gear. Problem was that it was bloody freezing which explains the quizzical yet hypothermic look that Helen captured in the photo. I like to think that in years to come it will become the cycling equivalent of the Mona Lisa with generations of riders staring up and asking "Why's that pillock riding summer shorts with winter boots?"

Shakespeare

I've concluded that I am incredibly jealous of William Shakespeare. It's not linked to his prose. I have no aspiration whatsoever to write fiction when there is so much surrealism evident in the real world. A number of my friends have decided to celebrate November by calling it "Movember", growing facial bum fluff and then begging for coinage in return. The Elizabethans would have been mystified, as their queen did it for free.

No. The jealousy stems from his work environment when compared to that within which I find myself. The post-noughties is simply not conducive to uninterrupted writing and I'd like to be transported back to the sixteenth century please to enable me to finish this book.

The week started reasonably well, by beginning with a Monday but it didn't last when my complex authoring and graphics production computer system had a bit of a spew. I'll not bore you with the detail but simply leave you with the immediate outcome which was me holding my head in my hands and repeating the phrase "*Why me?*". I stood to lose months of work if I wasn't careful and an extended period of flicking the "v"'s at the screen hadn't seemed to work.

Shakespeare's scrolls never "crashed" did they? He didn't take quill to paper and find that the only thing he could write was "Failed system dependency 44". Oh no, life was easy for him, he simply sat there and merrily copied Francis Bacon's homework into his little book. So I parked this problem, saved it for a moment when I was feeling saner and opened the word processor. Time for a few hours of increasing the word count which would have happened if only I'd had the sense to shut down my email.

"Ping!"
"Subject: Dave's Tax Return"

This year I'd made the huge mistake of abdicating the completion of my tax return to an accountant. A mistake that I will never make again. Wikipedia states that an accountant is defined thus:

"practitioner of accountancy, which is the measurement, disclosure or provision of assurance about financial information that helps managers, investors, tax authorities and others make decisions about allocating resources."

I would like to propose that the definition is refined further:

"one whose single role is to reduce their client's fiscal wealth by simply asking the same question in different guises whilst charging huge amounts by the hour and using a computer programme to do the real work in seconds"

The received email was the final straw in a process that has taken three months. Yet more questions that could have been answered from the information I'd supplied and yet more reasons why my return was "taking longer than anticipated" and "costing more than Greece". I properly lost it and redirected all of my creative efforts into the response to my accountant's boss. No doubt reading all of it will be added to my bill. And here's another area where our Will had it easy. The Elizabethan tax was dead simple. The Queen's men turned up at your door and pointed a sword at your chest. You simply handed over Dubloons until the sword was lowered and they went away. Five minutes effort and then back to copying.

Next, the shed began to collapse. Ok, I admit that is a slight exaggeration, but the blind above the door fell down (I'd put this up) and the halogen bulbs all decided that they'd had enough and committed suicide in unison. I was trying to ignore all of these events and concentrate on writing when the phone rang with an offer of work. It was too good to turn away as the job description went like this:

"Travel on the train to London and attend project meeting"
"Nod sagely at key points, stroke chin, occasionally ask for clarification"
"Go for a boat ride after meeting, give opinions, sing sea shanties"

Honestly, that was it. A few minutes of waffle followed by a dive into a canal tunnel near Camden lock. I don't mind admitting to a small portion of fear having entered that tunnel. This is what snakes must feel like when they are being born. It went on forever, was very dark and there was nowhere to get off. I had a concern that I hadn't stroked my chin enough and that my customer had found a strategic place to bump me off. Luckily he needed someone to open the lock gate on the other side hence I survived.

Now surely I had one up on Elizabethan Bill after this little jolly. Actually, no. The crux stems from the words: "travel on the train". Trains weren't invented in William's era so his only option for London to Stratford was to hop on a coach. If he was feeling a bit brassic, he could go public and share the coach with others. Maybe they would all be coming home from work after a busy day.

Well lucky old Will, the mobile phone was not invented then. If his fellow passengers had felt the need to inform their spouses of their travel situation, they'd have had to get out a scroll, write it down and hand it to the coach driver for delivery at the same time as them. In modern times it is far more painful as I shared a carriage with a hundred iPhone users who were:

"JUST ON THE...HELLO..HELLO..SORRY WENT THROUGH A TUNNEL..I'M JUST ON THE TRAIN".

Yes mate, she knows, you probably get the same train every day. You'll see her in about 20 minutes and you could inform her in person of your mode of travel that evening. There is no need to tell her, me and the other hundred iPhone users who are also *"JUST ON THE TRAIN"* as well.

Fortunately, there are exceptions. There are the twenty people who have already informed their wife, mother, grandparents, lawyer and doctor that they are "*JUST ON A TRAIN*" and so have phoned the office. "*JUST RINGING TO SEE HOW THINGS ARE GOING*". Well, I can tell you. Since you left things are going fine, everybody has got on with some work for once now that the loud-mouthed pillock has sodded off out for the day and isn't constantly pestering for updates.

I hate commuter trains with a vengeance. Why doesn't anybody text? Why can't they leave the office alone? Why can't they carry deodorant and give themselves the odd sniff to see if the fact they've had to walk a few steps have made them go a bit ripe? Why can't they eat sandwiches with their mouths closed? Why do I have to hear that as well? And finally, did your company fashion you with that laptop to play Minesweeper? Or did you lie to IT and pretend that you'd work on the train?

My resolve to not retreat to commuter land has been seriously strengthened. It's either the shed or the building site for me and I'm not very good with the hod so that narrows it down to the shed.

Reflection

Writing's hard, I'll make no bones about that. The act of sitting in front of some electronic gadgetry and distilling the thought process into electronic bits takes some doing. When I tell people that I'm spending the year attempting to write a book, I often hear the "Oh! I'd love to do that" retort. But would they? Admittedly writers are not required to clock in at nine am and toddle off home at five. They don't have to queue for the coffee machine or write a business case for entry into the stationery cupboard. There is a degree of flexibility. But the grass is never greener on the other side as they are required to sit down and write.

Sometimes this is difficult.

I was sent an excellent piece by Andy Kirkpatrick, a climbing writer, who has put together a web page with heaps of good advice for those resisting the temptation of authorship. I read it all and have nicked a few of his ideas but it has made me sit back and look inward at my approach and I've quickly realised that I am at the mercy of a mysterious spirit who governs my writing productivity. To exhibit this I'll let you into a typical Dave writing session, it goes something like this:

Firstly, I sit down at the desk, switch on the computer and fire up the word processor, determined to hammer out several thousand words. I'll confidently type the chapter title and lean back in my chair, pleased with progress to date. Then I'll save the document to the hard disk and prepare for a deluge of words. They won't come, so I tidy the desk a bit more and sharpen a pencil instead, who knows why I write with a keyboard? It's some sort of psychological effort to get me into the zone. In the absence of words, I'll reformat the title changing it to bold or a different font, then it's off to social media or Angry Birds for a bit of inspiration.

The writer's constipation will often continue for a while. A cup of tea provides a welcome distraction as does spilling it all over my desk and clearing it up with post-its. Looking out of the window occupies a few more seconds followed by some further desk rearrangement and chair height adjustment. I check my mobile phone, but no new texts have arrived, there are a few more social media posts to read but they are all about coffee, illness or another pointless, inane blog entry (usually mine). An inner voice shouts at me to return to the document, so I reformat the title again and save the document just in case.

This can go on for hours with words per minute measured in small fractions until suddenly he appears, Doppelganger Dave, my productive literary double. He's a sneaky bugger as well. I cannot summon him to order, he just turns up. I'm forced to the back of my conscious mind as Mr Doppleganger elbows his way in and takes over. While I sit in a synaptic reception he takes control of my fingers and thraps out several thousand words into the computer. Exhausted, he departs and I regain control of my conscious mind and survey the wordfest he's left behind.

Sometimes I have no idea where it came from, I can see what he was thinking but would love to replicate the chain of thought that led him there, but I can't as he's buggered off for a cup of tea. Occasionally the words make sense and I'm pretty sure he's been nicking my ideas. Once he'd simply written a shopping list consisting entirely of bike parts and I felt obliged to purchase them.

There's a problem though, this Dave is only available for a few hours each day. When he's not there progress is glacial and I'm forced to focus on other tasks. I'd love to be a word factory, but I'm not. I've read through some of the "forced" writing that I've tried and its bilge. Out of Dave and Doppelganger Dave, Doppelganger's the best writer by far and I'll be needing his services to get to the end of the book. This revelation leads to several conclusions that I'm happy to state. Firstly, a career as a professional author does not await. I'm productive in fits and starts and simply cannot focus on writing as a full-time job. I'm the luckiest bloke on the planet to have been given this year, but a year is all it will be. The next writing project will be a hobby rather than a vocation and will probably take me ten.

Therefore, I've got the calendar out and come up with a plan. It involves getting the book finished by April ready for publication then deciding exactly how I am going to do that. Simplistically there are two routes; self-publication or approach several publishers and see if any of them bite. I took route two tentatively early this year and gained a lot of useful feedback. Most of this was around personal hygiene and dress sense, but it was mooted that the book could have commercial appeal and there would certainly be interest. The main problem for me is commission. It was a real eye-opener to understand the kind of rates we're talking about. Think of a number close to 100% on one side and a fraction of it on the other and guess which side applies to the author?

My cunning plan is to rock up at their door with a finished product which I believe is unusual. Most authors are wizards with the word processor but leave layout and design to their publisher. I've put a lot of effort into researching competing offerings and working out the size, shape, layout and content I need to make mine stand out. However, German measles stands out as well, so this may not necessarily be a good thing. But it is a useful time filler for the hours that while away whilst Doppelganger Dave is out drinking with his mates.

Self-publication has its own issues. Mainly the fact that the word "self" applies to financing as well. I will have to bear the costs of printing, marketing, sales and distribution myself. This comes with the "How many copies can I shift" gamble along with who shall I shift them to and how shall I tell them that I would like them to act as shiftees? Therefore, I'll explore option one whilst keeping the door of option two firmly open in the instance of rejection or failed negotiations.

Earlier I said *"several conclusions"*, so here's another one. I need to develop some revenue streams that don't rely on books. This is countered by conclusion number three, no way am I ever getting a normal job again. Luckily opportunity presents itself to he who waits and as the year heads to a close I find myself involved in several discussions that all involve making a living whilst not wearing a tie. None, some or all of these may turn into opportunities but it's nice that they're there and hopefully, there'll be something for me to do that earns money.

Radio

I'm sure you're familiar with the name Fenton. If you are not, search for a video of a bunch of deer being chased around a park by Fenton the dog. The video's gone viral down to the owner's horror as to what his dog is up to. *"Jesus Christ"* he exclaims, as the pack of deer are loosely herded by what looks to be a black labrador.

Now, this video has really pissed me off. And this has nothing to do with coming from a generation that spent Sunday evenings glued to "One Man and His Dog" in the olden days of three channels on the TV. I could present a case against the "dogs of today", their lack of patience and unwillingness to serve an apprenticeship. Plainly the dogs of today simply dive in and herd things, whereas the dogs I used to watch on TV shepherded properly with lots of lying down and come-bys. They went through years of training before the reward of a TV appearance. Fenton simply acts like a dick in Richmond Park and millions are in awe of his antics.

But my beef is different, the reason I am pissed off is that it's gone viral with no effort whatsoever. The owner simply uploaded it and suddenly they're famous. I saw them on breakfast TV on Monday, a father and son team lauded by the presenters for their fantastic ability to press "Record", "Stop" and then "Share".

I am bitter, and I will admit to that. I sit in my shed day in day out trying to think of ideas for self-promotion and publicity. I'm going to need them if I'm ever to sell a copy of this book. I also need some help with research for my "Year Record" project and the more people that know about it, the more help I can get.

In April I had a brainwave, I'd create a Twitter account as a tribute to Tommy Godwin, from it I would tweet his daily mileage and cyclists all around the world could follow his progress. The cycling press would pick up on it and the whole thing would go viral. What could possibly go wrong?

On Sunday the account had nine followers. I'd sent links to the cycling press, tweeted various cycling celebrities, discussed it with journalists and they had responded by emailing me pictures of tumbleweed. Nevertheless, I maintained the account in the vain hope that one day somebody would see it and take an interest.

Last week I took a call from the BBC. A very nice lady asked me about my interest in Tommy Godwin as they were doing a short programme about him that would go out on Monday night. I waffled on a bit about how inspirational the year record was whilst ignoring her loud yawns down the phone. Then I mentioned the Twitter account. The yawns were eclipsed by scribbles, turns out she was from BBC online and I'd said a magic word.

We finished the conversation and I thought nothing of it, maybe I'd get one extra hit on the website as she made sure I was telling the truth. But on Monday I went viral. Well, maybe viral is a bit of an exaggeration, let's agree that on Monday my website and Twitter account did more traffic in a day than they usually manage all year.

I was getting "pings" every minute as people signed up to the Twitter account and all sorts of emails asking questions about Tommy and the year record. It turns out that the nice lady had written a story about it and put it up on the BBC website. The cycling press and journalists had read it as well and copied it to their websites (fascists, won't listen to me..but Auntie Beeb mutters and they are slathering). People were tweeting left right and centre about the year record account and telling their friends. Cycling forums were discussing it and linking back to my site. Traffic was at an all-time high.

Then I got a phone call from Lee Stone at BBC Wiltshire Radio, would I pop down to the studio now for a quick over-the-air interview? I pretended that I had all sorts of highly important meetings, but he persisted and I agreed to wander down to their offices at 5.45 pm. I told a few friends about this and one asked if I felt nervous about going on air. I nonchalantly waved him away with the information that I was joint winner of the Wootton Bassett School Drama cup in 1982. Secretly I had one overriding fear, I was scared that I'd say "fuck".

I am a little sweary. Evidenced by anyone who has passed within 500 yards of my garage. Walking down Victoria Hill I chanted a little mantra "Don't say fuck, don't say fuck, don't say fuck". But this made things worse. It was now front of mind and taking over all rational thought, I should have been preparing myself with statistics and unique insights into Tommy's rides but the front lobe was clogged with the word I'm not allowed to say.

A few minutes later I was buzzed in the door fully expecting to be whisked into a meeting room and fully briefed on how to act and behave on air. I imagined them giving me some sort of loose script and carefully reminding me that profanities are not to be uttered within BBC premises, especially the word "fuck". I was hoping for a green room similar to that enjoyed by the guests of Jonathan Ross, maybe with complimentary wine or a few M&Ms.

Things were rather different though. I was taken straight upstairs into a room full of recording machines and computers. A guy called Mark was twiddling knobs, talking to callers on the phone, typing into a computer and waving through a glass window at somebody. It was almost as if I'd walked into a multi-tasking seminar for men. Mark put me at ease, offered me a drink, told me I'd be on in ten minutes whilst simultaneously answering the door, programming two idle computers and writing the script for next week's show. I pretended to look busy by writing my name fifteen times into my notebook.

All too quickly I was ushered into an empty studio and sat near a microphone. The door was shut and I was left to my thoughts. "Don't say fuck, don't say fuck, don't say fuck". these were interrupted by a ball of energy that erupted into the air from nowhere and morphed into a Radio DJ. Like Mark, Lee had taken multi-tasking to a new art form. He shook my hand, welcomed me, went on air, cued the news, asked me a few questions, cued a desperately bad record from the seventies, introduced it, played it, gave the listeners a nice introduction to my story, smiled very broadly and then turned in my direction.

"Don't say fuck, don't say fuck, don't say fuck", was thumping in my ears as his first question came forth. I felt a mixture of mild panic mixed with curiosity. "What would happen if I did say fuck?". Would I get even more Twitter followers? Would this elevate me up to Fenton level?

This made things ten times worse as I'd moved from a quest to be polite, into a rude social experiment. But the temptation was there, nobody had told me not to say it, they only had themselves to blame. I paused momentarily, analysed his question, leaned forward towards the microphone and answered with "fuck".

No of course I didn't. I gave a relatively lucid performance and managed to keep the "umm" to words ratio in the low fifteen per cent. I wanted to say it though and it is only now that I can reveal to Lee that whilst he was showing an interest in my turgid blatherings about cycling, all I wanted to say was "fuck".

I'm sure a few people heard my interview, but Radio Four have not been in touch. So it was back to the grindstone for the rest of the week, bashing my head against chapters of the book and trying to understand the mad bloke on the voice recorder waffling on about sheep.

I went through my ride notes and realised that a set was missing. I'd ridden a route around the Isle of Wight before working out my book writing methodology. No notes, no photos, no GPS traces, only distant memories. I needed all of these to stay on track, thus decided to ride it on Wednesday regardless of the weather. Wednesday was set to be a national strike, we'll come to that in a bit.

Leaving the ferry at Yarmouth I noticed the wind. It was hard to ignore due to the lycra enema I was receiving from the unusually violent westerly gale. Stoically I threw myself onto my steed and bravely set off into the wind. The "don't say fuck" rule does not apply in these conditions. I said it a lot as the wind delivered a meteorological condition known in the trade as schizophrenia. Simplistically, the weather cannot decide what it wants to be, so it tries everything in an attempt to settle on a suitable personality. Rain, sun, cloud, a hail of frogs, mist, monsoon and calm all passed over in a single hour.

Turning to get the wind on my back was a mild relief, but the hilly coastline of the Isle of Wight negated that. Photos were difficult as the camera kept getting blown over and my lunchtime sandwiches had decided not to make the journey with me, the fridge at home seemed far too cosy.

After a well-fought fifty-five miles, I arrived at Cowes eagerly looking forward to a brief rest on the floating bridge. It was shut. "fuck, fuck, fuckity, fuck, fuck, fuck, fuck it". The bridge operators were out in solidarity with the workers. I sat forlornly and pondered my lack of pension. They were stood around braziers, eating chestnuts and shouting slogans to get theirs. Me, I had to ride an additional ten miles in this wind to have a hope of earning something towards mine.

The "fuck" rule was again disregarded as I desperately time trialled back to Yarmouth cruelly chased by the fading light. Three-quarters of the job was done, but a return trip was still required.

Countryfile

I had an almost rationale debate with my teenage daughter a few weeks ago that went something along these lines:

"Dad, why do you watch Countryfile? I can't see the point in it."
"Well Holly, it is an extremely valuable programme on several levels"
"Huh?"
"Firstly, I am regularly brought up to date with the best farming practices carried out by plumb voiced farmers"
"Mkay"
"Next, I get to see Matt and Ellie trying to make ramblers look interesting. This followed by John Craven getting over serious about some controversy that nobody can do anything about"
"Hmmm"
"But finally, and most importantly of all, I am told the weather outlook for the week"
"Dad, it's still pointless"
"Isn't"
"Is"
"Isn't, isn't, isn't, isn't, no returns"

Holly filled her ears with iPod earphones, mouthed "Pointless" at the television and flounced off upstairs for a skype session with Justin Beiber. Don't tell her this though, but she is mostly right. Fifty minutes of Countryfile are completely pointless but I have to sit through it to get to the forecast, which is the best on the box.

I know this because I have watched it all year. I use the Countryfile forecast to plan my week, deciding where to ride or whether to forget it and have some quality shed-time instead. Last week I'd planned a trip to Scotland to plug a few of the photography gaps. The tension built as the clock moved towards 7.15 pm Sunday, would Countryfile's weather forecast underwrite my trip?

Simplistically, the answer was "No". The forecaster dispensed with any charts, science or isobars. He simply pointed at Scotland and shouted "Run away! Run away!". I interpreted this to mean that a storm was coming. The BBC News channel was a little more lucid and calmly advised me not to travel. I turned to Helen and asked, "What do you think?". She told me that I would be fine, but she was holding my life insurance policy at the time so I discounted that. To make things worse I had been organised for once and packed for the trip in advance. I had to cancel and thus spent Sunday evening forlornly emptying well-packed bags of cycling gear onto the bedroom floor.

The cancellation meant I had to spend this week at home and in the absence of any other distractions, do some proper work on the book. Consequently, I don't have anything interesting to write about at all. This is not down to a complete lack of output, there have been loads. It's mainly down to the fact that there is only so much blogging you can do about hitting a keyboard a lot and wiggling a mouse. Which is all I've done for five days. But I will attempt to construct a few highlights as it distracts me from proper work for a while.

Firstly I've invented a new cycling diagram. I spent ages on this in Adobe Illustrator and then showed it to some cycling friends. None of us spotted the problem with it that we'll discuss later in the book. They all responded with the same phrase. "What the fuck is that Dave" (damn, I'd promised myself a swear free blog this week). I chuntered on about wind direction and route directional statistics but they were having none of it, so we'll be redesigning that one then.

Next, I laid out my route guide pages. This had already been done in a draft form but needed some proper precision and consistency adding to the pages. "Proper precision and consistency" comes hard to someone like me, so I spent days on it. I now have a new respect for graphic designers and arty/marketingish type people. Previously, I thought that all they did was wear niche T-shirts, eat Quinoa based salads whilst pressing a "Make this thing look much better" button in Adobe Photoshop.

Now I've been through it myself, I properly appreciate how hard and time-consuming consistency is. Making the slightest change over here and suddenly over there looks completely wrong. So you change over there to look right, but now over here is looking dodgy. So you spend ages working on over here and over there together, sitting back with a satisfied grin only to realise that whilst they both look cool the rest of the document is now a complete mess.

I've also been working on route statistics, both the display of them and the data capture. This comes with its own set of problems especially when you look at how I gathered them. Most route information has been captured using a GPS, this is a great little tool that logs your position every few seconds. I've carried one on all of my rides. The problem is that on these rides I've been taking photos using a process that goes something like this:

- stop
- set camera up on tripod and press self-timer
- frantically ride up the road
- ride back wearing gormless face
- repeat many times until an almost acceptable picture achieved

Now any sensible person would turn off the GPS logger during this process as you don't want the photo miles included in the route. Re-read the first three words of the last sentence and guess what I did? So all of my routes are a bit of a mess, which in turn blows my statistics and requires that somebody patiently edit the file and remove the errant logs.

More hours were spent clicking at the mouse whilst staring at the screen. I think this is similar to how Air Traffic Controllers work these days, I hope they've banned social networking sites and forums from their computers? I've been tempted to ban them from mine to elicit some focus.

On Thursday I cracked and sneaked out for an afternoon bike ride as only us freelancers can do. The wind had other ideas, consequently cranking itself up to "11" to deter my skiving. But after doing a little work on the Tommy Godwin story I felt obliged to persist. On that day in 1939, he had ridden 162 miles, so it would be rude of me to stay at home. I straddled the Cross bike (for any non-cyclists "cross" is a technical term, all of my bikes are, of course, delirious with pleasure) and sped out into the hills. Then I turned West and track-standed my way to Avebury in a gale. The wind was strong, cold and blustery which made things much worse, like pushing against a locked door that suddenly gives.

Riding past Hackpen Hill I spotted a Chinook Helicopter on low-level manoeuvres. I have no idea what it was trying to do, but how those pilots keep those great big things in the air in blustery gales is beyond me. I'm sure it's all done with computers, but so is most of my book and the previous nine hundred words are testament to it not being a walk in the park. The return journey would have been stupidly fast but the Cross bike is a single speed. So only my legs went stupidly fast, the rest of the body and bike ambled back pleasantly.

Sitting here on the forty-ninth Friday of my project I'm reasonably pleased with the week. I can print bits of the book out now and am almost ready to approach publishers with a "What do you think?". The spreadsheet says at least 35 more man-days are required to finish the content. That translates into 3 Dave months. The savings account is in denial about the impending date called Christmas and doesn't want to hear "3 months". Would anyone like to buy some bikes? One previous owner slightly abused (the bikes are pretty knackered as well).

Distractions

Spike Milligan has to be one of the greatest authors of all time. I am blissfully aware that that statement would probably be deemed heresy were it uttered within earshot of any academic concerned with English Literature. But it's true. Reading anything written by Spike should always be done either on the toilet or near one, as he littered his text with hand grenades of wit designed to force the reader to piss themselves on the spot.

Take this little snippet from Puckoon.

"Suddenly, nothing happened. It happened suddenly mind you"

Absolute literary genius that eclipses any "All the world's a stage, and all the men and women merely players" in my book. I've read just about everything Spike Milligan has ever written, listened to all of the Goon Show recordings and still remember scenes from the TV show "There's a lot of it about". Spike was an amazing musician, a comedy genius and a highly prolific author but reading his biography exposes a darker side of his character, he was plagued by depression.

In his worst periods, Spike would spend weeks on end in bed simply staring at the ceiling and refusing all contact with others. Out of the blue, a thought would trigger him out of his mire and he'd return to productivity as if nothing had happened at all. Reading these words I began to see Spike as a human curve. Spike appeared to oscillate regularly over time through a familiar pattern and in understanding this I began to empathise with Spike. We both share similar characteristics. I hasten to add that it is not "genius", "amazing" or "prolific" in my case, it's the oscillation. Some weeks I'm flying high at the top of the curve and extremely productive, others just seem to be seven days that passed while I appeared to be alive.

The last few weeks have been some of the latter. I'm sure I've been working on something as the Playstation has a coating of dust and the garden is in a right state. But I can't for the life of me work out what? Book progress has been glacial, an Arabian shoplifter would have typed out more words than I have over the past three weeks. So I sat myself down and asked, why?

A few minutes of staring at the floor and shuffling shoes ensued. Then I owned up to have been *"messing about doing other things that aren't the book"*. The inquest gathered pace and we began to catalogue just what it was I'd been up to.

Firstly, there's an extended piece of IT consultancy I have done for a client interfacing with Government IT systems. It should have been a "piece of IT consultancy" but I chose to ignore the word Government before I took it on. How foolish. What was supposed to be a few days worth of javascript hackery turned into ten days of hair-tearing frustration with civil service first line support technicians. I'd ask a simple question, they'd seek clarification from IT support who would respond with "tell him to switch it off and on again". This works in many cases I'm sure, but is slightly lacking when asking for further detail concerning XML interface specifications. I formed a special bond with my IT caseworker "Simon". He tried his hardest to track down answers. I suggested to him that some examples would make things a lot easier and received this:

"We did think about creating official examples some time ago, but the cost to us as a public body was deemed to be prohibitive in the current climate."

Well done the Government. "We would like to encourage you to use our electronic services as it would save us money. But helping you to use our electronic services would be too costly in the current climate, so we'll write some crap documentation and you can guess instead". I gave myself a stiff talking to over this one, invoking the "Thirteen years in Royal Mail, you should have known better clause". All IT consultancy is banned until the book is finished.

Next, there are business opportunities. Leaving a structured work environment goes a long way to freeing the mind. Ideas that were previously constrained by budgets, defined strategy, skillsets or common sense are now free to come to the fore. Additionally, many ex-colleagues believe I've finished the book and are getting in touch with equally mad paths to future wealth.

I confess I've been caught up in a few of them. Some are just discussions, others a bit of code hackery and one almost has a business plan. I've got to knock most of them on the head though We have an attic full of my unfinished Airfix models, a testament to an ability to start with enthusiasm but never complete.

Bollocking number two. "Dave, focus on the book, fanny about with business ideas in your spare time or when it's finished, and by the way, someone has already invented a mobile phone linked doorbell" (well they patented it, I thought of it in 2003).

Finally, I don't mind admitting that I have a little bit of the Spike in my makeup. Sometimes I'm bouncing around like an Italian cruise ship passenger. Other times I'm a little more introspective, wondering whether it's going to work, whether I'm up to it or whether anyone gives a shit either way. Self-doubt can be a huge driver, it can also eat away at a project until nothing remains.

I had a stern chat with myself. I've decided that the weapon of choice is obstinacy. The few friends that I have will argue that there's no shortage of that, it just needs application and focus, so that's what I'll do.

Numerous other distractions have also raised their head in the past few weeks. The car failed its MOT and a huge argument with the garage ensued as to cause and more importantly the cost of the remedy. We built a shed, yes, another one, ready for the next army of bikes that will make its way to my front door. I've done some more research into the Year Record and met a whole new bunch of fabulous people with amazing stories to tell. We've de-cluttered and downsized our life a bit. eBay is flooded with the contents of our attic and I've now got a large collection of "We're sorry you are leaving us" letters. This is partly due to looking at the bills we paid in 2011 and wondering how on earth we paid them with me out of work. The truth is we didn't. My savings account made up the rest and it's worked out that we can do without cable TV, heating insurance, contact lenses that are never used and subscriptions to magazines full of adverts for stuff that costs money.

Suitably chastised I've returned to the original plan. I've also returned to these musings. The benefits (to me) outweigh the cost as it provides a weekly tape measure of the distance travelled and the distance yet to go. Also, writing them allows me to vent a little steam. Nine weeks left to complete the project. We started with Spike so let's stay with him at the end and finish on a rather apt poem that tickled my spotty youth.

"The boy stood on the burning deck,
Whence all but he had fled -
The twit!"

The Time Machine

Anyone with the slightest interest in reading should stop at this sentence and run off to the library for a good nose into H.G Wells book "The Time Machine". It's a much better read than this, arguably one of the first science fiction books ever written. If you haven't read it already and are determined to stick with me instead then I will summarise the plot. A bloke invents a time travel contraption, goes forward in time, has a ding dong with some Morlocks, comes back, gobs off about it to his mates then disappears.

As far as I can remember he only nips forward in time. I don't think he used his machine to go backwards which in my view is a huge mistake. Going forwards simply provides a voyeuristic journey of the cock-ups you are going to make. Going backwards is far more useful as you can then correct the cock-ups based on hindsight and hence never make them in the first place. Now I am sure some smart arse will mention the Butterfly Effect. Put simply, if you go back in time and tread on a butterfly then the repercussions across history can be immense.

But who cares! I'd suffer a fourth term of Margaret Thatcher if it enabled me to go back and not say something dreadful that I said to one of my neighbours in the early seventies. It still haunts me today and I'd love to give that little me a good smack in the chops and send him on his way before he had a chance to offend. Then I'd move on to some of the clothes, haircuts, drunken trysts that weren't taken and some that were. Finally, I'd buy a few shares in Apple and life today would be peachy.

This chain of thought is not as random as you may think. It is driven by the practical experience of completing the writing of the book. Simplistically my workflow goes along the lines of; do some cycling, take notes and photos in some form, coerce them into a few meaningful sentences, edit and review for accuracy then lay it all out into the book. I am now in the final stages of "meaningful sentences" and it is here that I sit willing H.G Wells to visit me and deliver the much needed time machine.

Some of my ride notes are dreadful. They were shouted into a voice recorder, often breathlessly at the top of the hill and with scant regard for the bloke who would end up editing them into a rich and meaningful book. This week I was putting the finishing touches to a chapter concerning Yorkshire, this included a particularly spectacular climb that's almost iconic in cycling circles. I could just about remember riding it and was convinced that in my notes there would be sufficient material to support the construction of some perfect two-wheeled prose that would leave the reader enraptured.

"Difficult climb leading to moorland"

That was all I had down. The urge to nip back a few months and give the idiot on a bike with a voice recorder a right leathering was irresistible. How on earth am I supposed to work with that? The whole chapter hinged around this climb and the rider's quest to accomplish it and I'd only managed to provide a single adjective "difficult". "Difficult", here's a really interesting fact. Shakespeare only used "difficult" once in his entire works. That's how crap it is as an adjective. The "fluffy wank" quotient of "difficult" on a scale of 0-10 is about 2 which equates to "for use in local authority guidance material or drain clearing instructions". Interestingly Shakespeare uses "quo" more times than "difficult" if only he'd have heard the relentless three chord madrigals that were to come. He'd have got in the time machine, travelled forward and handed out a swift long-haired guitarist cull.

"But it's OK", argues the past-tense Dave, "at least we have the reference to

moorland".

Well actually Dave, it isn't OK. Yorkshire is one bloody great lump of moorland. There's more moorland than anything else in Yorkshire where the stock response to "Where is X?" is "They're up on t'moor" (where the dogs play football). As you can see, it's not all roses in the Barter writing shed at the moment. I'm having to fill in a few documentary gaps by staring long and hard at maps and trying to place myself back in the scene. Then I recreate the ride using Google street view which has proved to be a lifesaver on this project. Using street view I can carry out the ride from the safety of my shed gaining a 360-degree view of the road and landscapes around. Does it beg the question as to why did I even bother doing the rides at all? I could have plotted them on a computer screen and ridden them from the comfort of my office chair.

Adjectives are causing me pain in other ways as well. There are forty chapters in the book which require a unique flavour to prevent repetition. Given that each discusses cycling in some form many adjectives are required as there are lots of bits of Britain that need describing. I've used up the entire supply from the Oxford English dictionary and have now had to resort to inventing my own.

I'm proud to introduce the first use of "wibblemaker" to describe a climb, "wibble" being the only utterance you a capable of having ascended it. Then we have "smold", a shortening of "same old" to be used when the landscape has not varied for a while. Also a big round of applause for "phlatch" please. This is a conglomeration of "phlegm" and "patch" used to describe the mark left on black lycra when bicycle-based nose clearance has unfortunately been misdirected onto the rider instead. And, yes, I know it is a noun.

It's not just been words words words this week. I've also been on my travels. As I write the calendar recently clicked over a month and the year is now 2012. This is one hundred years from 1912, which is the year in which Tommy Godwin was born. I've written plenty about Tommy before and made no secret of the fact that he's my number one cycling hero for riding 75,065 miles in a single year. Last year I did 8,500 and I'm still shagged out, Tommy once did more than that in a month.

This week I met with Barbara his daughter, Neil whose parents were Tommy's greatest friends and Stoke City Council who have decided that given this is the Olympic year and would have been Tommy's centenary, it's worth celebrating the man's achievements.

My year record book project is gathering further momentum as I recently sat down with Joe Greaves the son of Walter Greaves. Walter's story is truly amazing, he held the year record a few years before Tommy but rode it in slightly different circumstances..he only had one arm. Joe passed me an amazing piece of writing that covers Walter's life and his record riding year. At first read, it seems like fiction as the things Walter did to get the record off the ground beggar belief.

It was amusing to read of how they conditioned Walter's saddle before he set out on his ride. It was spread with butter and then beaten about with a hammer. I imagined Helen's eyes going firmly up to the ceiling if I raided the fridge for some Anchor, slathered it all over my bike and then took to it with a mallet in fury. Thankfully for us modern cyclists those days are gone with computer-aided design ensuring that largely synthetic saddles are properly modelled to the bell curve of cycling arses.

There are seven main players and one rogue in the Year Record story. I now have enough material to cover Tommy, Walter and Marcel Planes. Ossie Nicholson was an Australian professional and I have some material on him. I mooted a trip to Australia to complete my research, but the response "Not without us" came quickly back from the family. The other riders are proving a little more elusive, particularly Bernard Bennett who rode the same year as Tommy Godwin. This stuff takes time. Naively I thought I'd be done in six months. The end of this year would be a more feasible projection.

Finally. I've been working on project "Obsessive Compulsive Cycling Disorder". This is hugely exciting as I've nearly finished it. It's a foray into publishing that I have been planning to do for a while but kept putting off. Seeing as I need to venture into some form of paid employment shortly, I thought I'd better get it out of the way, so evenings have been spent in front of the keyboard instead of Eastenders.

This requires another trip back in the time machine. I'd return to October 2010 and have a quiet word with the bloke about to hand in his notice and set out to write a book. I would suggest to the young fellow that he might want to consider options for self-cloning before he handed in his fateful letter. He'd point at the Morlocks and tell me to sod off.

Obsessive Compulsive Cycling Disorder

Testing. That final overlooked element of many failed IT projects. Usually left to the last minute and carried out in haste. Testing is usually carried out by "testers", wonderful people whose sole role in life is to present developers with a list of things that are crap about the project to which they have dedicated the last three months of their life. To become a tester you need to enjoy delivering bad tidings there is a clear career progression from tester to TV News presenter. I believe that Moira Stuart enjoyed nothing more than repeatedly crashing web browsers in a previous career.

I've worked with many testers over the years and whilst they are often perfectly friendly out of work, as soon as you enter the office the gloves are removed. Nothing is ever allowed to be "just about OK", everything must adhere to the "spec." or a defect report will be issued. This is essentially the same as grassing you to the headmaster as these defect reports are added up and presented to monthly meetings, where you are verbally caned for being a naughty boy.

As per everything at work, it occasionally gets out of hand. I've had defect reports raised for a missing full stop in some customer-facing text. This has created a chain of bureaucracy, delay and reporting akin to a court submission for corporate fraud. Made worse by the fact that the tester had access to the live system and could have made the change in a click. But processes are processes.

Cycling has "testers" as well. These individuals share many personality traits with IT testers. They often have "issues", speak in curt but cutting sentences and occasionally dabble in serious drug abuse. The cycling testers work in a different way to their IT counterparts, instead of trying to break computer systems, they attempt to break themselves by riding against the clock as fast as they can. These freaks enjoy nothing better than a good time trial. They don headgear that makes them look like an alien, add aerofoils to their bike and hammer up and down dual carriageways in search of the perfect "ten".

I've always been pretty crap at "testing" in both IT and cycling careers. Impatience has been the enemy of the former and a lack of muscles in the legs the latter. My cycling time trials have mostly been over a distance of ten miles. A perfect distance for me to get it completely wrong. My usual approach is to hammer off the line in a quest to get to my lactate threshold as fast as I can. For those who are unaware of this measure, it is 0.2 miles per hour slower than the speed required to make you physically sick with exertion. Common knowledge is that you can hold it for about a minute. But that doesn't stop me from trying to stay there for ten miles.

Hitting your lactate threshold has the downside of telling your body that it's time to stop and get off. It's not very efficient when time trialling, as your speed graph climbs to an impressive high and then rapidly drops to that of my Mum pootling idly to the shops on her Puch. Which is about the average speed I end up with at the end of the ten. Therefore, I gracefully retired from time trialling many years ago and stuck to simply messing about on the bike instead. Until this year that is.

My testing career on the bike has no future, instead, I'm testing for the book. I'm sure I've mentioned the torment between publishing via a traditional publishing firm or doing it myself. Both are complete unknowns and the first option will always be an unknown until I've done it once. My old testing colleagues will hold their heads in their hands if they see me going live without having some form of test. So I've created one.

"Obsessive Compulsive Cycling Disorder"

Or OCCD for short. Now you have to admit that it's catchy as hell. It's my publishing test vehicle that's almost ready for launch. What I've done is a little bit cheaty but should allow me to gain the test data I crave. I've taken thirty articles previously written by me and wrapped them into a book (oops I did it again). It's not just a cut-and-paste job as I've written a whole load of new text as well. But it is a quick avenue to publish something myself and understand how the whole business works.

I've written a long rambling introduction to the book and then a series of shorter pieces that introduce each article. The content is all cycling based. The short pieces attempt to put it all in a bit of context and you get a view of this idiot who bumbled into cycling, got a bit obsessed by it and then forced his obsession on others by waffling on.

The bridging text that I've written follows the style I have used in the "proper" book that is yet to come. Hopefully, some readers out there will feedback on their thoughts which in turn allows me to "tweak" the other offering against these defect reports.

I read through it again last night and it is a bit of a Frankenstein's monster. Rest assured that there are no other authors out there polishing their CV's in anticipation of this groundbreaking text hitting the market. It's pretty personal and selfish as most of the text centres on me and it's one hundred per cent cycling focused, so will only appeal to weirdos. Nevertheless, I am excited as the big project moves into the testing phase. There is potential that it could elongate things a tad but it's a price worth paying to get the end product right.

Self Publishing

Last week I failed to write a word. Which is pretty tardy given that I made myself a solemn promise last month to carry on writing no matter how many times people shouted: "stop!". Like a naughty schoolboy sitting outside the headmaster's office, I've been lining up my excuses. So let's see if any of them will stick.

We begin with a wedding on a Friday. Friday's an odd day for a wedding and I probably should have asked the happy couple why? But there was free wine at the reception and I made good use of this to try and forget my abysmal performance in the church. For a wide variety of reasons, I don't spend a lot of time in them. The main one is vicars who direct me vigorously towards the betting shop as soon as they see me approach. Consequently, I can only do the hymns that we sang at school, which were "Onward Christian Soldiers", "Bread of Heaven" (I know it's not called that!) and another one with a catchy tune that I hum a lot whilst cycling but can't remember the words.

Kate and David chose other hymns that never made it into my ancient religious curriculum. They also chose to get married in a bloody great cathedral and invite a select guest list. I got in purely down to my wife's family tree. So, large church, smallish congregation, unknown hymns, you can guess what I did. I mimed. Unlike one relative who shall remain nameless but should consider a tracheotomy. We all had a lovely evening which strayed off the beaten path a bit for me as I ended up in a detailed discussion about playing golf abroad. Weddings do test one's self-restraint as I hadn't the heart to tell my fellow converser that golf is second only to worm charming on my list of sports I'd consign to Room 101.

But the wedding isn't a very good excuse as I could have hammered out the blog on Saturday instead. I could try mentioning the weather? You may have noticed that all of that nasty easterly wind has gone and the temperatures have shot up into double figures. Surely a dosser like me would be out on the bike all day long every day of the week. But I am afraid that you would be completely wrong. I have been working very hard. Mainly because the bike is in a right state and I can only take it out under cover of rain in case a proper cyclist spots me.

Attention has been focused upon the creation of a new business plan for something quite spectacular. I know I should be finishing off the other book, and I am. However, the fact that the only monthly post we receive is Helen's wage slip means that the Dave-living-the-life-of-Riley situation just cannot be sustained. Equally the Dave-putting-on-a-suit-and-working-in-an-office scenario cannot be entertained either so I'm heading for the middle ground of attempting to set something up that can sustain a cycling lifestyle and buy a few fish fingers as well.

Fortunately, I am in cahoots with another cyclist who has a similar aim although he may have set his sights higher than fish fingers. Don't ask what it is we're going to be doing as we're not one hundred per cent sure ourselves. But we've drawn a few flow charts and written a few lines of computer code so hopefully, it will all come together in the end.

The business stuff isn't an excuse either. The truth is that my little side project entitled OCCD has robbed me of all available spare time. OCCD was meant to be a test that would allow me to discover the practical issues that need to be overcome to publish. I thought it would be quite straightforward to tidy up a few of my old articles and publish them as a Kindle book. And to be fair the writing part of it was. All I had to do was write some filler text and an intro to the book. This was about 15,000 words in total and took a few evenings sitting in front of the telly in my pants.

Next came document assembly. I pulled the whole thing together using iWork Pages, importing some of the articles from my website and others from the depths of my hard drive. This introduced problem number one as there was a huge inconsistency in font sizes, line spacing and paragraph formatting. Sorting all of this out took hours as Pages does not have a button entitled "Unwind the mess Dave has created and make it all look nice".

I moved on to the creation of the eBook formats. I had chosen Amazon Kindle as my primary channel and assumed a quick Google of "export from Pages to Kindle" would liberate thousands of options.

It turns out that Pages isn't the greatest tool to use when writing for the Kindle it ranks right down there with chalk and slate on the scale of usefulness. This was compounded by the fact that I wanted to create a paper version as well. Pages does not offer much control over the creation of PDF files that printers require. So I had made a huge mistake by spending hours formatting my text in completely the wrong software package.

I decided to spend some time on a bit of proper research and so headed to Google again with the query "Kindle and print publishing using software that Dave owns". The biggest hit was "Adobe Indesign" which made sense as it is used by just about everyone in the industry for laying out books. I am even writing my main book using it, so please tell me why I decided to follow an alternative path with the Kindle project?

I fired up Indesign and searched for the menu item entitled "Import from Pages", it was on holiday with Lord Lucan. Indesign imports from everything bar Pages, it probably imports from Jet Set Willy, but iWork Pages is not on the list. More torture as I exported from Pages into Microsoft Word format and lost most of my reformatting work in the process. The shed reverberated to the sound of a man pleading with his computer to give him a break.

Finally, I got Indesign to accept my text (by importing it into Jet Set Willy) and then stared at the resulting mess on the screen. More hours and much more pleading passed as I wrestled with the deep recesses of the software to bring my masterpiece back into line. My Google search history for that evening looks something like this:

"How to automatically create new pages in Indesign when importing large text files"
"How to change the font size for paragraphs only"
"How to undo deleting all text after changing font size"
"How to fix broken iMac screen"
"Suitable forehead plasters"

I'll spare you the rest of the story, but many, many, many hours and late nights later I had the text under control and was ready for my first export to Kindle. Amazon provides a plug-in that gives Indesign a "Wizard" to help you with this. Well, Indesign's Amazon Gandalf can fuck right off as he was about as useful as a spoiler on a milk float in getting my text exported.

The Wizard had a "create a table of contents" button which I thought would be useful for users but no matter how I pressed it, it wouldn't work. I tried a straightforward click, nothing. So then I pressed a bit harder, still no table of contents. I tried using the keyboard to do it instead, nada. I even sneaked up on it, hovering over the "Cover image" first before clicking it and pressing "Export" before it had noticed. But the button had wised up to that trick and deftly removed the table of contents.

Hours more searching liberated the answer. The Wizard would only create a table of contents if you had already added one in the first place. Of course, completely logical. How could I ever have considered any other path? I then had to work out how to add a table of contents which took a few more hours of frantic internet searching to get right. Stupidly I thought the Wizard would format the table of contents as I had created it, so I spent a long time getting it right. Only to discover that what it does is delete the one you have formatted and replace it with its own.

Eventually, the Kindle walls came tumbling down and I managed to get a version loaded upon my device. It looked bloody awful. So another night was lost to a valiant fight with Indesign as I reformatted the whole thing, changed fonts again and struggled hard to make bullets display properly on the screen.

In parallel, Helen had been proofreading a printout of the text. I'd anticipated a few little tweaks, she presented me with hundreds of spelling mistakes and errors. More hours were spent dicking around with the text I was growing to hate. Even more pain as my dicking around changed the formatting causing pages to disappear out of sight.

Finally, we all called a truce. It looked like the document was ready to go. It looked fine on my Kindle and I'd made all of the changes that Helen had marked. Publishing via Amazon was a relatively painless process as their website Wizard was a damn sight more friendly than mine.

On Sunday the 19th of February 2013 I published my first book. Helen patted me on the back and paid the huge sum of 98p. She downloaded it to her Kindle and it opened at the wrong page. I'll own up now. I acted like a child as I buried my face in my hands and tried not to cry. So much time had gone into getting the format right that I'd neglected to check the opening page. This, of course, was set by Amazon's Indesign tossing stupid wizard and it turns out that it does this where the table of contents was FIRST placed, not where it actually is.

To make matters worse, Amazon takes twelve hours to accept changes to published books. My book was in a "being checked" status which meant it could be bought but could not be suspended or altered. The rest of the family avoided me that evening as I let the stress filter from my brain into my facial expressions. These varied from bottom lip extended by three inches to the glaring maniac who probably shouldn't be near knives.

Much later that evening I was able to resolve the problem. But feel bad for the ten people who had bought it so far as the Introduction is supposed to set the reader up for what is to come. Without it, the book is just a series of weird articles about not very good cycling.

So here you have my excuse. The reason for zero writing output was no time. The reason for no time was a vanity publishing project gone slightly tits up. But I got there in the end. Sales have gone relatively well I think? My expectation for purchase was; my Mum, Helen and a few friends who felt bad for me. I have now sold more copies than I have friends, so I await the Amazon feedback process with trepidation.

I've now made proper friends with Indesign when I found out that it makes the print-ready stuff a breeze. Today I published a print version of the OCCD. It uses an On-Demand printing service which in turn restricts the formatting and layout of the book. But the copy I bought seems to be OK, well it's readable!

I spoke about this being a testing process and it has certainly opened my eyes to the pitfalls ready to trap the self-publishing author who doesn't think things through. I've made changes to my schedule accordingly but also had a load of new ideas that need discussing with others. In the meantime, I'll just sit here waiting for the first review. I am a bit nervous as my Mum diligently second checked the text and found another two pages worth of errors.

A Mess

"Pick up your bloody mess will you!", emotive words shouted at generations of young people by disapproving elders. A constant reminder that the litter issue we suffer from in urban and other areas is always the fault of the youngsters. Nobody would dare drop anything in the old days for fear of a naked birching by the local bobby in view of all on the village green. The fact that there was nothing to drop in the first place is immaterial to the argument. "If we had have had plastic wrappers, we'd have eaten them for nourishment" would be the elderly refrain.

The problem is I am equally as guilty as the elders. I'm constantly shouting this very phrase at my children, always with me standing outside of their bedroom and them cowering within. Mess bloody annoys me and they know it. Yet this does absolutely nothing to dissuade them from liberally scattering all of their possessions and half of the kitchen cupboard across their bedroom carpets. They say things like "It's my room, I like it like this" and then get the arse when I empty the vegetable recycling bin onto their bed. My daughter even tried to construct a lucid argument based upon the fact that the mess had gone that little bit too far and was therefore beyond her capability as a child to rectify it. I disconnected the internet and within an hour she had mended her ways.

Clearly, I am mess intolerant. Slightly hypocritical as areas of my life are all over the place including my computer hard drive, bike bits box and the magazine pile next to my bed. But that doesn't stop me from appreciating a semblance of order. I'm dead jealous of those with tidy houses, neatly arranged tool boards, cars that are absent of dust/chocolate eclair wrappers and gardens that could host Antiques Roadshow. I do try hard though and feel that a quest for order is as noble as actually achieving it. This is why I have disdain for farmers.

Even I have to admit that this is a bit left field. Beginning an article berating your messy children and then leading immediately into a distaste for those of an arable disposition. However, there is sound reasoning behind this as every other road cyclist will tell you. Let me explain further.

As of the beginning of this week, three rides were all that was needed to complete the information gathering for the book. The oracle of Countryfile spoke and informed me that the approaching clement weather would allow me to tick off two of the three in a period of a few days. I hastily stuffed my bike and riding gear into the car and headed up to Telford to knock off ride number one, a hilly epic winding through the Shropshire hills and over the Long Mynd. Things were looking good as I left The Wrekin and rode unhindered through Coalbrookdale. The rain was absent and roads dry, my freshly clean bike almost shone in the sunlight that forced its way through the thinning cloud.

But then I ventured onto the smaller roads, into the territory of the farmers and within minutes all was not well. This is the time of year when our farmers decide that tarmac is all a bit passé and needs sprucing up a little. So as a public service they drive from the shit strewn fields onto the roads liberally doling out copious amounts of mud/cowcrap to paint the surface a seasonal brown. Some of them take a more organic approach and dispense with the tractor wheel as a distribution device preferring to spray from the cattle direct. Lakes of warm bovine piss lurk between mounds of steaming half-digested grass ready to catch out the unwary cyclist often known as Dave.

Within fifteen minutes of hitting the lanes, I was covered from head to foot in crap. My bike was unrecognisable, it looked like I was riding a frame made from slurry and to make matters worse it began to properly clog. The Easton forks have clearance issues, it only takes a few millimetres of mud to cause an annoying rub on the tyre. The only cure is to stop and frantically shove twigs deep into the fork and try and dislodge it.

This was spoiling an otherwise epic ride. I began to fume about the farmers. Why the hell can't they bloody well clear their mess up? Why do we scream blue murder at an errant chav who drops a Snickers wrapper, yet doff cap and salute the "way of the country" to a farmer who distributes four tons of cow shit down a scenic lane? Things get worse when you look at their farmyards. The places are littered with broken-down machinery, old tractors, cars from the seventies and all manner of fertiliser bags/drums/pallets/farmers wives/chickens/EU subsidy receipts.

But like my daughter, the farmers when confronted would come up with the "difficulty" repost. "Well you see it'd be too expensive to clear them roads my lover", they'd reply, "The EU don't have a subsidy for that and we'd actually have to pay for it". I'd then counter that they could always travel from field to field on their own land, but they'd argue that this would spoil the nice hedgerows they'd cultivated or get more mud on their VAT free tractor that they'd have to clean.

Surely it wouldn't be too hard to fit some sort of brush to the back of the tractor? Or failing that there's the old fashioned way of getting out there with a hose and a broom. And don't go giving me all of that "You don't understand the ways of the country, farmers work all hours and cows won't milk themselves" bollocks. Because I've listened to the Archers and all farmers ever do is gossip about Beryl then get killed falling off roofs. It just needs some innovation to sort out the problem. How about attaching the brooms to the cows as they are led to the milk shed? Or adding huge great doormats at the field entrance so the tractor can wipe its virtual feet?

I finished the ride in a bit of a sulk, packed the bike and most of Shropshire's topsoil into the car and mooched off to Norfolk for the second ride. This was a whole different kettle of fish. The Norfolk farmers have much better manners and the roads were remarkably shit free. Furthermore, there was a huge absence of hills to boot and the sun made an appearance for most of the day. That doesn't mean that I wasn't able to inject some form of stress. This was perfectly achieved due to the ferry at Woolbastwick.

I'd planned a loop that crosses the Bure Marshes, for those in the dark this needs a ferry to achieve due to the lack of a suitable bridge. The ferry runs all through British Summertime, other times of the year you are advised to ring and check. On Monday I rang them and a salty old dog informed me that they would probably be running on Thursday when I planned to ride. But best ring and check on the day. No problem. I wrote the number on my map and duly called it after 30 minutes of setting off.

No answer. It was 9.30 am and I imagined that they were having a late start so left it another 30 minutes as I cycled ever closer. No answer. A tinge of stress began to appear as the alternative was an extra fifteen miles on top of a route that was already eighty miles long. I kept calling and kept getting no answer. I rode closer and closer to the point of no return and eventually after 30 odd miles I rode over it. An inner voice told me that all would be OK. The reason they weren't answering was that they were out in the boat busily ferrying passengers across the river.

Ten miles later the awful truth became apparent. At riverside I found a complete absence of ferry, I called one final time to receive the traditional no answer. I then said the traditional "fuck it" and looked for alternative options. An old couple were messing about with a boat on the other side. I shouted a ferry based enquiry at them, hoping that they would sense my plight and offer a lift. They just shook their heads in a mixture of confusion and (possibly) derision. I then stared hopefully at the sign advertising the ferry, maybe there was an alternative number. But the number that I already had stared back at me. Or did it?

Frantically I dug out the map. Some idiot had transcribed the number incorrectly. A "5" and "6" had become switched in the journey from mind to pen. I called the number on the sign and guess what...a salty old dog answered and happily agreed to come and pick me up.

The rest of the ride continued without hitch. I probably picked the best day of the year to cycle the Norfolk broads. If I'd omitted the arm-warmers I could even have cultivated a touch of sunburn. The only other minor annoyance was my misreading of the wind direction from the weather forecast causing me to end the ride with thirty miles of nagging headwind.

Proofreading

This weekend I was at a presentation where the oft-abused act of "please introduce yourself to the group" was initiated. This is often a recipe for disaster as certain loquacious attendees suck the will to live from the room with their long rambling tales of previous achievements and conquests. These can range from a name-checked list of celebrities that have graced their presence to a strictly chronological list of tasks they have completed which begins from birth and is documented by week.

Fortunately, verbosity was not in attendance at this particular meeting we were asked to describe ourselves in one single word. I was there with a friend and had to act fast to prevent him nipping in with "tosser" when it came to my turn. But the truth is I found it incredibly hard. Many options sprung to mind ranging from caucasian (nicely flippant) through geek (not cool anymore) to hammerfore (come on catch up, what's a hammerfore?).

This then triggered another line of thought concerning "perception". I began to wonder what others would say if asked to describe Dave in one word. I would hope some would be suitably polite and maybe stick to physical descriptors like blond, skinny, twig-like or odd. Others might stray into a few more cutting areas concerning how I act. I'd probably have to prepare for adjectives such as gobby, argumentative, forthright and even naked (based upon some previous misdemeanours carried out in the area surrounding Stafford Street). But what of those who have never met me and have only read the stuff I've fretted out over my keyboard, what would they think?

This is a tricky one. However, I have got some sort of idea as I've been re-reading my ebook which hopefully you know is all about me. I had to do this as I made two monstrous mistakes in publishing it, and before anyone states that one of them was "publishing it" I'd like to point out that I made that joke first.

The first mistake is the most heinous of all and I struggle to understand how it happened in the first place. I missed a chapter out of the published book! This is me holding my hand up right now. I've been a very silly author and stuck an anthology of 30 articles on Amazon that only contains 29. It must have been a slip of the mouse between wordprocessor and Indesign. Regardless, the damage has been done and I only managed to correct it this weekend with a new version uploaded.

The second was proofreading. Despite recruiting an army of unpaid volunteers (Mum and Helen) a few little mistakettes slipped through the net. So I've spent every free moment possible re-reading the book and hopefully ironed the vast majority of them out. The weirdest one was the substitution of "relativity" for "reality". I blame this on spell check but the sentence in question talks about the ills of watching "relativity TV". Readers must have been thinking *"What the hell is relativity TV? Is it some sort of new digital channel for physicists? Or does it vary its content based upon the position and speed of the viewer?"*. That one is fixed. I also spelt "Ventoux" wrong and missed a few apostrophes. I'm dreading that the book has been sold to one of those Amazon reviewer grammar pedants and I'll end up with a review along the lines of:

"I feel disgusted and ripped off for a whole 77p by this disgusting mess of un-proof read diatribe with the occasional unnecessary use of really naughty words"

Back to the question. What impression of Dave would an unfamiliar reader construct having dragged themselves through the book? I imagine they would think the bloke was a slightly disorganised, reasonably cheerful chappy who seems to enjoy his cycling. And they'd be mostly right. But there is a darker side to authorship that I visit regularly. It's the issue of "self-doubt". What if they are not getting that impression? What if they imagine some scarecrow-like egotist who lords it over his wordprocessor with a mission to tell the cycling world "how it is". Or worse, a desperately sad attention seeker looking to fill the childhood gap created by not getting Flight Deck for Christmas.

This eats away particularly as I've thought long and hard about it myself. My driver for writing is probably a subliminal combination of both of the above (I never did get Flight Deck, I had to buy it second hand from a Blue Peter Bring and Buy sale). However, no matter how far I dig I struggle to answer the question. Why on earth do I do it? I honestly don't know.

Then I look around and see some of my friends writing and publishing as well. One of them draws and sticks his pictures up for all to see, my daughter does this as well. I have no idea if they are any good or not as my artist ability runs out as soon as the etch-a-sketch is taken away from me. I was thinking about this whilst cycling the other day and came to a conclusion that I didn't expect. The truth is I have no idea as to the motivation behind those who publish, no matter what. Musicians, writers, artists (apart from the "piss" ones), poets and even the geeky scientists who write obscure papers about theories concerning strings.

But I do know one thing. I'm proud of every single one of the little tykes. Because what they have done is taken the brave step of putting something out there to be critiqued. And, boy how we love to critique don't we? I've seen it all over the web, read it in papers, heard it in pub conversations and done a fair bit of it myself. If the creator is not there to defend their work, then no holds are barred. We're happy to let rip yet forget the critical phrase "Fair play to them for putting it out there, at least they had a go".

So now I've joined the legions of the published I'd just like to turn to all of those who went before me and those who will follow and offer a bloody great round of applause. No matter how great or awful your work is, I'm now one hundred per cent on your side. Let's celebrate our works with the mantra that "a seat in the auditorium may be a comfortable place but all the real action happens on stage". Finally, let's return to my answer to the one-word question, I apologise for taking a tortuous route. I answered "Dave". I think it's all-encompassing really because were others to describe a slightly mental, weird-looking, cyclist type who obsessively bangs on about it online they'd say "Oh that pillock, he's like Dave".

The Publisher

I'm at week seventy. Just to recap if you've still got the will to live I resigned from a proper job with a suit, tie, pension and as many bullshit bingo business phrases as you can fit in a large suitcase. The grand plan was to spend the following 52 weeks writing a book about cycling and then become a millionaire upon the proceeds. Like all grand plans, some tolerance needs to be applied. So if we take objective number one, I'm about 38% out on that already and objective number two is in a bit of a sorry state as well, hanging around the 0.005% mark.

Sadly Obsessive Compulsive Cycling Disorder does not count as the book about cycling, as I'd written half of it before I even started and it's mostly a series of chapters taking the piss out of me. A proper book about cycling needs to be all serious with lots of nice photos, interesting diagrams and some stern words about being safe and wearing helmets. But proper books about cycling are hard. I learnt a lot from self-publishing OCCD which can be summarised in the sentence, "Writing a book is about one-third of the work necessary to get it published".

There are loads of other tricky things that need doing once you've got the words typed. You've got to lay it all out in a design package, then proofread it, then lay it all out again after you've busted your layout in fixing the myriad of spelling mistakes. Facts have to be checked, fonts have to be made consistent, photos need cropping, processing and editing to get the idiot's thumbnail out of the shot.

Now I'm not scared of the odd bit of hard work, if you don't believe me, I'll point to the fact that I still live under the same roof as two teenage children and the case will immediately be dismissed. But doing all of this and trying to be all entrepreneurial at the same time was causing a few conflicts of interest. On one hand, I know that I should be swearing at Indesign, but business priorities meant I'm required for swearing at javascript instead.

A few weeks back I had a bit of a cold sweat when it became clear that there was a scenario whereby I'd park the whole project and wait until I had more time to finish it. The thing is there's never "more time" in the Barter household. Even if I made that million pounds mentioned earlier, it would soon be spent on tradesmen to complete the scroll known as "Dave's DIY, gardening and general administration to-do list". It became very clear that if I was going to get this cycling magnum opus to market I'd need quite a lot of help.

I've dithered before about publishers, naively put off by a fag packet calculation that showed I could make a better return publishing myself. Well OCCD taught me a stark lesson to the contrary. I've sold a fair amount of copies to date but the royalty share is shocking. Amazon hand me a mere 22p for the 77p list price of the Kindle book and even worse 53p for the £7.75 they take for a paperback. I need to sell millions of copies to pay for the groundsmen and plasterers I require.

Raising prices won't work at my stage of the game either, *"Who the fuck is Dave Barter?"* narrowly loses out to *"Oh, only 77p what can go wrong?"* and people will take a punt which is what you need to do when your marketing budget only stretches to a lot of gobbing off on social media.

I decided to revisit the publisher dilemma. I wanted to find out whether they could help me with layout, proofing and marketing and what the commercials would look like compared to striking out on my own. Being a bit of a fussy bugger I spent some time looking around for the types of books I'd like to buy along with the authors that I rated. The thinking was that these people and products would be attached to publishers who would understand my cycling quest. One name popped up across several books, Vertebrate Publishing, so I took a punt and dropped them a long email going on about me and my various projects. Luckily they employ a resident psychiatrist and he was despatched to find out what this idiot was going on about and whether he had any good ideas they could nick.

We met in a cafe frequented by outdoor types. The owner nearly hugged me when I ordered the most expensive shortbread as everyone else was sat there with bread, jam, tea and body odour. I arrived first, all keen and eager with a few sample chapters and photos on my iPad. I kept this hidden under the table just in case any of the outdoors types were to spot it and make it known that these new-fangled gadgets were unnecessary when all one needed was an elastic band, a few dead pigeons, the neighbours pigs and a rickety shed.

Vertebrate's psychiatrist saw through the pathetic beard growth and pronounced me relatively sane. He seemed to like the photos and the concept hadn't driven him to go and join the walkers for some jam. I was dead surprised when we loosely shook on a deal. Surprise turned to shock when this week an agreement dropped through the letterbox which read along the lines of:

"We the undersigned slightly mental publishing company hereby promise to layout and check Dave's book fairly pronto as long as he finishes the photography, dots the "i"'s, crosses the "t"'s and finishes off the statistics pages he's been dicking about with. When it's done we'll make it and sell it and give Dave some cash"

I stared at the thing for ages. In the detail section was a deadline, I stared at this for even more ages but it was the deadline that convinced me to sign. The royalties and revenues section was all very nice but I needed a proper kick up the arse to get the project completed. Here was a bit of paper offering some help in return for a share of the spoils. Some furious calendar action showed that as long as I gave up weekends in June the photography could be done. Malcolm-over-the-road has been recruited for a long weekend of Scottish photo-bitching in May and as I type this the long-suffering Helen is working on diagrams on the computer in the kitchen.

The liberation comes from the designer/proofreader working in the mad publisher's office. He/she/it will do all of the really hard work for me that I'd convinced myself I could do but reality turned up with a big wet fish round the face and stated the contrary. My lot is done by

August, then it's over to them. We're planning to have it published in October/November this year. It allows me to go back to what I do best, gadding about the place taking quirky pictures and writing some associated lunacy whilst some poor mug tries to format some sense out of it.

The fiscal objective is still clearly out of reach as the agreement had a set of percentages, the largest of which was not mine. But at least the publishing one is now achievable and it also allows me to be that annoying twat who comes out with the phrase "I was talking to my publisher the other day...". Does anyone want to be my agent?

Bed and Breakfast

I now consider myself to be a connoisseur of British bed and breakfast accommodation. The year and a half I've spent chasing around the country has allowed me to develop a nose for the different varieties on offer and an instinctive ability to judge the contents based upon the exterior. Stick me in front of any B&B and I'll quickly be able to tell you the girth of the proprietor (proportionate to the garishness of curtains), their sex (female in all cases), the likelihood of getting instant coffee in a fancy pot at breakfast and whether you're going to get the full life story or extended commentary concerning a particularly nasty operation that their husband is about to have.

The British Bed and Breakfast must be some kind of illicit care in the community scheme that the government will never admit to. Based upon my random selection of over forty establishments in the past year, I can categorically state that without exception their owners are all ever so slightly mad. This was driven home over the past couple of weeks as I fought hard to complete the Scottish photographs and the last northern English route for the book. In an alcoholic stupor, my neighbour's wife had agreed that her husband could be freed from the garden for a weekend and allowed away with me to act as a model. The two of us publicly made all sorts of convoluted photography plans whilst privately plotting a shed load of illicit mountain biking as well.

We piled my car full of every known variety of bike and camera, blew kisses at the wives and farted our way northwards as forty-something-year-old males will do. We nearly killed a family at Tebay services when I opened the car door and the green cloud escaped to envelop their Ford Focus. Luckily they had the windows up, but their once black car is now a mucky shade of grey. I blame the majority of it on Malcolm who had consumed a Tupperware full of leftover meatballs and couscous. Then digested it for most of the M6.

Our first destination was Newcastleton where we had booked a couple of nights' stay in a B&B run by Sandy. It only took us one missed turning to find it and we were welcomed by Sandy herself and her husband. Thirty minutes later we were able to return to the car and unpack. Flippin heck they could talk. From "Hello" they quickly went on to cycling, then Wiltshire, then horses, then jam, a quick diversion into some gossip about the neighbours and finally a lengthy dissection of the entire local community. Malc and I tried all manner of conversation killers but to no avail. Malc's farts fell on deaf noses, my foot tapping went unheard and a lengthy series of yawns were interpreted as "Please tell us more about Molly's horse's fit of dysentery"

We made the fatal mistake of asking Sandy for directions to the pub for dinner. An hour later we were fighting our way through a bush completely lost in the near dark. Typical men. Sandy had been struck with a rare fit of conciseness and a clear set of directions had been delivered. We had listened to the first instruction and completely ignored the rest. After I'd led Malc through a proper peat bog into the near-impenetrable forest he proposed the motion that we were lost and should retreat to the road. I asked him if he'd listened properly to the directions and he confessed that he'd "got the gist". I too owned up to hearing the odd "right" but not taking it in. Somehow we made it, got slightly pissed but still managed to sneak back into the B&B skilfully avoiding the risk of an extended conversation with Sandy whilst nursing an overflowing bladder.

But Sandy was not easily beaten. Breakfast the next day was 5% fry up, 95% musing upon the state of the nation and other philosophical matters. Malc and I did more nodding than eating as Sandy leaned against her Welsh dresser and regaled her audience of two. It took an hour and fifteen minutes to get through the first meal of the day, at home I can manage it in five. Sandy said "I must let you get on" about two hundred times but then remembered some other snippet of information that hadn't quite left her head. To be fair she was very nice and her B&B was fantastic value with great food, it's just that she bolsters the value with additional vowels and consonants that aren't necessary given the price. We were sad to leave, especially Malc who was given the job of paying. This really did take forty minutes as I sat tapping my foot in the car whilst Malc and Sandy discussed the Countryside Alliance. But we didn't mind, Sandy's gaff was well worth the cash and if you're chatty it would be the perfect holiday destination. I give her five stars for value and three for lunacy.

The next stop was Blair Atholl and the Glen Tilt Hotel where I walked confidently in and asked if they had a room for two men. Eyebrows were raised slightly but a vacancy was found and we were asked to return later when our room would be ready. This worked for us as we duly slipped off up Glen Tilt on our MTB's for five hours of the finest sun drenched Scottish mountain biking. We returned and collected our keys. The hotel manager had thoughtfully placed us at the top of the building which proved slightly troublesome as my calves had been given a stern talking to by the myriad of bloody great climbs on the route. I struggled up three flights of stairs with heavy bags and pushed open the door to our room.

Well, "room" is probably an overstatement. "Cupboard" might be a bit more apt and I think to fully comply with the Trades Descriptions Act it should have been labelled "cubicle". Two beds had been squeezed into an impossibly small space. Even worse was the heat. The room was in the roof of the hotel and took the full brunt of the rare visits made by our wonderful sun. Malc and I felt like we'd paid for a prison cooler. It was impossible to move around the room without placing an arse in the other's face. The correct tactic was to announce a need to shift position to give the other companion time to hide under the sheets.

We took solace in dinner, but I had clear reservations given the state of the hotel furnishings, carpets and staff. The hotel manager's suspicions were confirmed when I ordered two lime and sodas at the bar. A couple of food-stained menus were proffered and I scanned the list looking for the item with the lowest probability of food poisoning.

Roast of the day is often a good bet as one would hope it is potentially the freshest item of food. I plumped for that and Malc went for fishcakes with a side order of chips.

The food came pretty quickly and can only just be described as edible. My fatty lump of pork lay stranded upon an island of mash potato surrounded by a sea of greasy gravy, bizarrely I had been given a side order of both boiled and roast potatoes. Malc's chips completed the potato top trumps and we tried in vain to eat our way through this feast of King Edwards. Whilst this was all going on the fat waiter was deftly serving other guests in the room using his gut. He'd developed the enviable skill of balancing a tray of plates between the bar and his flab leaving his two hands free to unload ready for delivery to the table. Who needs topless waitresses when you have Scotsmen with moobs?

After Blair Atholl, we shot up to Inverness and took advantage of another day's sun nailing some stunning photos. Lunch was eaten in yet another lunatic run establishment where we plumped for the Monday special. I'd hate to see the rest of the week given the insipid piss week soup we were served. It was as if pumpkins had been dropped into water for a few seconds and then removed, the consistency was so thin that any spoon dipped into it came out dry. Added to this was the miserable candour of the cafe owner and the even more miserable portion size of the bread and cheese we were promised. We left twelve pounds lighter but not a lot heavier and made our way down to Peebles for the final day of the trip.

The plan was to stop in a B&B for the night and then hit the Glentress trail centre the next day. Accommodation proved to be a bit tricky as a whole load of bikers were in town for the Tweedlove festival. After several circuits of the town, we spotted a sign pointing towards a farm B&B. A twisty road through trees brought us to a bungalow on a hill where we were greeted by the wonderful Sheila. At this point, we were pretty knackered and all the two of us craved was a room and then some food. Sheila insisted on the full tour so we acquiesced and followed her around. Like all B&B owners, she's completely barking mad and seemed to have no idea as to the unique selling points of her particular abode. I wish I could remember her complete script as it was hilarious, the highlights were:

"This is the tap, the water from it is completely fresh"
"Here we have a great little shaving socket, which works"
"Here's the bathroom, you can use it on your own"
"There's a mirror there" (really! I thought it was a doppelganger?)

Finally, the two of us were ushered into the breakfast room where two solitary chairs sat in the middle of the room. We plonked ourselves down like guilty schoolboys and submitted ourselves to Sheila's breakfast requirements interrogation. It was really hard not to laugh as Sheila was pretty deaf:

"What's your names then?"
"Dave"
"Joan?"
"Dave"
"Steve?"
"Dave"
"William?"
"DAVE!!!"

We gave up on the chairs and shouted into Sheila's ear for ten minutes whilst making sure that she wasn't writing "curry" on the breakfast order pad. Finally, we were able to make our way into town and liberate two burgers from the back of a local pub freezer. We returned to Sheila's B&B and spent the rest of the evening reading on her veranda. As the light began to fade we decided to return to the room. But the front door was locked and we'd left our keys inside. You know what is coming next. I rang the doorbell, hammered at the knocker, rang the bell again but to no avail. Malc went round the side to investigate options for climbing through the window when finally Sheila's husband answered the door semi-dressed minus his teeth. He told us we were lucky he was in as Sheila would never have heard the bell. A fortunate escape as the barn was full of chickens.

The next day's mountain biking more than made up for the

madness. Glentress was dry, fast and more importantly empty which meant I could mince down the descents out of view. The only drama came in the last few miles when we met a bunch of lads staring at a taco'd wheel. I confidently stepped in with my multi-tool and wielded it about for a bit in a poor attempt to straighten the wheel. Ten minutes later it was just as bent as before and many of the spoke nipples were now rounded. I blamed it on the cheap wheel as Malc and I made our excuses and left the poor buggers to it.

It was a long drive home. After a morning's biking and energy bar consumption the car's atmosphere was probably 40% methane by the time we arrived in Wiltshire. But, that's another two chapters in the bag and I'm still on track for my end of July deadline. I typed this in the car at Keswick having completed the final route for the book and then nipped over to the lakes for a week's camping with the family. It was a working holiday as there were more photos to take and a lot of writing to catch up on. I'd say that there was a tinge of sadness as I finished the final ride, but that would be utter bollocks. It was so hard that I rode around the car park at the end looking for someone to help me off the bike. I'm definitely getting old.

Audio Book

As a young lad, I had a whole series of dreams and aspirations. A few of them shall remain undocumented as they involved Clare Grogan, but I don't mind admitting that I often lay on my bed listening to scratchy old records and wondering what it must be like to be famous and receive fan mail. As I grew older, I took a few tentative steps towards this objective by picking up a guitar and attempting to mimic my musical heroes. A slightly problematic approach as Alien Sex Fiend is probably missing from any sensible musical curriculum given that their songs contained about three notes.

Like my cycling, my musical career has been defined by an inordinate imbalance of enthusiasm versus ability. As you can guess, I have a house full of guitars, all of which I am unable to play very well at all. Thirty-one years after first picking up the guitar I can still make mistakes on the intro to "Smoke on the Water" and cannot play "Every Breath You Take" without being asked to stop by anyone within audible range. But this clear lack of talent has never been a barrier and I've even stood on stage making mistakes publicly. The highlight of which was being informed by an unfortunate punter that whilst I was *"the worst guitar player they have ever seen technically"*, they had, *"quite enjoyed the unusual sounds I'd managed to make and were intrigued as to how I had managed it?"*.

The guitar playing was the wrong path to fan mail. Thirty-six years, three bands and absolutely no letters. Well, apart from the warning we received from Brighton Borough Council in our student house, in hindsight, Simon and I were a bit unsociable jamming Subhumans songs in my bedroom at 2 am on a Tuesday.

Acting proved equally futile. Despite many appearances upon the hallowed stage of Wootton Bassett Comprehensive assembly hall, my prodigious childhood talent remained undiscovered. I blame this on Mr Cook our music teacher who made me sing a solo during a school production of Sweeny Todd just as my voice had finally decided to break. The audience got the full operatic range in a single song and the talent scouts sodded off to Sean Bean's school instead.

In my tender youth, I'd never considered writing as a path to fan mail. Let's be honest, teenagers don't often have posters of great literary masters upon their walls. I had Toyah, Beki Bondage and Clare Grogan, George Orwell, John Steinbeck and Sven Hassel were notable in their absence. However, teenagers are usually wrong about everything, I proved to be no exception as I'm now receiving a trickle of emails after publishing OCCD. The problem is that the majority of it comes from men in their late forties with a penchant for wearing lycra.

I've got my dreams and aspirations strategy wrong. If I had thought it through I would have spent the last year working on a project that nubile young ladies would relate to. I would not have written a long rambling introduction about getting fat and subsequently battering my arse on a bike for many years hence. This is going to put them right off from the start and will only encourage middle-agers like me to continue reading. However, it's too late now and if I'm honest it's gratifying to know that others like me have been in a similar boat. The mail I am currently getting conforms to a fairly standard template:

"Dear Dave,

Just finished reading Obsessive Compulsive Cycling Disorder. Managed to ignore the typos (YES I KNOW I SPELT PELOTON WRONG). Like you, I picked up cycling again after [getting fat/losing fitness/realising that if an idiot like you can then so can I/being told to by the Mrs]. Can I have a copy of [your LEJOG route/a properly edited copy/your wife's therapist's phone number]. Interestingly I am [over the age of 80/using you as an excuse to buy more bikes/attempting LEJOG/C2C/RAAM and blaming you if it goes wrong]

Sincerely
Cycle Bloke"

I shouldn't take the piss though as it is proving to be a huge motivator. Every single email has offered a little lift when my head has started to drop as the daunting task of book number two completion marches on. I've been devious and used a number of the emailers to offer feedback on some sample chapters and most of what they said is good. My absolute favourite was:

"There are a few patches which didn't feel quite as polished in 'Daveness'"

Which is a perfect analogy for my saddle.

Then last month out of the blue I received an email from a chap named "Simon". His intro labelled him as a "voice artist", which I had a short giggle at wondering if voice artistry had traversed similar periods to physical art. The Renaissance, where voices went back to grunts instead of all of this new fangled modern word rubbish, Romanticism, where all words were dramatically emphasised and emotionally charged and finally the abstract period where Birmingham accents came to the fore.

Anyway, Simon offered to create an audio version of my book and market it for me. All I had to do was say "yes" and agree to a royalty split. Given that Simon's percentages were nearly half that of Amazon I was pretty damned interested and the sample text he provided was clear and well-spoken, two words that have never been applied to my speech patterns.

I took him up on his offer and the poor man has spent a month reading my typo-ridden text back into a microphone and pulling an audio version of the book together. It's been interesting listening to his sample chapters as Simon doesn't sound like me at all. At first, I found this very odd, but speaking to others it appears that audiobooks should be read clearly with proper pronunciation, the last thing any listener wants is an audible typo.

I learnt something completely new. One of the chapters is entitled "The Tao of Singlespeeding". Simon pronounced "Tao" as "DOW", I thought he'd had a momentary bad cold and advised him of the mistake. Simon pointed me to the internet and, blow me, he was right. How many of us have been mispronouncing this word?

Simon finished the book this week and I've recorded a brief intro so that listeners can properly understand why I am not reading the rest of the book. My dreams and ambitions have come full circle as well because some royalty-free music was required. In a massive fit of egotism, I sent Simon an MP3 of some poor guitar composition/ playing of my own. He has foolishly agreed to use it as bridging music between chapters of the audiobook. I just know where this is going to lead:

"Dear Dave,

I very much enjoyed SIMON reading the audio version of your book Obsessive Compulsive Cycling Disorder, but please can you edit out the desperately shit guitar player who pops up between chapters and the idiot at the front with a complete lack of accent."

Hopefully, the audiobook will be out before the end of the month. It will be very interesting to see what people make of it. I hope I do not end up being sued by drivers who've fallen asleep at the wheel with my book in their CD player.

New Forest

Have you ever thought long and hard about what will end up written upon your gravestone? Being a slightly morbid sort of bloke I must admit that I have given it some cogitation. The optimist in me always hopes that it will be something along the lines of "Here lies Dave Barter 1966 - 2070, Literary genius, Tour de France winner (vets Singlespeed category), Inventor of the world-famous mobile phone doorbell before that kid who patented it". However, my mind is governed by realism and the truth is that I think my gravestone will hold a simple epitaph that will state:

"Here lies Dave....he tried"

And I do try very hard at most things. Writing's one of them and my trying encompasses attempting to bash out some relatively original words that are devoid of the usual stereotyping. I've read a lot of other cycling articles and get a bit fed up with hearing about burning thighs, pain barriers, soaring heart rates or fights with gravity. They all stereotype cycle rides and are, to be frank, a bit boring as we've heard them all before (especially from me as one of the four appears in many of my previous writings). But sometimes it's hard to avoid the stereotype and this week one made itself known to me as I fought valiantly to complete the photography for the book.

Scratch one stereotype, let's make it two, as the stereotypical British weather pattern of relentless rain during summer reared its ugly head (wahey a cliche!) and bit me on the arse (ok, that's enough). I had a clear plan for book completion pinned to the wall of the shed which stated "All photography complete by the end of June". This meant giving up every free weekend to a road trip with a bike, camera and child photographer stuffed into the car. Driving to some nether region of the UK where I would ponce around on the bike and the child would attempt in vain to get a photo of me looking slightly competent. There are complex family reasons as to why it had to be a child their diaries are fuller than mine and each weekend was booked with some event that meant Helen had to stay at home and ferry an alternating child to it. This left a remaining child that could be reluctantly seconded to photography duty with Dad.

The weekend before last had "Available child" and "Lake District/ Northumberland" pencilled into it. The British climate had other ideas, it had "Lake District/Northumberland" and "Jetwash" written on its calendar. The weekend after had "Wales" with four sub-locations written optimistically next to it. British climate reached for the blue marker and simply coloured in the whole weekend whilst simultaneously phoning Michael Fish and warning him not to get it wrong this time. In desperation, I scurried around the BBC Weather website looking for a ray of hope which was delivered in last Sunday's forecast. There appeared to be potential for a modicum of sun in the New Forest. I needed to take photos there so I bribed daughter Holly with the promise of a can of coke (sugar deprivation works wonders in our house) and the plan was hatched.

What I hadn't realised was that every other occupant of the British Isles had also seen the same forecast and subsequently decided to descend upon the New Forest on Sunday for a nice bit of forest mixed with scattered clouds and sunshine. This adds a new dimension to our road-based photoshoot, especially given that I'm trying to portray the cyclist riding in good light on an empty road. Holly and I found the perfect location deep in the forest area where the speed limit is forty miles per hour. I set the camera up for her and we agreed that a zoom shot would showcase the road which required me to be some distance away on the bike. There was a lot of clouds but equally a decent amount of wind which meant waiting for the right moment when the clouds parted and the sun lit up the road. Now, if it was just me, Holly, the road and the clouds then the whole process would be relatively straightforward. However, add the entire population of Britain driving across the scene and it all becomes fiendishly complex.

I would sit on the bike by the side of the road waiting for the sun to come out. I'd then have to wait for this to coincide with a gap in the traffic from BOTH directions and pedal towards Holly who'd get the shot. It's sounding complex already, but throw in some ponies. The New Forest is littered with them, they're pretty wild and don't give a hoot about cars (or maybe they don't give a neigh, I'm not sure?). These ponies wander wilfully into the road causing the traffic to slow and bunch up which in turn fills my road with cars ruining my shot. It gets worse.

Every cyclist in the world had also seen the forecast and made a beeline for the New Forest for a rare day's rain-free pedalling. Not only did I have cars leaking into my frame there were cyclists as well. Which would have been OK if they weren't all wearing garishly coloured fluorescent waterproofs and pushing their bikes up moderately graded hills. I cheerily said "Hello" to a couple of pushers glad that the ability to translate the fire behind the eyes doesn't exist as "Get the fucking hell on with it please you're ruining my shot" would end up with my being reported to the CTC. After a whole series of failed attempts, I was about to suggest we give up and go elsewhere when stereotype number two wandered into the scene. He didn't wander, he floored it. Yes, the silver BMW driver.

Much of the New Forest has a forty mph speed limit for a good reason as described above. It's stuffed full of bends, humps, horses and pushing cyclists. Travelling at faster than forty is always going to end in either tears or a collection of bikes and human/equine body parts upon the windscreen. Although I hated all of the drivers interrupting my shoot with a vengeance I did grudgingly respect their adherence to the limit. However, Mr Stereotype didn't, he attempted to pass most of them as I watched in horror up the road. I knew that on passing me he would encounter a group of horses that were distracting traffic and also some more pushing cyclists in the distance. So feeling both scared and public-spirited I made a "Warning! slow down" signal by raising and lowering my arm.

The problem is we are dealing with a stereotype here and he responded as stereotypes will by reaching out of his window with his left arm and pointing clearly to the sky with his middle finger. He just about had time to swerve over to the right side of the road and miss the horses, the caravan he was overtaking, the pushing cyclists and the gasp of horror from my mouth. What happened next has caused me to lose all faith in the British public. A four by four that I can't identify travelling in the opposite direction passed me. The passenger window was wound down and I heard the time-honoured phrase, specially reserved for sanctimonious cyclists, screamed at me as the car passed by. "Caaaaaaaaaannnnnnnnnttttttttttt"

And let's just say he didn't mean the opposite of "can". This is what it has come to on the road. Warn a motorist of a hazard ahead whilst holding a bike and you're scum worthy of the highest form of both visual and verbal assault. If Jeremy Clarkson had made the same warning gesture, the car would have meekly pulled in and then returned for an autograph. But a cyclist, let's simply stereotype them as sanctimonious overtaker haters. There's no way they could have been trying to save a life.

Holly and I moved to a quieter spot and took loads of photos that were only pissed about by ponies. To be honest I didn't mind as they can't say "caaaaaaaannnnnttttt" and also they live there so have every right to stroll into the frame and hold a hoof over the subject's head. As we sat slurping our cans of coke and eating lunch I told Holly that I genuinely despair for all of us, not based on Mr Stereotype, but "Mr caaaannnnnnttt instead". She was about to reply when a marauding pony intervened and tried to nick her sandwich. Now I despair for the ponies as well.

Reviews

I'm jealous of a lot of people. Men with six-packs, anyone who can draw, kids who can wheelie for miles whilst smoking/texting and proper mountain climbers who aren't scared of heights. The list could go on and on but the last entry in bold would state "those with thick skins". And by thick skins I don't mean the kind cultivated by McDonald's, I'm talking about those who can let any form of criticism gently waft over their head and away with the wind. Frankly, I'm the opposite. As soon as any product of mine is called into question I spiral into a tornado of self-doubt worrying that the whole world probably holds a similar opinion. Therefore choosing the temporary career of authorship was, in hindsight, a precarious path to take. Literary criticism abounds with the advent of the internet. Sites such as Amazon actively encourage reviews and ratings regardless of the reviewer's qualifications or critical ability.

There is a wealth of advice for authors on dealing with reviews of their work. It all boils down to a simple mantra. "Ignore them, ignore them, ignore them, don't react, ignore them". This probably stems from the motivations of one posting a negative review. They've read your work and didn't like it. Nothing you can say will make them change their mind. It's like eating a pasty tasting of dogshit. If you returned to the shop and were told that admittedly there was an overtone of canine faeces, however, the owner worked long and hard on its construction, it doesn't remove the fact that you didn't like the pasty. Pointing at a legion of previously happy customers will not sway your opinion. In fact the more the owner bangs on about your misguided critique of his dog egg-based vat free snacks the more you'll solidify your hatred of his product. The best strategy is simply to accept that we live in a very diverse world full of diverse opinions that are often unbending. I present the success of Genesis with Phil Collins as the frontman as evidence and rest my case.

Given all of the above, I had carefully prepared myself for the publication of my first book. I had no idea as to how well it would go down and resolved to embrace the first poor review in the name of diversity. I'd even written a mental list of areas that would probably cause a reader duress. Grammar was high on the list, but I seem to have gotten away with it so far. Next came swearing, the book has a fair quotient of "fucks", "bollocks" and "pisses" but these seem to have been ignored as well, probably because cycling is a pretty sweary pastime and they are deemed necessary nomenclature. Finally, there's the writing style. I can't believe there is a way with words that embraces everyone equally. Although it appears that the vast majority of the country will read anything as long as it contains rich people engaging in bondage punctuated by helicopter rides. I'm not bitter at the success of "Fifty Shades of Grey" I'm inspired and have been working feverishly on a cycling variant that includes plenty of spicy chapters peppered with tyre sealant, track pump-action and a particularly gruelling bedroom scene where the main character services a bottom bracket.

So this week I was properly put to the test when I received my first negative review. Here's the full text, kindly posted by Tom on Amazon.com:

"If this had been written 10 or 15 years ago I might have found these stories interesting but in 2012 these stories are rather mundane and have been told an untold number of times by an endless supply of authors. For ex., the story about getting drunk and generally doing dumb things before a hill climb is fantastically unoriginal. If you are new to cycling you might find the stories entertaining but if you've been around probably not."

Now, my initial reaction was to immediately comment upon his review. Did he not realise how much time and effort I'd put into the 85,000 words? Did he not realise I am self-published and did this all off my own back? Surely 77p is a throwaway amount of money in this day and age, and does he not realise that I only see 22p of it? But luckily I held back. These things wouldn't matter to Tom as his kindle book tasted of dogshit and there's nothing I can do to change his mind. Instead, I'll seek solace in my dissection of TomV's review.

Firstly, Tom states that I am a little late in publishing my book. Apparently, I've missed the boat by 10 to 15 years, the basis of which appears to be that he would have been younger and been of a more receptive frame of mind. As he has aged, cycling literature has worn upon his eyes and in the intervening period, he's heard it all. This also causes me a slight quandary as 10-15 years ago I was a fat bastard who hardly cycled at all, the book documents this. If written at that time it would have documented a few London-Brighton rides with huge amounts of filler text describing beer and dogshit tasting pasties.

Digging further and quoting Tom directly the stories have been told, "an untold number of times by an endless supply of authors". I found this quite interesting. Firstly, an "untold number of times", really? If I have got this right there are libraries full of tales of riding mountain bikes at night in Wiltshire, crashing at 40mph on alpine descents, riding steep switchbacks in Sardinia or drawing sexual allegories with titanium bike purchases. So I phoned the local library and made a few enquires, "We've never heard of and would never stock such drivel" was the curt reply, "But we might be interested in the titanium sex story if it's got helicopters in it".

Then I moved on to the "endless supply of authors", this tickled me a lot. I guess it is a real problem in cycling that is now further compounded as the sport gains in popularity. Every event spawns untold numbers of words that hammer at the eyes of seasoned cyclists ten to fifteen years ahead of their time. The endless supply of authors is akin to a verbal British winter drowning the internet with their unnecessary words. What we need is a cull or maybe some regulation to ensure that only a select few are sanctioned to write about things that haven't been done before.

To be fair to Tom I can probably see where he is coming from. He's an American, it's a much bigger country. He's doubtless ridden stuff similar to my meagre achievements and read many similar blog posts over the years. I can imagine that the self-effacing British humour might have grated as well, especially the fact that the only use of the word "awesome" was in a text taking the piss out of an American cycling blogger.

Then I stumbled across this, "generally doing dumb things before a hill climb is fantastically unoriginal". I have to agree with Tom. This is a major failing on my part and I've fallen into the stereotypical trap that all hill climbers find themselves snared by. The done thing in cycling is to keep quiet, ride the hill climb, log it upon Strava and tell everyone you were awesome. Whatever you do, you mustn't ever be found guilty of the oxymoron "fantastically unoriginal". I began to wonder what would have been original? Maybe I should fatten up before a hill climb? or work years on a theory disproving Newton's gravitational laws? or look for events with poorly described courses, ride downhill and use pedantry to win the prize?

Face it, all of this dissection serves no purpose. Ribbing Tom will not change his opinion of my book and rightly so. The real frustration is that I'd like to give him his money back but there's no way for this to be achieved. Fortunately, there appears to be a few others who had opinions to the contrary, interestingly many of these are those who've "been around" and write telling me that the book has inspired them to get out and ride once again. But the whole episode has been a good test of authorship restraint. Unless you count the publication of fourteen hundred words moaning about a bad review and pulling the reviewer's text to bits? I'd never do that, it would be a fantastically unoriginal thing to do.

Competing

Project yourself back in time as long as necessary until you reach that point at which you first decided what you wanted to be when you grew up. I have to go back nearly thirty years and look down upon a young lad who sat in one of the chemistry labs in Wootton Bassett Comprehensive. He'd just placed a small grain of sodium into a test tube half full of water which had subsequently exploded. Projecting myself into this young lad's brain I can remember his thoughts at the time. *"Bloody hell, this is brilliant. I love chemistry, it's all explosions and funny smells, this is what I want to do when I'm older"*

And so at the tender age of fifteen, I decided that I would become a research chemist. Three years later I deliberately failed chemistry A level in protest after disillusionment had set in. I hadn't realised that chemistry was not as easy or interesting as first impressions had implied. Firstly the explosions had been replaced with slightly tedious experiments. Mixing resin with colours and stabilisers and then observing it was like watching paint dry. Additionally, I found out that the 'O' level chemistry syllabus was all lies. Those nice diagrams of atoms with electrons neatly orbiting around protons turned out to be an oversimplification. The truth involved charge clouds and all sorts of complexity that I struggled to cope with. In the end, I chose to study maths and aspired to become a BBC cameraman. The BBC firmly rejected me in 1989 based on no photographic experience whatsoever and the fact that my Dad bought the Daily Telegraph.

Several things happened recently to remind me of these youthful aspirations, all of them cycling related. Firstly Britain suddenly ruled the world at cycling. Paul Weller's brother, Bradley Wiggins, held off a skinny Italian to win the Tour de France. The first time a Lambretta rider had made the transition from scooter to bicycle successfully. Bradley achieved this despite suffering from a reverse form of alopecia that seriously affects his cheekbones. Wind tunnel testing clearly showed that Brad would lose two watts per decade to his bum-fluff, yet he continued unbowed to destroy his rivals and win by several minutes. Then our Olympic athletes took up the mantle and won everything else. Mark Cavendish did a splendid job of lulling all of the other nations into a false sense of security by letting Borat's uncle win the road race. The track riders then turned up and carved "Britain Woz 'ere" into the boards of the Velodrome with their cruel cycling knives. Secondly, I received an email from one of the youngest readers of OCCD. He'd actually enjoyed it, despite a complete lack of references to bitches, bling or the X-Factor. His email ended with this paragraph. *"Finally, I have very big dreams as a cyclist that are laughed off by everybody. These are to ride the tour and be world road race champion and wear the rainbow jersey as well as representing my country in the Olympic games"*

That's a pretty big aspiration for a fifteen-year-old lad. However, I very much doubt that he's the only youngster in the UK thinking along these lines. I can imagine that at this moment in time countless dusty bikes are re-emerging from garages as their owners reacquaint themselves with this cycling lark. I bet there is a large vein of parents who've dragged their kids screaming away from the computer and shoved them on two wheels demanding they become the next "Hoy". I'll also wager that bike shop door hinges will need an extra drop of oil as an influx of portly men struggle to open them in a quest for a new carbon bike.

Now let's be clear. This is a very very good thing. It's always easy to deride fat blokes buying carbon bikes, but they are one step ahead of the fat blokes not buying bikes at all. By owning a carbon bike they've increased their probability of riding it and therefore potentially decreased their longevity as a fat bloke. There's always a slim chance that a child thrown off Facebook and onto the bike will remain seated and pedalling, as they realise that whilst country lanes don't come with "Like" buttons they do create experiences worth socially networking about.

What scares me is that the nation will return to cycling and then rapidly retreat again in a similar manner to my experience with chemistry. The reason is that they're drawn in by iconic images of British cyclists winning (the explosions) without realising just what is required to make it to that point (the charge clouds). It all looks so easy. Shave off all hair below the waist, look good in some skin-tight clothes then mount an assembly of space-age materials and all that's needed is to practise the no hands celebration for the victory at the end. However, cycling holds a dark secret that's rarely mentioned in bike shops or displayed upon healthy living posters. Cycling success is down to mastery of a simple equation:

Winning potential = [power] x [ability to suffer] x [tactics]

Power and tactics are the same as in many other sports. The strongest and wiliest will more than likely become the winner. It's the "suffer" bit that is so important to the cycling equation. For example, a casual observer of the Olympic time trial will have wondered what all the fuss was about. Bradley spun his legs up to "fast" and stayed there for twenty-seven miles. He sweated a bit and produced the odd gurn but made it all look quite easy. Compare this to a Premier League footballer receiving a small tap to the knee in the penalty area. He'll be rolling around on the floor wailing in pain as if a leg based Chinese burn has been administered by Geoff Capes.

The contrast is down to the fact that Bradley has learned to suffer properly. Riding at 30 miles an hour for an extended period hurts no matter how strong you are. Your body is designed that way as it's not meant to do it. So the legs pass a few quick notes to the brain along the lines of "I don't think she'll take any more captain" but the elite cyclist's brain is trained to tear up these notes and demand warp factor eleven instead. These special brains know how to eke every single watt out of the dilithium crystal as they've trained that way for years.

Commentators mislead us when they talk about suffering as they only ever seem to apply it to the cyclists going out the back. All cyclists in all races suffer. It's necessary to do well and the more suffering you can put up with the greater advantage you will have over your rivals. In football, this only applies to the fans. As a Swindon Town supporter, I've suffered greatly over the years whilst my team have ambled about the pitch casually letting goals in and then recovering in nightclubs. Competitive cycling and suffering go hand in hand. Yet it's one of the upgrades that is not sold on the shelf or reviewed in the cycling mags. I propose that this should change and bike shops could offer a new service to aspiring Tour de France winners.

"Hello, I'd like to upgrade my bike and win the Tour de France"
"Certainly sir. Just squeeze through the door and we'll see what we can do. Now, how about this Pinarello that weighs less than your wallet and costs more than your neighbour's extension?"
"Yes please, can I have a saddlebag as well?"
"Certainly sir. Now you'll be needing some Team Sky kit and a Rapha man bag. Would that be XXXXXXXL or XXXXXL?"
"XXXXL please as I need to get some sun on the muffins"
"No problem. Now, this week we are recommending suffer pack five, which consists of ten rapid smacks to the bollocks with a pedal spanner. Or you could go for the subscription suffer pack where we ship a weekly Bargain Hunt DVD to your house along with a bouncer to ensure you watch it"
"Hmmm, I think I'll start easy and go with the iPod that only loads Mark Knopfler songs"

You can see where I'm coming from can't you (I hope). It's wonderful that competitive success is inspiring many to take to cycling but will quickly become tragic if the reality of competition bites those who turn up at the door of the sport. My fifteen-year-old reader is an exception, of course, he suffered thirty of my chapters and clearly shows he can take the pain. I've filed his email for ten years when he stands on the Champs-Élysées and I can wave it about whilst claiming that I inspired him on the way.

But what about the others? What they need is a book extolling the virtues of cycling in the UK without the need to compete. A list of "must-do" rides with suffering set to "Knopfler" rather than "spanner-to-bollocks". This tome can lie in wait for those who decide that growing sideburns whilst suffering like a dog is just not for them. Hopefully, it will act as a net to catch some of the inevitable fallers making their way back to the TV with pizza and beer in hand.

Fortunately, I'm still making progress towards this goal. A recent hiatus in book writing will shortly be ended as my publisher has been in touch to say "Dave, where's this book then and can we start printing it". The weather/photography excuse has now faded as the sun's come out and the roads are tourist-free as the kids have returned to school. I've finished writing it and just have to read the words again and make sure they're correct. This is particularly important given the recent review I received from Chris. It was mostly nice and I particularly liked; *"This book is probably not for you if you are a tricyclist responsible for tourism in the Grimsby area and are easily offended by Anglo-Saxon expletives"*. It made me wonder what book WOULD be for you if you sat in this niche?

Up North Again

"He wants to come across as a humorous, somewhat bumbling, everyman."

So wrote a recent reviewer on Amazon when describing yours truly. He couldn't be more wrong. I want to come across as a "lithe, superhuman, devastatingly fast climber with world-class organisational skills, a model of efficiency and dedication". The problem is that I can't, as I'm a "somewhat bumbling everyman". I could attempt to mask the bumbling-ness in my writing, but all that would be left is a few descriptive paragraphs about some trees coupled with some cycling statistics that the morbidly obese may find slightly impressive. I'd love to be able to leave the bumbling-ness behind, it drives me insane as its presence is felt in almost all of my cycling expeditions. And whilst it may seem endearing to readers, I spend a large portion of my life cursing the little things that I always seem to get wrong.

This fact was waved firmly in my face over the past week as I headed north in an attempt to tick off a large amount of photography. Complications arose as I packed the bikes. A night stop in central Glasgow meant they needed to be locked in the boot out of view. This required bike dismantling, which in turn required that specialist tools be used, and crucially, packed for subsequent reassembly. I found this frustrating as I attempted to tessellate wheels, frames, saddles and suspension forks into a rectangular boot. They almost fitted about five times. During the sixth attempt to get them in I fetched a lump hammer. Only the combined cost of the two bikes prevented their remodelling.

As usual, Helen bore the brunt of my packing frustration. The tally of "Where the fuck is my…" outbursts quickly shot into double figures as I stalked the house attempting to track down cycling accoutrements, guidebooks and things generally right in front of my face. The car filled to comedy proportions. How can a single man have so much stuff? Where does it all come from and what is it for? I'm genuinely envious of prehistoric men and their simple needs. A pointy rock, some fur and a couple of coconut shells in case they encounter Raquel Welsh.

The whole exercise was curtailed by exhaustion rather than completion. Sometime close to midnight there appeared to be more stuff in the car than the house so I assumed everything was in. An assumption I would regret a few days later. Monday morning I trundled out of Swindon and made my way up to the Peak District. My friend Andy had agreed to model for me for a few days and as a result, we managed to get some decent shots on the Cat and Fiddle climb. Andy pulled out his best northerner smile for the occasion which southerners like me often mistake for "daggers" but Andy assures me it is a look of glee once one passes the Watford Gap. He's clearly the Mona Lisa of cycling photography.

The next day we optimistically headed for the Lakes and nailed a few more shots in between dodging deluges of rain. So far things were almost going to plan. The weather could have been kinder, but a decent wind was shuffling the clouds/showers along so we were blessed with sporadic patches of sunshine into which Andy would be despatched. Somewhere close to 4 pm we parted and I headed East to Northumberland. I'd decided to use the evening light to compose a few arty self-portraits high on Chapel Fell. A 7.30 pm sunset meant this was achievable without caning my poor overladen car.

An hour later I was ambling up Hartside when I came upon a lone cyclist pushing his bike up the hill. His head was down, as was his rear tyre. The devil on my left shoulder advised that it was his fault. The light was fading, I didn't have much time and he should have set out better prepared. Maybe he was fatigued by the climb and had deflated his rear tyre as a visual excuse? I nearly sped past until the angel on my right shoulder made me wind down the window and enquire "Alright mate?"

The answer was "No". The lone traveller was a coast-to-coast rider who'd used up all of his patches on a nasty pinch flat. I parked up and we inspected the damage. He'd attempted to plug the hole in his tube with a self-adhesive patch combined with puncture repair glue. The tube had somehow been doubled over into the tyre and it all looked a right mess. Empathy flowed as I remembered the years I'd spent bodging puncture repairs. So I offered to replace the tube with one of my spares. I carefully checked his tyre for thorns, carefully set the tube within the tyre, carefully inflated it to 100psi and immediately deflated it as I managed to unscrew the valve inner whilst removing the track pump. Out came the hammer and ten minutes later he was on his way.

A cursory "thanks" along with no offer of compensation for the brand new tube was offered. Motoring samaritans are ten-a-penny in the north. However, the glow of helping a fellow cyclist was payment enough until I summited Chapel Fell just in time to watch the sun line climb up the hill and disappear over the other side. The evening light was gone, I'd missed it by minutes.

Tail between my legs I skulked off to Scotland. This included a brief diversion to Kirroughtree, a mountain bike trail centre that includes a mini-Moab section of rocky trail. I'd wanted to ride this for years after experiencing the real thing several times on the Slickrock Trail. Rain and a severe lack of talent detracted from the experience a little. After dabbing for the hundredth time I was thankful for the lack of other riders able to witness this perfect display of formation mountain bike mincing. I rounded the ride off with a wrong turning down a mile-long climb before heading out to Glentrool on a forty-mile fire road epic more suitable to my ability.

A day later I reached my most northerly point. Lochinver. Conditions were perfect for cycling photography as late afternoon sunshine threw broody shadows across the rocky Assynt landscape. I parked below Stac Pollaidh, set the camera on its tripod, attached the remote release sensor and reached for the cable required to attach it to the camera. My hand closed upon empty space. Meanwhile, the cable cuddled up to a cute little USB printer connector back in Swindon.

Bumbling isn't the word for this packing omission. Downright utter incompetence gets closer but is not strong enough for me. Everything else was in place, the scenery, the light, a functioning bicycle, tripod, the correct cycling attire and a complete lack of motorists to ruin the shots. All I needed was a small thin cable, no longer than six inches in length to relay a message from the sensor to the camera saying "NOW". I made a half-hearted attempt to get the shots using the camera self-timer, but Nikon in their infinite wisdom set this to a maximum length of ten seconds. After four shots of my arse heading away from the camera, I gave up and took panoramas instead. The evening was spent alone in a hotel room chanting "You stupid bloody pillock" over and over again.

Things were made worse by the weather forecast. I'd hoped for a week's worth of Indian summer which would allow me to get pictures done in at least four more locations. But the jet stream had other ideas leaving me with one final day of reliable sun. I decided to nip over to Torridon and ride the Applecross peninsular with my compact camera. This has a thirty-second delay on the self-timer, slightly more conducive to an arty self-portrait. The sunshine obliged once again so I stopped several times using a mini-tripod to catch myself in cycling action. Things seemed to be going well and from what I could see the pictures had turned out OK. I stopped at Applecross for a quick drink and reviewed the pictures I'd taken so far.

All was looking good. The composition seemed fine, with nice colours, a blue sky and a lovely orange date stamp on the bottom right-hand corner. This was taking bumbling to new levels. I'd moved beyond the simple omission of a necessary item, gone through poor weather planning straight into complete inability to operate a necessary work item coupled with total lack of review of output results. I'm currently classed as self-employed so took immediate action by dismissing myself on the spot. I subsequently took myself to an industrial tribunal and lost as befits my bumbling nature. The camera sat nervously during this process, unsure whether it was destined to be hurled into the sea. I convinced myself that Photoshop would have a "Remove date stamp from image" menu item and thus set off up the Pass of the Cattle.

Occasionally anger can serve a valid purpose. I used it to beat the climb into submission. The ascent from Applecross to the Bealach Na Ba is 2000 feet high and not very long. It's a demanding ride, one of the toughest in the UK but the severity passed me by on Saturday. I set about it like an idiot who has just cocked up his photos and soon found myself in the rhythm of a bumbling cyclist determined to at least get one thing right. The metres began to fall as I forgot the poisons left in my legs from the previous day's ride. The climb gets ever more serious as the height is gained culminating in a long steep twenty per cent ramp that leads to a false summit. It didn't bother me. I just rode at the bloody thing, unleashing frustration upon it, determined to keep a high pace that would see me burst rather than grovel onto the summit.

Thirty-six minutes later, it was done. I reached the summit with all traces of bumbling left beside the road. This was a decent climb, the second-best according to Strava and the perfect tonic for a man starting to wonder if anything was destined to go right. I coasted down the other side and returned to the car ready for the long journey back home. On the way, I rationalised the bumbling into a positive. I'm not a bad plumber these days mainly because I have made every possible plumbing mistake once. From improperly fluxed solder joints to over-tightening compression joints, I've done the lot.

It's the same with my cycling and writing as well. Looking back over the past few days, I may have forgotten some important stuff and cocked up the camera settings but hopefully, that won't happen again. I am a veteran of poorly executed puncture repairs and these days can usually fix anything quickly and effectively. These bumblings must serve some sort of purpose to make me a better cyclist, writer, photographer or person in general. The key is to accept them a little more gracefully than I currently do. Looking at each minor bumble as a learning experience rather than a reason to dig deep into my sack of profanity. I'd just about come to terms with this when I reversed the car into a large rock in a service station car park.

Club Dinner

Writer's block. The dreaded two-word sword of Damocles hanging over the head of every author. Those of us who decide to inflict ourselves upon the eyes of others via the literary word all fear its appearance. There can be no more awful fate for an author than to sit in front of a blank page that steadfastly refuses to fill itself with meaningful words. For those who don't write, imagine the sneeze that just refuses to happen, the squeezed spot that liberates nothing at all or the long lonely sit on the loo when the digestive system refuses to say "goodbye". Writer's block is normally related to inspiration. The author knows that something should be described but can't quite put their finger on what that something is or how they should go about painting their literary picture.

There are many and varied explanations for the condition. Wikipedia cites some interesting cases. I quite enjoyed that of George Orwell's character, Gordon Comstock, who struggled to write a poem about London as it was "too big". I'd have sorted him out in no time at all. A pair of binoculars turned the wrong way round and he'd have been good to go. It gets a bit more serious when you consider William Shakespeare, who suddenly stopped composing great plays and sonnets. One minute he's banging away productively at his scrolls. The next minute, nothing. All inspiration gone, a complete lack of words, a load of relieved geese. After much investigation, I found out that this was down to the fact that he had died, which came as a relief. There was me worrying that a form of scriber's cancer existed, able to afflict even the greatest of writers. So what hope for a mere scribbler like me?

I haven't written much for well over a month. I've fallen victim to this terrible affliction. There is no doubt that I have been suffering terribly from writer's block but in my case, the block is different from the norm. I have a head full of ideas and inspiration, that's never a problem. Surreal experiences never cease to find me whilst I'm out cycling. For example, the dead badger lying peacefully by the side of the ride on a loop I ride twice a week. After a few rides, I noticed he was putting on some weight. A week later he was pregnant, then a couple of days after that he was flat. He'd exploded in a massive post-mortal attack of flatulence. It made me almost glad to be human, partly as I won't be gassed for getting a bit of a cough near cows, but mostly down to the fact that even if I do pass on in some hilarious fashion my dignity will be returned after I'm scraped up and gently placed into a wooden box. I'd hope that my mortal remains will not end up being publicly defiled by a fart from beyond the grave.

Anyhow, all this talk of exploding badgers does nothing to explain my block. As stated, it is not an inspirational blockage, it is simply down to the Babylonians who proposed the 24 hour day. In hindsight, they made a bit of a mistake by not including quite enough hours. If they'd added say six or seven more per day I'd be able to get all of my stuff done and find some time for a nice bit of blog writing. This Babylonian foresight would have ensured that the world had a much greater understanding of exploding badgers than it currently does. My writer's block is down to stuff that I have to do which is preventing me from writing. This stuff falls into three distinct categories; work, my UK route guide and things I commit to doing that I really shouldn't.

Work has been particularly stressful as it is currently unpaid. My friend Andy and I have been beavering away at a technology start-up based around mapping. It all sounded so easy when we drew a few diagrams on a bit of paper. All we had to do was import some data, fiddle with it a bit and chuck out some maps and stuff on screen. Customers would then flock to our door, awe-stricken by the maps we had created and hand over their account/sort code details. I decided to focus our minds by booking us into a conference where we could launch our product. In September that conference seemed a long way away. With less than three weeks to go, we've upgraded our business plan status to "actively shitting ourselves". Andy and I have a conference call every day at 9 am. It usually goes along the lines of:

Andy: "Here's the list of things you broke yesterday that I have fixed. I've added to it the list of things I didn't get done as I was fixing the things you broke yesterday"
Dave: "Thanks, I've had this new idea do you think we could...."
<screen goes blank, call disconnected>
<Dave reinitiates call>
Dave: "OK, message understood. What needs doing today?"
Andy: <reels off list longer than a queue of snakes>

We've both been working ridiculously hard for months to build a new product. It's so nearly there, but as with all traditional IT initiatives we're constantly tripped up by unforeseen snags. In Andy's case, the snag is working with Dave. In my case, it's usually down to the fact that the programming code I copied from the internet doesn't quite work the way I thought it should. Days are long as I do battle with SQL, javascript, PHP, C++, Mercator projections, geometric unions, Unix command lines and something called XSLT which I don't really know what it is but it feels like we should be using it along with everyone else.

The small portion of the day that remains should be a time to relax and write blogs. Sadly every hour of that is commandeered by the quest to finish my proper book. Nearly two years ago I set out to write the bloody thing (within a year) and still I haven't finished. To be fair, the writing is done. It's the detail that takes a huge amount of my current minimal spare time. The book has forty chapters (the next one's going to have two). Each chapter has descriptions, maps, route instructions, photos, diagrams and statistics. Many of these are produced by a computer program, but it all needs to be checked. Route instructions are particularly hard as I read through my notes whilst following the map on the screen. Each turn has to be described accurately, often in tandem with Google Streetview to make sure the directions are correct.

I spent one evening cursing the Google van that had gone down a back road in Wales and picked up some leaves on its camera. These leaves blocked out a road sign that I needed to check. I noticed a pub on the road and nearly called them to go out and confirm that the sign really did say "Cymtlyingpwthdoggrty", however, a leaf was covering up its full name. A chapter takes me nearly ten hours to complete. That's four hundred hours required that the Babylonians failed to account for. Fortunately, my publisher has been patient as the book arrives with them in stages. We're so nearly there, a week or two more and it'll be done. It's morphed into a family production with Helen aiding on the maps and routes along with Holly helping out on graphics. Two years ago I announced that I was leaving my job to write a book. Not many "we's" in that sentence.

Then there are the things I simply don't have time for but commit to anyway. A review of GPS units for a magazine sounded easy but took several weekends to complete. My objectivity was tested to the limit by a manufacturer who shall remain unnamed but could be referred to as "FagAshLil" limited. The test unit they supplied had been used by the smoking department to track down cigarettes. On opening the box I was reminded instantly of my Dad during his sixty a day phase. The unit was superbly protected by a liberal coating of nicotine, as an ex-smoker, I fought hard against the urge to lick it all off.

Finally, there's the Barrow Central Wheelers. They are a Lakeland cycling club that must surely be described as slightly unhinged. Earlier this year they asked me to come and speak at their annual dinner. For some reason, they imagined I could vocalise my passion and knowledge of the Cycling Year Record in a manner that would befit their Christmas do. At the time of asking I was pretty keen. I enjoy giving presentations, mainly because it is formalised showing off. Inadequate forty-something males like me need to grab as many showing off opportunities as possible. Once past thirty they are pretty thin on the ground. I can't wheelie, my guitar playing is awful, the only joke I can remember starts "knock-knock" and everybody has seen that silly hand thing where it looks like your thumb is split in half.

The week of the presentation was prefixed by months of

procrastination. I reassured myself that everything would be fine and it'd only take an hour or so to knock up some good looking slides. Three days before the event I opened up my presentation software and realised that it hadn't seen the light of day for years. I had completely forgotten how anything worked. It took thirty minutes to find the "New slide" control and as for adding in photos, how had I ever managed that? The next few evenings were spent mostly shouting "Why? How? Please Help!" at the computer. It patiently obliged by doing everything it was told to do, and nothing more.

In other families, Mum has a word with the kids to advise that "Daddy is finding it tough at the moment as his manager has loaded him up with an unfeasibility large amount of work so cut him some slack". Mine simply acknowledge that the bloody idiot has left it to the last minute again as a smelly, unshaven wreck storms about the place banging cupboards whilst ranting about projector screens.

Preparation for the big day couldn't have gone worse. A particularly difficult work problem converged with several other external factors pushing my stress levels over the edge. My body reacts brilliantly to this by switching on the insomnia button. This is why evolution has to be a load of old bollocks. Surely the best way to react to a mental crisis is a good night's sleep. We've been on this earth for quite a few years and I cannot believe that those who had only 30 minutes sleep the night before were able to best dodge the sabre tooth tiger. Hunters look for weakness, and if I was hiding in a bush spotting the best human to nibble on, I'd pick the yawner. He'd still be rubbing his eyes as I jumped out whilst his mates had legged it into the jungle.

So why has evolution invented insomnia? What is the point of it other than to thin us out by getting rid of the worriers? It's surely the product of a vengeful God who sees it as a nice opportunity for us to get in a little more praying as we lie there begging to be overtaken by a little sleep. I reckon I had about two hours the night before my big performance. The drive up to the Lakes was taken slowly and carefully with biblical downpours fuelling stress levels further.

I tried to convince myself that all would be OK. Many years previously I'd been asked to present at a postal conference in Prague. A colleague and I took advantage of a foreign travel expenses policy that did not appear to have an upper limit. The night ended with us trading blows in Wenceslas Square before making up and retiring back to the bar. We were put into a taxi and got back to the hotel purely by mime. On arrival, we didn't have enough cash to pay the fare so Richard sent me to my room to get some more. I managed to open the door and woke up the next day on the floor. Richard had no idea how he had paid the remainder to the driver and didn't want to know. At breakfast, we were the greyest men walking the earth, zombified by our excesses with livers desperately searching for instructions on what to do next. We commandeered all of the free water in the conference centre and cuddled it until it was our turn to speak. I have no idea what I said but the resulting minutes thanked the British contingent for "their interesting contribution to the event".

So with this track record, I'd hope to muddle through. I made it to the hotel unscathed and met Allen and Glen from the club. They fretted for a while about projector screens whilst I stressed further over the enormity of my task. Speaking at a cycling club dinner is a different league from a business presentation. You're supposed to inject some humour, chuck about a few anecdotes, give out some pearls of wisdom and tell the audience a few little snippets that they didn't already know. I had some slides along with a fatigued brain that was just about managing to keep bodily functions to spec.

Fortunately, Barrow Central Wheelers are an incredibly welcoming bunch. Allen and Glen went out of their way to make me feel relaxed and at home. We settled down to dinner and bantered about cycling as us cycling types do. I kept my alcohol consumption in check and did my best to eat with elbows in and not lick peas off the fork. I'd almost managed to relax when the club chairman, Mike Speight, announced that it was time for the guest speaker.

A microphone was placed in my hand and I arose to a sea (well fifty) of expectant faces all awaiting an hour's worth of witty, informative cycling based entertainment. Not a good moment for the mind to go completely blank.

My brain decided to go on a mini-lock down just at the time when I needed it most. Information was drip-fed to my mouth which began to talk. But I felt like a detached observer to the proceedings wondering when the presenter was going to get into some sort of flow. I'd prepared loads of notes, a few jokes and some interesting little snippets but many of them refused to appear. Fortunately, I had my slides as prompts and managed to navigate myself down this verbal canal with the presentational boat lurching from side to side.

The audience were either too kind or too pissed to point out my predicament. It may have been that the words came out in some sort of order and made some sort of sense. I'm self-critical and halfway through was keen to stop and request that I start the whole thing again. It was like one of those races where you've put in a big effort to prepare but on the day it just doesn't translate. You want to get off and go home but there's a crowd, people who aren't riding but are looking at you expectantly. You have to keep going, you have to make it to the end by letting each expectant look nudge you a little further down the road.

I made it to the end, a quick check of the head showed no bottle impacts and I hadn't spotted any sleepers. Everyone was very kind and appreciative, I even got to hand out the trophies to the prize winners. Like all good cycling clubs, almost all of them were won by the same bloke. The rest of the evening passed in a blur of conversation, Peroni and whippets. I made the whippets up but was very disappointed to be in such northern company without even a sniff of one. The Barrow Wheelers blew away all of the northern stereotypes as they were generous, humorous and all drank lager. The evening ended with me very much buoyed up by their company, more than adequate payment for the ordeal. Later that evening I collapsed exhausted onto my hotel bed and fell into another deep bout of insomnia.

Mistakes

One week on and the writer's block has disappeared, as a result, my parents have reinstalled the swear filter on the broadband connection and my wife is busy updating her "why did you marry Dave" FAQ. The intensity of work vs book writing continues, however some bugger is shining a bloody great torch down the tunnel entrance. It's very nearly written. I've submitted thirty of forty chapters to my publisher and this laptop contains the final ten, four of which need a few tweaks, six of which are just about finished. I'm days away from completing this project with an overrun of approximately eleven months. Now, to the casual observer, this may seem to be a little late.

However, I come from the IT industry and a 100% overrun on the estimate is what we hackers refer to as "just in time". In my defence, I can point at projects with much higher levels of funding that have lateness quotients similar to evolution. Take the NHS patient record system for example. This has received billions of pounds to date all of which have gone towards the funding of an argument as to who's fault it is that the project is late. My defence is simpler in that I just don't have one. One year to write and publish a UK route guide was riding a wave of optimism that even the gnarliest of surfers would have run from. Two years is pushing it. The next book will require that I retire.

The publisher is now patiently wending their way through the mass of stuff I've emailed their way. I'm receiving a weekly list of questions concerning the text most of which can be answered with "Yes, you are right". To give some background, something happened to me in my youth that destroyed my natural sense of direction. I am completely and utterly left/right dyslexic. This is why I don't lead group rides anymore. Even with a GPS attached to the bars we end up swerving all over the road as I shout, "left, no right! no left actually". These days I've given up giving directions unless I can point and shout "that way". This dyslexia translates into other languages and nomenclatures as well. I am not properly sure which is port/starboard, links/rechts, droite/gauche.

In compiling route directions for the book I've made loads of left/right mistakes. Tom patiently emails me for clarification as he checks the routes himself. He needn't bother, the answer is always that I've got it wrong, even from the luxury of my shed sat in front of a map with plenty of time to make the right decision I cock it up. As I complete the final set of routes I've become conscious of this and end up miming the directions whilst attempting to orientate my body with the map. From the house it looks like I'm pretending to fly planes, the family don't bat an eyelid at this madness, round our way it has become the norm.

This wouldn't be Dave without a few other mishaps to pepper the way and I've made a corker with a few of the photos. As stated elsewhere I'm having to take a lot of self-portraits. Sadly the country is not awash with handsome, lithe roadies with no jobs and a willingness to be photographed countrywide at short notice riding small lengths of tarmac. The only one I know of is me, as long as we can agree that "quirky" is a reasonable substitute for "handsome", "skinny" will do for "lithe" and "unpaid" replaces "no job". Therefore I have to use my tried and tested technique of camera on tripod and remote release to get my pictures.

A few weeks previously a weather window opened delivering some rare winter sun to the UK. I was able to knock off the remaining Welsh pictures required for the book. One set needed a trip to the Irfon valley, on arrival I noted that conditions were not just good, they were utterly perfect. There was a complete absence of traffic, the sun was low and casting moody shadows down the shallow valley, the autumnal colours lit the scene with contrast and I'd remembered to bring everything. The only problem was the direction of the sun. It blasted down the valley throwing out long shadows from everything that got in its way. I needed a shot of me riding up the valley as it told the story of the road which followed the Irfon's dash down through the Welsh geology. I set up the tripod attached lens and squinted down the viewfinder. The picture was framed perfectly so I grasped the remote and rode up and down over twenty times. For every fifth shot, I varied aperture and/or exposure to practise a crude form of bracketing. For the non-technical camera users out there (including me) this means "take loads of pictures using loads of settings and hopefully one of them will be OK".

Things were going swimmingly. No cars to interrupt my shoot and all of the local sheep were giving me a wide berth. Looking at the small preview on my camera LCD showed some lovely shots and I packed up anticipating a job well done. Like an excited child, I scooted home and plugged the SD card into my computer. It took an age for the images to upload, finally, the screen pinged into a maelstrom of vivid Welsh colour. These were some of the best pictures I had ever taken apart from the tripod.

Oh shit, oh fuckington bollocksy shite. The tripod had thrown some beautifully long shadows of their own which had bled wonderfully into the frame. There's me looking almost normal in the saddle, wearing a coordinated kit and riding in one of the most perfect places in the UK accompanied by a tripod. I visualised this as a centre spread in the book. The reader opens and is momentarily awestruck before the giggles begin. What's that funny three legged intruder? Has Dave stumbled into a Welsh version of the War of the Worlds, please save us from Jeff Wayne!

I've given up facepalming. My forehead is far too worn. Instead, I used the power of the internet in a plea for help. King Richard was offering a lot of land for a nag. I had some beer and need of photoshop. He vainly asked the surrounding air for a horse, I tweeted "Can anyone out there fix this?". Many of the replies contained the words "no" and "twat". One wag simply cropped the scene to include only me, therefore reducing its impact by about 95%. Fortunately, my publisher came to the rescue with a few deft swishes of the digital eraser. I should have widened the brief to include more muscles, a manly tash and Claire Grogan cheering with glee from the side of the road.

A combination of winter, over-busyness, lack of daylight and drug revelations have conspired to limit my cycling. The weather and lack of hours keep me from venturing outdoors and the drug revelations force me to read about cycling non-stop rather than doing it. Normally I'll scour the newspapers in a vain search for a small clip about Mark Cavendish. However, recent months have filled the press with the Lance revelations whilst Tyler's "Race in the Dark" has occupied a portion of my Kindle's silicon bookshelf. At first, I joined in the outrage against Lance. I'd cheered this bloke on from the side of the road whilst the French chalked syringes. How galling for them to be right all along.

Then Tyler's book overtook mine in the Amazon charts and my focus switched to him instead. Now whilst it is admirable that he's fessed up and spilt the beans I'm feeling a little disgruntled. He's outselling me by a mile, yet the only cheating I've ever done is to play Indian poker with a mate whilst facing a mirror. Then I dug back a little further to the Etape de Tour 2005. The stage results read something like this:

Dave Barter (amateur): 8 hours 49 minutes
Tyler Hamilton (cheat): 5 hours 47 minutes

Admittedly Tyler was in the race proper whilst Dave was tootling his way over a sportive. But the route was the same and Tyler's drugs gave him a three-hour head start. His drugs are also giving him an unfair advantage in the Amazon world. Without them, his book would be a boring list of races ridden followed by a brief bit of emotion when Tugboat bites the dust. David Millar did it to me as well, took a shed load of drugs, lied, owned up, wrote a book and nailed the sympathy vote. Therefore I have asked Amazon to create a new category within sporting literature called "Cycling - drug cheats". Hamilton, Landis, Millar, Armstrong and Bez (if he ever gets on a bike) will all be moved into this list to fight it out amongst themselves. The rest of us whose only digression has been a slight over-application of Deep Heat can stay in the proper chart.

Resolutions

Tomorrow is the last day of the year and the eve of New Year's resolutions. Many people scratch their heads thinking of new things that they can resolve to do. For most of us mere mortals, the resolutions usually involve eating less, exercising more, increasing the personal congeniality rating or becoming a little more productive. In an idle moment, I wondered what the Queen resolves to achieve coming into a brand new year? Does she come up with normal things, such as walking the corgis more often, laying off the pink gin a bit or delivering harder backhanders to Prince Philip every time he farts during Hollyoaks? Or maybe they're a bit more fitting of her position, coercing David Cameron to invade China, declaring herself head of the Jewish religion or removing the phrase "people's princess" from the Oxford English dictionary.

But whatever they are, I bet the Queen is making some. As are the vast majority of her subjects. The cyclists will be staring at their post-Christmas wobbly bits and resolving to spend January on the bike. Resolutions such as these will be made from a warm living room as they watch their Bradley Wiggins 2012 DVD from the comfort of the sofa. They'll forget that in the UK cycling in January is simply not feasible. Slithering around all over the place on knackered roads, dodging snow, ice, water, potholes, slurry and hungover motorists is just about possible. But proper cycling is out of the question.

Some will retreat to the turbo trainer but let's face it, the turbo trainer is damage limitation. Anyone who can suffer more than an hour of going nowhere whilst listening to the sound of a slightly broken Magimix deserves a mention in the New Year's honours list. It's riding on the flat with your brakes rubbing. My turbo trainer simply serves its purpose of reducing the volume of air that I have to heat in the house. One year I tried a different approach and signed up for spinning classes. This was essentially the same as turbo training but with the added novelty of being shouted at over techno music whilst smelling the farts of the bloke on the bike next to you.

As you can see, I hold a deep cynicism for New Year's resolutions. I've made plenty in my time and broken every single one of them. Since the age of 14, there's not been a year in my life without a cigarette, yet I gave up nearly twenty years ago. Alcohol has featured in a consistent monthly volume and I still look like Lofty from Eastenders despite pull-up bars and various press up regimes. My cycling performance has been consistently "the same" since about 2002 despite numerous years where I've resolved to race or time trial or get stronger/faster/better.

Maybe I should work harder to stick to these resolutions. I could conjure up a new one along the lines of resolving to work harder on my resolutions. But then I'd need one to resolve to work harder on and thus enter an infinite loop. So this year I've prepared a new proposal that I am going to take to the New Year's resolution committee. It's based upon a full analysis of my performance in all areas throughout the year. I have outlined strengths, weaknesses, opportunities for improvement and threats to target achievement. A myriad of key performance indicators has been assessed along with a set of monitoring protocols to back them up. All of the evidence gathered and personal analysis carried out has led to a simple resolution that stands a chance of getting a tick in the box. I've decided that next year I'm going to be a little bit less shit at everything that I do.

Now there's a lot to live up to in that previous sentence as my catalogue of shitnessis thicker than Mark Cavendish's thighs. This may seem harsh, however, looking back things have not quite gone to plan. The early part of the year started well and I managed to publish a book. Unfortunately, a little bit of shitness crept into it, or maybe that should be rephrased as "shit loads of typos and a mound of poor grammar to add some extra spice". I resolved to sort all of these out and republish it ready for Christmas. Neither of these was achieved. Therefore I'm still actively selling something that is ever so slightly shonky, which reminds me of the seven years I spent running my previous business.

Speaking of businesses, I was meant to be creating one of those as well. Helen reminds me of this fact daily by shaking an empty piggy bank next to my ear and pointing to the savings account statement. Andy and I created a grand proposition, business plan and investor pitch in a huge surge of momentum. Then quietly binned it to do something else much more sensible. This will turn out to be the right decision. It's just a bit shit that we happened to launch it in the middle of office party season. I can't tell whether or not we are on the right track as most of the feedback we're getting is typed with one finger and a hangover.

Cycling has not escaped the shitness. It has been the main symptom. I've not done anything at all this year apart from pedal round the same old loops and nick some Strava KOM's from pensioners. Every single bike in the fleet is battle damaged and there's one that's not even built. This is surely a cycling crime? To prioritise "other stuff" above and beyond the construction of a new stead. I've not explored anything, I've gone about the same speed as I always do. The only real achievement has been to end the year under ten stone in weight.

Then there's the book I was meant to publish. The book I spent a whole year researching, or dallying around the UK on my bike as my friends like to call it. When asked in November last year I confidently replied that it would be out before the Olympics. This then became Christmas 2012 and now it's looking like March 2013. Fortunately Vertebrate are driving the whole project forwards but it is taking longer than expected, mainly down to my shitness and the amount of stuff that needs checking. To offer me some form of personal consolation it's worth stating that the weather chucked in its own little bit of shitness and stymied my plans for taking photographs.

So the year hasn't exactly gone to plan, but let's be frank these are the sort of problems that many would like to have. The less shit 2013 has a lot going for it. My first proper book will be released, properly proofread and properly laid out. The only downside is that the odd photo of me has slipped into it (thankfully not the cover).

Then there's the new business, I've got a whole host of meetings to go to and a whole lot of funky new technology to show people. We're being much less shit on direction and strategy which should hopefully result in a much less shit bank account balance.

Finally, we have the less shit cycling. I've entered the Fausto Coppi Gran Fondo again after too many years away. So I'll have to be less shit at cycling by quite a lot, otherwise, I will expire upon the steep slopes of the Fauniera. My bike is destined to become a lot less shit as well. In a moment of utter madness during October, I bought a second hand Campagnolo Record groupset. It has sat in its box for months but shall emerge and make my decent bike just a little less shit than it is currently.

The Compass

Two great literary events happened to me as a child. The first was the discovery of the ladies underwear section in Mum's Freeman's catalogue which coincided with the onset of puberty. The second was reading of the Total Perspective Vortex located on Frogstar World B. This evil machine was conjured up by Douglas Adams in the Hitchhiker's Guide to the Galaxy, it placed the subject in the context of the universe with a clear pointer showing themselves in perspective. The sense of utter disproportion destroyed the subject's mind as they realised the futility of their existence within a universe so vast. I loved the concept of the Total Perspective Vortex, only a truly great imagination could conceive of such a thing and more so allow Zaphod Beeblebrox to leave it unscathed.

"In an infinite universe, the one thing sentient life cannot afford to have is a sense of proportion." - Douglas Adams, true brilliance.

Now I'm not sure that the Freemans catalogue is published anymore and anyway I've moved on to Altered Images posters. But the Total Perspective Vortex has stayed with me for the rest of my life. I've yearned for it in business meetings when aftershave doused consultants have told me that I must have got it wrong as we didn't buy it from Microsoft. If only it was there waiting at the end of every red carpet, VIP lounge or Amstrad boardroom.

But the machine is not purely fictitious, variants do exist. I know

236

because I've stepped into them and this meandering blog post is about to explain the results of Dave's entry into the Cycling Total Perspective Vortex.

Let's begin with the publication of Great British Bike Rides. The whole reason why I started this blog in the first place. It hit the streets at the beginning of April, I'll never forget the moment that a large box arrived at the house with my 30 copies contained within, mainly because I was out riding in the rain and yet again failed to get the king-of-the-mountain on the steep bit of Clyffe Pypard Hill. Opening the box and levering out the freshly printed copy was a dangerous moment. I'd told anyone and everyone that the reason for writing this book was to give my pallbearers something to throw in the hole after me with an accompanying "Well at least he managed to finish something". That first copy was another tick on the celestial list of criteria that need to be met before Dave's foot meets the water carrier.

A few days later the book was available for purchase from Amazon. Therein began a period of hugely unbridled stress. The first reviews. I've had plenty for Obsessive Compulsive Cycling Disorder, some of them were great others almost personal in their disgust that I ever laid a finger to keyboard. One, in particular, rang in my ears "Go back to the day job Dave". What day job? I'd burnt my bridges there I'm afraid, they've replaced all of my stuff with Microsoft Excel and told the remaining staff to smile politely but firmly lock the door if I ever return.

Then it came, strangely from a 60-year-old grandmother, *"I had thought I was buying this as a present - but NO WAY - I'm keeping it for myself!"* she wrote. Five stars, my first review was a goodie and I had no idea who they were at all. The stress subsided somewhat as further reviews were added and it seemed that most purchasers got the concept and were impressed with our design and the photography. These were key elements that I had wanted to work when I first envisaged the book.

A launch had been planned at Cotswold Cycles and I spent days fretting over slides whilst worrying that there'd be no interest at all and I'd be rattling on about B roads to a room devoid of humanity. Fortunately, we got a decent crowd and despite some fat fingers on the slide controller and plenty of "ums" the talk seemed to go down well.

After the final slide, I asked if there were any questions? This is normally a cue for the crowd to look at their watches, cough politely and use telepathy to threaten all assembled with torture if they dare let this idiot linger in front of them any longer.

An older cyclist stood up. "Here we go", I thought, "He's now going to put me right on the routes, my nomenclature and berate me for the photo in Wales without a helmet". He cleared his throat as I was about to clear my colon.

"I'd like to thank you", he kindly intoned, "thank you, you've done all the work".

The colon stayed full.

"I'm coming to the end of my cycling life and it won't be long before I can't ride anymore. I've been thinking about what to do and where to go in my twilight pedalling years. You've done that for me now. I can take this book and go to these places and ride, you've done all the work".

Now my eyes were full. I don't think anyone will ever say anything to me about cycling that means as much as his words that evening. It would have been the perfect end to the book launch had I not later inspected a flash carbon bike with the shop owner and commented that it was light because it had no back brake. The owner patiently pointed to the bottom bracket mounted rear calliper, as all of those who had purchased a book on the night immediately sought refunds.

However, my inability to comprehend modern cycle design was not the only cringe-worthy incident of the evening. That came with the fellow who ran over and excitedly pointed to page 19. "Seen that, seen that, oh dear!" were his words, his finger pointed squarely at the compass wind diagram.

At first, I had no idea as to why he was so excited, maybe he'd sneaked a few caffeine gels from the bike shop shelves. Then it hit home. I felt the bike shop close in around me as my vision tunnelled down to the compass diagram. I could hear my heartbeat, my mouth went dry as he flicked from ride to ride and we saw that the error had been compounded throughout the book. I'd got East and West the wrong way round. How could this have possibly happened? We'd checked every ride countless times. I had proof copies with notes on the compass to change figures where rounding had caused errors, yet I hadn't noticed the East/West swap. The error is hidden somewhat by misdirection. The compass is ingrained in the minds of many from an early age. When you glance at it the arrow says "West" even though the label's marked "East".

Later I found the culprit, two lines of code with the labels entered the wrong way round. This code was used to generate every single compass diagram in the book (41 of them) and this is the code that got every single one of them wrong. The matter was further highlighted when the "Dave go back to the desk job" reviewer bought a copy of the book and took great delight in detailing this error in his next review, along with a few others he'd spotted. At least he'd doubled his stars though and added some nice stuff.

After the launch, I went through another set of "firsts". First time seeing the book on the shelves in a shop, first royalty cheque, first carbon frame purchase, the first talk booked in a London bike shop, the first talk cancelled due to lack of interest, first review that directly referred to my body mass and first-ever bike crash during a filmed author interview (the "unclipping fail" incident up Winnats Pass was dropped from the cut).

I even ended up on the proper telly after the BBC One Show commissioned a piece concerning Tommy Godwin's year record. A production company contacted me and asked for some help with the research and possibly a stint in front of the camera. I supplied them with facts and figures, spoke at length on the phone concerning Tommy and dutifully drove a 300-mile round trip to spend a day filming for the show.

The piece was shot at Tutbury Castle and as I climbed out of my car I bumped into Iwan Thomas, who wasn't looking as he was tweeting. We cycled around a bit talking, then did a staged piece in the castle cafe concerning food and Tommy's diet. Two days later I had a call from the producer, the filming had looked good, but couldn't be used as we weren't wearing helmets. Cycling film without helmets breaks the BBC's postbox. So it looked like the filming needed to be done again. One month later, 300 miles more driving, same location, Iwan still tweeting this time furiously as he'd spotted a gardener dressed like Steven Seagal. I met a different producer (the previous chap seemed to have "left" the company). Again we filmed all day which liberated enough footage for five minutes on screen.

I awaited my call to sit on the sofa and banter light-heartedly about the record. It never came, some bloke called Chris Hoy took that honour, but I did get to see myself on prime time TV, talking posh, with a mouse stuck to my cycling jersey and the wind blowing my hair to reveal a massive great 46-year-old spam forehead. In hindsight, I'd fallen into the typical TV idiot trap. I gave up two days, provided two bikes, drove 600 miles and provided clear detailed research material and consultancy for free. Iwan got paid, Chris got paid, the cameraman got paid, the two producers got paid, the production company got paid, the company hiring the food props got paid, the castle cafe got paid, I got a bacon butty for lunch and of course, the DVD promised by the production company will never materialise. Since the TV appearance, the calls to my agent (Helen aka wife) have consisted of two attempts to sell us a government grant for insulation and a modelling agency who appeared to have the wrong number for Twiggy. And so I've stepped out of the Cycling Total Perspective Vortex with a clear indication of where I sit within its universe.

The cycling TV punditry career is not going to happen (too thin, ugly, spamhead, inability to ask for money, no celebrity cycling mates). The renowned cycling author career won't happen either, this is largely due to economics, Great British Bike Rides has a retail price of £25 and after all the various commissions have been deducted I see approximately £2.50 per sale. Doing my accounts a couple of months back showed that the book cost in the region of £30,000 to write which means I need to sell 12,000 copies to break even. This is going to take a long time to achieve and is probably unrealistic in the short term. However, that's not why I did it in the first place. The whole point of Great British Bike Rides was this:

"Dear Dave,

We just returned from a month in the UK and made a pilgrimage to our favourite bookshop-- Stanford's on Long Acre-- while in London a few days ago. Imagine our surprise when the book we dreamed of finding jumped right out at us on their "Cycling" shelf! I have only written once before to an author, but had to write and tell you what a wonderful surprise it was to stumble on your new book, "Great British Bike Rides." If we made a list of everything we wanted to find in a book to help us plan cycling holidays in Britain, yours has it all-- and then some! It is an unbelievable wealth of information, and we can hardly wait to start planning our first holiday focused on cycling (rather than walking; since 1997, we have been coming to the UK to do long walks, and just re-walked Wainwright's 'coast to coast' route 2 weeks ago to celebrate my retirement). I pushed aside my novel and devoured your book on the long flight back to California!"

That's worth every single penny of my investment and negates every single quibble highlighted by a tetchy reviewer. In that email is the pointer that places me clearly upon the cycling map. I'm not a mainstream cycling pundit who will appeal to the masses. I'm not an encyclopaedic Velo-historian who can present a deep analysis of cycling racing icons. I'm not an amazing endurance cyclist who has an incredible set of tales to tell about my feats of endeavour (although my escape from a locked hotel room during LEJOG deserves a film all of its own). I'm not a great writer with beautiful eloquence in turn of phrase, you won't find many "fucks" in William Fotheringham's books.

What I am is quite simple. An ordinary, skinny British cyclist who loves riding his bike around his country and having ridden it around a bit, can't help but tell everyone about it. This is what the Cycling Total Perspective Vortex has told me. Stick to what you are and do what you love. This is what I am and this is what I love. Great British Bike Rides underpins this. There may be the odd mistake but it shouldn't distract from the art as a whole. The book lays out a man's passion for trogging out on his bike around some of the hardest yet greatest cycling loops in the country.

The compass points may be the wrong way round, but I think I can hold my head up high. This book was not commissioned for money, I received no advance for writing it, I paid for the cover shot and purchased every single piece of equipment to take the photos within. I drove and rode around the country twice to get the rides done and documented, covering all of my costs. I sought out a publisher who would understand this mission and do the concept justice, rather than one who had the best deal/greatest distribution network. I'm clearly the Mother Theresa of British cycling, selflessly nursing turbo-sick riders back out into the hills for little personal gain.

This simple, yet bleedingly obvious revelation has taken a while to sink in. The past six months have been some of the most difficult of my life as I've struggled to properly discover Dave and fit him into the humanistic jigsaw. Mix in some huge difficulties within my small business, some family illnesses add a tinge of bipolarism and you've got all the ingredients to kill the urge to write. Being the kind of fellow I am, a new project is required and next week it begins. The working title at the moment is *"Dave you idiot nobody will want to ride those routes?"*.

I've been looking at maps again and started to see some new lines. I've been riding a different set of bikes as well and think I've come up with the next set of challenges to lead on from Great British Bike Rides. One reviewer commented that GBBR was the cycling equivalent of the Munros, he looked forward to undertaking the "Barters". Well when he's done, I'm hoping to have the cycling 8000'ers ready for him to take on. The first ride begins on Thursday from Cardiff and ends in Fort William. Three mountains intervene and for purity, I feel the bike needs to accompany me to the top of them. However, the ticks of Snowdon, Sca Fell and Ben Nevis are the lesser objectives. I think the route I've planned between them is where the joy is to be had.

I have no idea how this whole project will pan out or even whether it will make it to completion (similar to the ride planned above). In tandem, I need to get the business to a point where I can get paid and repay in droves the support I've received from Helen to date. Equally, I owe a lot of micro-debts to readers who have stayed with me this far. I've been incredibly lucky to have the support from a certain vein within the cycling community, this might be you reading this very paragraph if you managed to get thus far without scrawling "self-indulgent twat" on the page and marking it D-. If it is, then thank you. I've come perilously close to packing the writing in at times but then someone emails me and blames me for another bike purchase they have made, and all is good in the world again.

Epilogue

Typing these final words I realise that were I to repeat the actions laid out in the previous chapters I would be breaking the law. How could any of us have imagined that a pandemic would lead to our governments curtailing the ability to ride our bikes? I've always known that many consider long-distance cycling to be madness, but never conceived of a day where it would become illegal. Yet here I am in 2021 stuck in my house looking back in envy at a guy who was able to dally about all over the country without having to drape his face in cloth and slather his body in sanitiser. CoronaVirus proved to be the impetus for pulling these witterings together as I reflected on a magical time in my life when I was able to do what I wanted, wherever I fancied without having to check a myriad of rules whilst distancing and frantically washing my hands.

Lockdown number three hit me the hardest as I was about to set out upon another cycling/writing journey when the government said *"Sorry Dave, no book writing for you, stay at home, protect the NHS and save lives"*. I find it easy to protect the NHS as I'm shit scared of hospitals. I'll happily dodge anywhere frequented by the ill or people trained to cut you open and poke about a bit. These buildings are full of tubes designed to go up your private parts and they put full-fat milk in the tea. Their entrances are frequented by chain smokers and you have to apply for a car parking space a year in advance. Saving lives is also top of my agenda. I do this well by avoiding a career as an electrician and choosing not to fly aeroplanes. It's staying at home that I really struggle with. I can handle it for short periods but it comes with baggage. Homes are a constant reminder of the annoying things you should do but can't be arsed. Such as cleaning, settling bills and being genial to your neighbours. When you share a home with a partner an acceptable level of decorum must be maintained. Whilst cycling I can empty my nostrils onto the road, scream Bon Jovi lyrics into the wind, swear loudly and gesture at motorists then eat peanut butter from the jar with my fingers. All of these would be frowned upon whilst at home and there's only one motorist to swear at which gets tedious after a while.

I'm not good at staying at home. This is the fault of Great British Bike Rides as I discovered the joy that not staying at home could bring. And in a monumental self-indulgent fit of sulking, I returned to that time and banged it into this book to make me feel better. Which it has. I realise the privilege of having the time, resources and good health to spend a prolonged period chasing a vanity project. Others in this world don't have it so easy. The manager of the Katie Hopkins fan club must struggle with boredom and let's have a minute's silence for Boris Johnson's fact-checker.

The final chapter of my journey into authorship ended with two books published and a vague idea of a ride over the three peaks. That was written in 2013 and I feel the need to tell you what happened since. There are some lessons in my journey that are worthwhile sharing and a few pieces of advice to anyone thinking of doing the same. Indulge me in a few more words while I bring you up to date.

Let's start with the ride over the three peaks (Snowdon, Scattered Fell and Ben Nevis). It was a ridiculous idea and should have remained at that. Instead, I had the most wonderful 9 days of riding interspersed with three pointless carries up mountains. I'm not sure it had been done before and I can see why. This was underlined by the fell runner at the top of Sca Fell Pike who curtly asked me "Why the fuck I'd carried my bike up there as I'd be carrying it down the other side?". She laughed a lot and left me to it with the parting thought that she would tell her husband what she'd witnessed as he was a bloody idiot and would probably attempt the same.

Continuing the theme of ridiculous ideas we move on to my

decision to leave my job and write a book about cycling. On the face of it not the smartest of career moves. My salary nosed dived and never recovered. 2010 was the last time I was employed. It's been eleven years in the wilderness of non-corporate life devoid of company cars, pension schemes and having to suck up to the receptionist. But every Friday Helen and I chink glasses and celebrate that step off the ladder. It liberated us from the angst many face when making life-changing decisions. As a result, we both embrace the unknown and are unafraid of upturning our lives and heading off into something quite different. A few years back we sold our house, downsized and moved to the coast. This decision took minutes, we both felt in need of another reboot so just did it. The business I started is still going and I enjoy the work we do. The pay's not great but that's probably down to the owner constantly being distracted by spurious cycling projects.

To be clear that (in my case) writing cycling books was never going to be a sustainable career. Obsessive Compulsive Cycling Disorder achieved sales that I could never have dreamed of. Self-published via Amazon it quickly took off and in 2015 spent nearly a year at the top of the cycling book charts. I was stunned to see what was a test project sell more than 50,000 copies across all formats. I was equally stunned to receive almost fuck all in royalties. Each copy sold gained me several pence. The Amazon model requires unknowns like me to price low to make it in front of potential buyers. The low price point comes with lower royalty percentages. Nevertheless, it bought me a new bike and a few accessories. More importantly, it reached an audience of cyclists similar to me. Those who had grown an obsession with bicycles and wanted to celebrate every aspect of it, including mishaps and suffering.

Since publication, I've received many messages from those who have empathised with my struggles on the bike. The best by far was from Sylvia, an 84-year-old lady cyclist from the Wirrell. Sylvia berated me for my course language, ageism and misogyny, but then went on to tell me that she had enjoyed the book and might even buy a copy. Turns out she'd found it on the shelves of the Eureka Cafe, a well-known cycling haunt. Sylvia was attempting to ride 1000 miles in a year as her own little challenge. We corresponded for a while and I looked forward to her emails which mixed a stern telling off with our shared love of the bike. Sylvia is why I write and will continue to do so. It's certainly not for money. It's for the people you discover who think like you. Who see through the constant denigration of cycling as a red light jumping lycra fest that acts to inconvenience others. Who are spirited away from normality by two wheels.

And now on to "Great British Bike Rides" the whole point of this book in the first place. It's been a huge success. To date my publisher's highest-grossing guidebook with over 16,000 copies sold since publication. I was able to fix the compass after the first print run sold out. Three editions have been printed and it occasionally stares down at me from the shelves of a reputable bookshop. I think I hit the market at exactly the right time, with the middle-aged men all donning their lycra and looking for hard things to do.

Mission has been accomplished. The book and its writing acted as a perfect watershed in my life between that of a salaryman and one who is a bit more self deterministic in life choices. The truth is that I was lucky, I had the resources to make the jump and it mostly worked out OK. I'm under no illusions that my path is open to all. However, the fact remains, I'm a cyclist and I really did get out of there. Cycling does that, it gets you out of situations and places. It may not allow you to leave your job, pick the right moment to buy bitcoin or find a life partner who doesn't mind the toilet seat being left up. But it will get you out of there wherever "there" may be.

Thanks and acknowledgements

This book could not have been written without the love and support of my amazing family. Helen my wife, Jake and Holly my two amazing children. I am also incredibly grateful to Dave Winterborne, Stuart Wright and Chris "Reg" Stevenson for reading the first draft and egging me on. I must also mention my old friend Steve Green who read the very earliest draft and thought it might be a goer. If you didn't like it I can give you their addresses. I'd thank Mum and Dad in person, but they both passed away recently. I miss them and without their genes and encouragement (mixed with occasional face palming) none of this would have happened. Finally thanks to you for reading this far and being a part of my ongoing therapy. I'll shut up now and leave you to go ride your bike. If you'd like to hurl any form of abuse my way please feel to email me at dave@phased.co.uk any time. I deleted all of that social media malarky years ago and feel much better for it.

Dave Barter
Brixham - England
December 2021

Printed in Great Britain
by Amazon